"YOU MADE THE DECISION.
HERE ARE SOME MORE 'POWER' TOOLS."

Dr. Phil sent you a major, scientifically based wake-up call. Now, here are even more daily tools for living the ultimate choice to take control of your weight—instead of letting your weight control you. You can do it—and Dr. Phil has some important nutritional plans to make it even more manageable.

In this essential companion to *The Ultimate Weight Solution*, Dr. Phil takes his groundbreaking weight loss plan even further by giving you a wealth of handy, accessible advice for every food situation and decision that you face. Here are the hands-on tools to help you identify

WHAT TO EAT
WHEN TO EAT
WHERE TO EAT
HOW TO EAT
WHY TO EAT OR NOT EAT

and essential, straightforward information on
THE CALORIE COUNTS FOR HIGH- AND
LOW-RESPONSE COST FOODS

UNHEALTHY HUNGER-DRIVING FOODS TO AVOID
WHILE IN THE WEIGHT LOSS MODE

AT-A-GLANCE FOOD COMPARISONS

HIGH-RESPONSE COST,
HUNGER-SUPPRESSING FOODS

TAKE-OUT & RESTAURANT FOOD STRATEGIES
and much more!

ALSO BY DR. PHIL MCGRAW

Life Strategies
Life Strategies Workbook
Relationship Rescue
Relationship Rescue Workbook
Self Matters
The Self Matters Companion
The Ultimate Weight Solution

The Ultimate
Weight Solution
Food Guide

Dr. Phil McGraw

DOUBLEDAY LARGE PRINT HOME LIBRARY EDITION

POCKET BOOKS
New York   London   Toronto   Sydney

This Large Print Edition, prepared especially for Doubleday Large Print Home Library, contains the complete, unabridged text of the original Publisher's Edition.

POCKET BOOKS, a division of Simon & Schuster, Inc.
1230 Avenue of the Americas, New York, NY 10020

Copyright © 2004 by Phillip C. McGraw

ISBN: 0-7394-4171-X

POCKET and colophon are registered trademarks of Simon & Schuster, Inc.

Cover photograph by Danny Turner

Manufactured in the United States of America

*This book is dedicated to the millions
of people who are using* The Ultimate Weight
Solution *and changing the epidemic of obesity
in America, one life at a time.*

Acknowledgments

One of the best decisions I have ever made was to ask Maggie Robinson, Ph.D., to be a part of my crusade of tackling obesity in America. Maggie is clearly the preeminent nutritionist in America today, and her tireless work on content, organization, flow, and writing was an invaluable asset to this project. Thanks Maggie for lending your expertise and passion about nutritional science to *The Ultimate Weight Solution Food Guide*. You have taught me a tremendous amount and I am proud to call you a friend.

Contents

INTRODUCTION   1

CHAPTER ONE: 9
Putting Your Weight on Project Status

CHAPTER TWO: 33
High-Response Cost, High-Yield
Nutrition: A Three-Stage Plan to
Weight Loss Freedom

CHAPTER THREE: 63
The Ultimate Weight Solution
Menus

CHAPTER FOUR: 105
No-Fail Solutions: Food Strategies
for Success

CHAPTER FIVE: 139
How to Use the Food Guide

THE ULTIMATE WEIGHT SOLUTION FOOD GUIDE   173

High-Response Cost, High-Yield Foods   174

Beef   174
Beverages   194
Breads, Bread Products, and Crackers   200
Cereals   208
Cheeses   220
Condiments   222
Eggs   234
Fast Foods, Allowable   236
Fats, Oils, and Salad Dressings   246
Fish and Shellfish   264
Fruits and Fruit Juices   282
Grains, Grain Cakes, Pasta, and Noodles   304
Lamb, Veal, and Game Products   310
Lunch Meats and Sausage   320
Milk, Milk Products, and Yogurt   326
Nuts and Seeds   330
Pork Products   334
Poultry Products   338
Soups   346
Soy and Vegetarian Foods   360
Sugar-Free Foods   364
Vegetables, Non-Starchy and Starchy   366

Low-Response Cost, Low-Yield Foods   442

Beef   442
Beverages   452
Bread Products, Crackers, and Muffins   462
Cakes and Pies   474
Candy   486

Contents

Cereals and Cereal Bars 500
Cheeses 512
Cookies 520
Dinners, Canned and Frozen 534
Donuts and Pastries 544
Eggs 560
Fast Foods 562
Fats 594
Fish and Shellfish 606
Frostings and Toppings 610
Fruits, Fruit Drinks, and Punches 614
Grains, Pasta, and Noodles 630
Gravies and Sauces 634
Ice Cream 640
Lamb, Veal, and Organ Meats 644
Lunch Meats and Sausages 648
Milk, Milk Products, Cream, and Yogurt 654
Nuts and Seed Products 660
Pancakes and Waffles 668
Pizza 674
Pork Products 682
Poultry Products 686
Puddings 692
Snacks: Chips, Pretzels, and Popcorn 698
Soups 706
Sugars, Sweeteners, Jams, and Syrups 714
Vegetables and Vegetable Products 720

MEDICAL AND NUTRITION REFERENCES 733

Introduction

Get excited.

What you are holding in your hands is a powerful tool for change, one that will help you take your nutrition, and your eating, to an entirely new level of self-control. If you take what I have to say about nutrition and food in this guide, learn it, and put it to use, you can keep your momentum going in the direction of permanent weight loss. I know that is the result you're aiming for, so let's plan to further that momentum of success right now.

If you have read or are reading *The Ultimate Weight Solution: The 7 Keys to Weight Loss Freedom,* then you have taken a very important step toward success. You know that losing weight and keeping it off are not simply matters of eating less and exercising more (although both are crucial), but of changing the particular psychological, behavioral, and environmental factors that cause you to overeat in the first place. You know you must build a way of life that supports healthy weight management on every side. Everything you will find in *The Ultimate Weight Solution,* and in this companion guide, is based on the premise that the power to change your weight and your health lies solely within you.

And if you are among the millions of people who are using the seven keys to weight loss freedom, then I am happy for you and proud of what you are doing to maximize your life. You are on the path to living a life that is infinitely more healthy for you, with an outpouring of positives because you have had the courage to do something significant and rewarding for yourself.

When you use the seven keys, you begin to: rid yourself of wrong thinking, heal yourself of emotions standing in the way of a healthy relationship with food, create a no-fail environment, shape your eating behavior into what you need for lifetime weight control, get real about nutritional choices that worked to your detriment, change your priorities to include exercise, and plug into a circle of support for encouragement and accountability. In short, you are changing how you're living.

Part of this process involves getting real about all those fad, "flavor-of-the-month" type diets you tried in the past—diets that promised you a short-cut but sent you down a dead-end road to failure instead. These diets can leave you weighing in much heavier than usual, with a pileup of not just pounds, but discouragement over your repeated failures. The promises made by fad diets can be seductive, and I assure you that caving in to them is a short drop back into the frustration and weight from where you came.

The current preoccupation with ultra low-carbohydrate dieting in this country is of deep concern to me as a clinical and medical psychologist. What is so troubling from both a psychological and nutritional perspective is that most of these diets advocate eating less than 100 grams of carbohydrates a day, when in fact your body requires nearly double that amount for normal brain metabolism and muscle function.

When you deny your body and brain sufficient carbohydrates, it can damage your inner psychology. It can bring on fatigue, irritability, and mood changes. Why? Under normal circumstances, your brain uses roughly 500 calories' worth of carbohydrate a day for optimal functioning, including the production of brain chemicals responsible for feelings of mental well-being. So without carbohydrates, your mental and emotional edge is gravely affected. Think of the consequences if you are an emotional overeater who decides to follow a low-carbohydrate diet. You already have a habit of medicating yourself with food. Then comes the double whammy: You choose to diet in such a way that it makes you feel worse emotionally and now you are more vulnerable than ever to bingeing and overeating. You are, in essence, conspiring against yourself by choosing a diet that without question sets you up for failure by further weakening you where you are the weakest. You are creating obstacles for yourself that you don't need.

It is time for all this health-defeating, behavior-defeating pseudonutrition to stop. Nutritionally, the solution for successful weight loss is not ultra low-carbohydrate dieting—far from it. What can genuinely help you lose weight and keep it off is *moderate* nutrition across the board—moderate carbohydrates, moderate protein, and moderate fat, and this current, accurate information comes straight from nutritional scientists, not from weight loss gurus or food faddists.

So with *The Ultimate Weight Solution Food Guide,* I am back with more to say about diet and nutrition—what to eat, how to eat, and why, in order to help you do what no fad diet has ever accomplished, and that is: achieve lifelong weight control. In this guide, you won't be relying on bad nutritional information, but rather on sound techniques and principles for shedding weight permanently by taking a moderate, balanced approach to eating.

In the first part of this guide, I have set out for you an effective, highly structured three-stage food plan, including weeks and weeks of menus, that takes you from initial weight loss right through to maintenance. It includes:

- **My Rapid Start Plan,** a specialized 14-day approach to eating that activates early, immediate weight loss in order to reinforce, and create for you, a pattern of success that sets the stage for continued weight loss. In this stage, you'll be eating foods in their pure, mostly unprocessed state (raw fruits, raw vegetables, vegetables cooked from raw or from frozen, and certain whole grains). This helps clear your system of processed sugars and refined carbohydrates in order to restore better metabolic control and recondition your taste preferences for healthier, more wholesome foods. Your body will begin changing for the better in a matter of days.

• **My High-Response Cost, High-Yield Weight Loss Plan,** for sustainable, consistent weight loss without deprivation. This stage liberalizes your eating plan, while remaining effectively calorie-controlled to ensure steady weight loss. There are no holes in your nutrition, either, only moderate, balanced eating with foods that offer built-in protection from gaining weight, some of which you can eat to your heart's content.

• **My Ultimate Maintenance Plan,** in which we will work through a number of critical steps so that you can learn how to live in your new body. With this plan, you'll be able to stay at your newfound thin, fit self for a lifetime as long as you do what is required.

The second part of *The Ultimate Weight Solution Food Guide* is devoted to a comprehensive listing of the nutrient content of thousands of foods, divided into my classifications of high-response cost, high-yield foods and low-response cost, low-yield foods. For you to make healthier nutritional choices, you need to know what's in the foods you're choosing, from calories to carbohydrates, from fat to sodium. This part of the guide provides that information, in one easy-to-use reference.

This guide is designed to be used along with *The Ultimate Weight Solution.* The hardcover book provides the keys and their corresponding steps to help you create a new lifestyle for yourself that is consistent with whatever it takes to support long-term rather than quick-fix weight loss. The guide helps you keep your nutritional momentum going, building on and adding to the book, with action-oriented answers and clear-cut instructions on exactly what and how to eat.

Throughout this guide, you will be introduced to even more behavioral and nutritional strategies, in order to support you when you're not in the mood to stick to your plan. Successful weight management isn't about willpower. It's about creating a life program by controlling, among other things, your environment, your schedule, and your self-destructive behaviors. The more strategies you can plug into your life, the more successful you will be.

You know from personal experience that there is nothing more frustrating, or more disheartening, than the struggle to lose weight and keep it off. Probably more than anything right now, you want to put that part of you behind you—and start piecing your life back together in such a way that you can respect and like yourself for who you are and what you do. And if you haven't said so to yourself, let me say it for you: You deserve more out of life than the way you have been living.

I am here to tell you that this want is worth having, and that you are worth whatever it takes to get it. This guide is thus a worthy resource for a worthy cause—you! The information on every page will help you, if you choose to help yourself to what it has to offer. It will not make you lose pounds or trim inches. Only you can do that. You have within you everything you need to transform the life you've been living, and become the healthy *you* that you want to be. Now is your chance to make a better life for yourself. It's a chance you don't want to miss!

ONE

Putting Your Weight on Project Status

You have made the important decision to lose weight, and you want to do it right this time. But to do so, you must be willing to put your weight on what I like to call Project Status. This means that you must consciously decide to actively, purposely work on improving your weight and your fitness level each and every day. Putting your weight on Project Status means giving your health and vitality a new, higher priority in your life, such that they become of conscious importance to you. You stay committed to working on them, disciplining yourself by working on all seven keys to weight loss freedom. (I've summarized the keys for you in the box on pages 25–26.)

You get out of this project—your weight—what you put into it. It will be from your commitment to set a personal standard for yourself—one that says you will not quit and you will not push aside your goals for a trimmer, healthier body—that your success will follow. You must be willing to reach for what you want and reach right now. To be in Project Status means that you do not neglect to take care of yourself first, and now is the time to start doing that.

Before beginning the nutritional plan in this guide, you must take some essential first steps that will help you reach the peak of your effectiveness, and lay the groundwork for constructive, lasting change. This is very important—don't hurry through these initial steps or avoid this part of the process. Take it seriously, and I promise you that you will have the foundation for the most effective and dramatic changes you have ever made in your weight.

STEP 1:
DETERMINE YOUR GET-REAL WEIGHT.

Your get-real weight is the healthiest and most realistic weight for you, based on your height, your bone structure, and your sex. It is not necessarily the weight of your youth, but rather a state of health and well-being that is congruent and in harmony with how you are physically and genetically configured. It is the weight that is "right" for you— a stable, comfortable weight, at which you look good, feel good, and lovingly accept yourself from the inside out.

You can figure out your get-real weight by using my Body Weight Standards, a system I developed for my patients; it is a modified and more realistic version of height-weight tables. Though not perfect, these body weight standards are more reflective of what can be achieved and certainly a better measure of where most people should be, weight-wise.

Using the Body Weight Standards chart below,

DR. PHIL'S BODY WEIGHT STANDARDS

Height	Women	Men
4' 10"	90 – **100** – 110	114 – **127** – 140
4' 11"	95 – **105** – 116	119 – **132** – 145
5'	99 – **110** – 121	123 – **137** – 151
5' 1"	103 – **115** – 127	128 – **142** – 156
5' 2"	108 – **120** – 132	132 – **147** – 162
5' 3"	112 – **125** – 138	137 – **152** – 167
5' 4"	117 – **130** – 143	141 – **157** – 173
5' 5"	122 – **135** – 148	146 – **162** – 178
5' 6"	126 – **140** – 154	150 – **167** – 184
5' 7"	130 – **145** – 160	155 – **172** – 189
5' 8"	135 – **150** – 165	159 – **177** – 195
5' 9"	139 – **155** – 171	164 – **182** – 200
5' 10"	144 – **160** – 176	168 – **187** – 206
5' 11"	148 – **165** – 182	173 – **192** – 211
6'	153 – **170** – 187	177 – **197** – 217
6' 1"	157 – **175** – 193	182 – **202** – 222
6' 2"	162 – **180** – 198	186 – **207** – 228
6' 3"	166 – **185** – 204	191 – **212** – 233
6' 4"	171 – **190** – 209	195 – **217** – 239

My get-real weight is: _____

identify where you should be, so that you can move forward from where you are now. The lower end of the ranges are for small-boned people; the upper end, for larger-boned individuals. Be honest here: Don't subjectively say you are small-boned, when in fact, you are just the opposite. Your get-real weight is your target. Record it in the space above.

STEP 2:
CHECK AND RECORD YOUR CURRENT WEIGHT AND WAIST MEASUREMENT BEFORE YOU START.

Do two things: First, step on the scale to weigh yourself to determine your starting point. Then, measure your waist with a tape measure positioned one inch above your navel. Taking waist measurements is important because weight distribution—where you carry weight on your body—can affect your health, for better or for worse. A too-large waistline circumference, for example, places you at greater risk for heart disease, diabetes, and certain cancers.

A waist measurement of 35 inches or more for women and 40 inches or more for men is cause for concern and may indicate that you are at risk for heart disease or diabetes. Keeping tabs on this simple measurement can protect you in some important ways.

Write your weight and waist measurement in the space below, along with the date.

Date: _____
My weight: _____
My waist measurement: _____

Although I do not advocate obsessive weighing and measuring, you do need to monitor your progress toward your get-real weight with some regularity and reasonable frequency. You should weigh yourself at least at one- or two-week intervals to stay on target; then record your weight in a notebook or journal. The scales should show a weight loss that may be quite dramatic in the beginning, eventually tapering off to a steady, even loss of a few pounds each week. If you aren't dropping pounds at a steady rate, or if you gain weight, you should be motivated to course-correct some aspect of the weight loss plan to make it more effective, including changing your behavior so that it is harder for you to cheat.

Weigh yourself at the same time each week, because your weight fluctuates throughout the day, and you can weigh more at night than you do in the morning. Promise yourself you will not self-destruct if the scale moves up a few pounds, but instead make this a priority for action-oriented repair.

At monthly intervals, remeasure your waist and

record these measurements. Watching your pounds and inches diminish will help reinforce your resolve and keep you moving in the right direction.

STEP 3:
CLEAR YOUR ENVIRONMENT OF "LOW-RESPONSE COST, LOW-YIELD FOODS."

The presence of food is one of the most insistent of all triggers to eat or overeat, and you know this yourself if you have ever tried to sample just a few healthy items from a buffet table. This step is thus about removing tempting foods from your environment, including your home, office, car, or anywhere you store food. After all, you can't eat what is not there.

Specifically, I would like you to take an inventory of your environment, looking for and tossing out what I call "low-response cost, low-yield foods." So that you understand the terminology, these foods require very little *response* from you when you eat them. In plain terms, they are foods that you just gulp and gain—easily ingested, overly convenient, and requiring little or no preparation on your part.

An excellent example of a low-response cost food is a microwaveable bean burrito. You zap it in your microwave in a matter of seconds, no preparation required. When you eat it, you don't even have to chomp on the burrito; it just slithers down your throat in a few quick gulps. What happens is that you consume an incredibly high number of calories and fat in a very short period of time.

Most low-response cost foods are also *low-yield foods.* That means they provide very little in the way of good nutrition, with a lot of calories packed into a very small amount of food. Sugar is an example of a low-yield food. It is very high in calories but practically devoid of nutrition, and for these reasons, it is best kept off-limits if you want to successfully control your weight.

Low-yield foods are engineered to be addictive; loaded with sugar, extra fat, calories, too much salt, and unhealthy additives; and of questionable nutritional value. What's more, they are processed and refined; that is, they have been milled or altered in some fashion that devalues their nutrition by extracting fiber and other nutrients.

To sum up, low-response cost, low-yield foods:
- Invite and promote fast, uncontrollable eating.
- Need little or no preparation time.
- Require little chewing or effort to eat. The food slides down your throat, and you barely have to chew it.
- Melt in your mouth.
- Can be too easily eaten straight from a package or container.
- Are highly processed.
- Are light on nutrition.

One of the most offending characteristics of low-response cost, low-yield foods is that they are *hunger drivers.* These foods do not keep you satisfied for very long and may make you hungrier later. Here's why: After you eat these foods, your body's natural stop-eating signals don't even have time to kick in. It takes about twenty minutes from the time you eat something until the hypothalamus in your brain shuts off your appetite. There's absolutely no way that burrito can offer any satisfying effects when it's overly easy to wolf it down in a matter of seconds. So you keep eating more and more of this stuff until you've eaten way beyond the point of fullness; and the unfortunate fact is that you're overfed with unnecessary calories and fat.

On pages 418 to 707 of this food guide, you'll find a comprehensive listing of low-response cost, low-yield foods by category. These are foods you want to limit or avoid. For now, here is an abbreviated list that will give you an idea of what to toss out:

- Cookies, candy, and any high-calorie, sweetened snack foods.
- Salty foods such as potato chips, pretzels, taco chips, nuts, and other packaged munchies.
- Sweet rolls, pastries, and doughnuts.
- Cakes, snack cakes, pies, and other baked sweets.

- Presweetened, sugary breakfast cereals.
- White bread, white rolls, white buns—anything that is not whole grain.
- Crackers that are not whole grain.
- Cold cuts.
- Ice cream and high-sugar frozen desserts.
- Quick-fix prepared foods such as pizza, fried entrées and dinners, and microwaveable sandwiches.
- Syrups, jams, and jellies.
- High-fat spreads, peanut butter, and dips.
- Sugared soft drinks and beverages, including flavored coffees.
- Alcoholic beverages.
- Any packaged food in which sugar is listed as one of the first three ingredients.
- Any food that can be classified as "junk food."
- Any food that you habitually binge on.

Ridding your environment of low-response cost, low-yield foods is one of the best moves you can take toward setting yourself up for success. It helps you get past needing to feel motivated all the time over trying to lose weight. When your enthusiasm flags and your willpower conks out—which it will—you need to have your environment set up in such a way that it supports you. This crucial step of eliminating low-response cost, low-yield foods does this for you.

STEP 4.
STOCK YOUR KITCHEN WITH
"HIGH-RESPONSE COST, HIGH-YIELD FOODS."

By "high-response cost foods," I mean foods that require a great deal of work and effort to prepare and to eat. The work output, or *response* on your part, that is required to ingest these foods is high, whereas the calorie payoff—although healthy—is low. A good example of a high-response cost, high-yield food is a ripe, juicy apple. It is coarse and takes a lot of chewing and grinding to get it down. It is also packed with fiber, which keeps your stomach from emptying too rapidly.

Why is this important? The fact that you must take time to prepare these foods, and that they take effort to chew, eat, and digest, is a real advantage to weight control. Why? *Because high-response cost foods defeat the urge to eat on impulse and therefore support better control.*

High-response cost foods are thus *hunger suppressors,* meaning they can control and curb your hunger. Because they take longer to eat, your body has more time to receive stop-eating signals from your hypothalamus. By the time you chew and ingest these foods, you're starting to feel full, so there is little chance that you will overeat. You will be amazed at how little food you'll eat, yet how full and satisfied you'll feel after eating it.

Most high-response cost foods also happen to

be "high-yield foods." High-yield foods are those that supply a lot of nutrients—in the form of carbohydrates, protein, fat, vitamins, minerals, fiber, and other food components—relative to the low amount of calories they contain.

High-yield foods are generally those of a more pure, basic variety and are closer to the state in which they are found in nature. They have not been critically changed during food processing, and thus are not usually laced with added sugar, fat, additives, and other health-defeating ingredients. High-yield foods are abundant in fiber, a weight-control ally that promotes feelings of fullness, stabilizes your blood sugar, and thus keeps your hunger at bay so that you're less likely to overeat.

High-yield foods such as fruits and vegetables are colorful too, a sign that they are plentiful in important food factors that reduce your risk of disease.

To recap, high-response cost, high-yield foods are those that:

- Take time and effort to fix.
- Require a great deal of chewing and ingestion energy.
- Cannot be eaten quickly.
- Suppress your hunger and curb your cravings.
- Are not "convenience foods" in any sense of the word.
- Supply a healthy balance of vitamins, minerals, fiber, and other nutrients.

For successful weight control, stock your kitchen with high-response cost, high-yield foods. There is a comprehensive list of these foods starting on page 150, and you should become very familiar with them because they form the centerpiece of nutrition for healthy weight control. For now, and as you begin this plan, make sure you have these foods on hand:

- Poultry, such as chicken and turkey breasts (prepared without skin).
- Fresh, frozen, or canned seafood (nothing that is breaded, however).
- Lean cuts of meat.
- Fresh eggs.
- Fresh fruits and vegetables. Frozen is fine too, since they've been chilled immediately after harvesting and may contain more nutrients than fresh produce that has been sitting on the shelf or in your refrigerator. Canned fruits and vegetables are acceptable, but may contain high levels of sodium.
- Whole grains and cereals such as brown rice, bulgur, oatmeal, rice, barley, and millet.
- High-fiber cereals. Although a packaged product, these cereals are specially formulated with added fiber—a hunger-suppressing ingredient in high-response cost grains and cereals.
- Reduced fat or fat-free dairy products such as skim milk, low-fat milk, sugar-free yogurt, and low-fat cheeses.
- Healthy fats such as olive oil, canola oil, and

nuts and seeds. These fats appear to delay hunger and help you feel more satisfied after eating a meal that contains them.

(For a comparative look at hunger suppressors and hunger drivers, refer to the chart on page 24.)

STEP 5:
PRIORITIZE EXERCISE INTO YOUR LIFE.

The fit, in-shape people of this world are doing something right—that something is exercise. Exercise burns calories; in fact, you can lose a pound of fat in ten exercise sessions of approximately forty-five minutes to one hour each, provided you do not take in a surplus of calories. The more food you burn off through exercise, the less you store as fat. Exercise also accelerates your metabolism, the physiological process that converts food into energy, so that you are burning up more calories even at rest.

There's something else at work, too: Food behavior and exercise behavior are highly interactive, with a powerful connection operating between the two. If you exercise on a regular basis, a rather amazing phenomenon occurs: You'll begin to experience a weakening desire to overeat. Your food behavior will begin to change almost automatically, and you'll make healthier food choices as a matter of routine.

For effective weight control, it is best to start an established exercise program that involves three to four hours a week of aerobic activity such as brisk walking, biking, jogging, aerobic dancing, playing tennis, aerobic exercise machines (treadmill, stair-climber, and so forth), or swimming.

Added to your aerobic exercise program should be weight training, at least two to three times a week. Weight training just happens to be one of the most powerful ways to rejuvenate and speed up your metabolism. It helps burn body fat (nearly 100 percent of the weight you lose is pure fat if you weight-train). And it builds firm, well-developed muscle while you're losing weight. More muscle translates into a faster metabolism. The reason for this is that muscle tissue demands much more oxygen and calories to sustain itself than fat tissue does. Fat tissue, by contrast, is relatively inactive, while muscle is constantly burning fuel at a rapid rate even while you're at rest. When you add muscle to your body through weight training, your metabolic rate goes up and stays up twenty-four hours a day.

Weight training also makes maintaining your weight loss much easier and more automatic. In fact, a number of studies have found that weight training stands out as a proven lifestyle strategy for keeping excess weight off over the long term. So for healthy, ongoing weight management, you need to consider weight training.

Supporting your weight loss by exercising is a real chance for you to get permanent control of your weight, no matter how long it has been since you last exercised.

STEP 6:
CREATE ACCOUNTABILITY.

The next important step before getting started requires that you make yourself accountable with regard to your get-real goal weight. This means enlisting someone who will serve as your "teammate," someone to whom you commit to make periodic reports. This person should come from your relational circle of support (explained in key 7): family members and friends who you consider to be the closest people in your life—the people you trust and value most. Figure out who would most strongly support what you want to accomplish and who would be willing and available to act in this capacity. Your teammate will be the person to whom you will have to confess if you fail to do what you plan to do.

At least once a week, if not daily, report on your compliance with your food plan, your exercise progress, the number of pounds you've lost, or other measures of progress. Knowing that you will check in with someone tomorrow keeps you on track today.

YOUR PERSONALIZED FOOD DIARY

When you start this plan, keep a "personalized food diary" in which you accurately record everything you eat and drink, as well as other elements of relevance, such as your energy intake (calories). Whether you like it or not, calories still do count when it comes to weight control, so you do need to pay some degree of attention to how many calories you're taking in. Now don't lock up on me here. I am not asking you to become tediously preoccupied with counting calories. What I am suggesting is that you keep track of your calories for perhaps just a week or two, in order to make sure that you are not overindulging on overlooked calories.

Becoming knowledgeable about the calorie counts of foods you typically eat helps keep you on track in terms of how much you're eating. The calorie information in this food guide will provide valuable, at-your-fingertips reference material for doing that.

Use the Food Diary to Plan Your Meals

One important way to use the personalized food diary below is to preplan what you will eat and drink each day. By this, I mean that you commit to paper your menu for the day, including three meals and two snacks, then eat only the foods on that menu. The significance of having a food plan, prepared ahead of time, is that it frees you from making last-minute decisions about what to eat and prevents you from caving in to sudden impulses to overeat. Planning your eating in advance eliminates any doubt about what you will eat and removes your fear of losing control. With a food plan in place for the day, you can and will regain greater control over your eating. So use this diary as a meal planner, above all.

Use the Food Diary to Monitor Your Eating Behavior

But you do not have to stop there. You can use this diary to record important information about your nutrition and eating habits. For example, you can record the time of your meals, the place, what you were doing at the time, or, in some cases, the emotional states (happy, sad, lonely, bored, stressed, angry, etc.) that may have triggered you to eat "off plan."

This information can help you see, in unquestionable black and white, precisely which eating habits you need to adjust or high-risk situations that are sabotaging your efforts. Maybe you find that you mindlessly reach for foods such as cookies, cake, candy, or ice cream—the so-called comfort foods—when you feel tired after a long day at work. Or that being in certain places, like your car or office, triggers the impulse to eat.

Then you can thoughtfully review your entries,

looking for red flags. Assess the obstacles that can have an impact on reaching your get-real weight. This means anticipating the times, places, circumstances—even people—that typically make it difficult for you to stay the course. That way, you can work out an advance strategy for avoiding these pitfalls, or at least outlasting them. You're in a better position to avoid them by changing your routine, changing your schedule, or changing your environment.

You can also plan very carefully what you are going to do at those moments when you have the urge to binge or overeat. This should involve "incompatible substitutes"—activities such as exercising, relaxation, listening to music—any activity that cannot coexist with eating. For example, when you feel compelled to soothe frustrations with a bag of chips, pick up your knitting needles instead and start knitting. Knitting is incompatible with crunching down on chips. Or take a walk. Walking around the block is incompatible with bingeing. Incompatible substitutes also take your mind off food and eating. So as soon as you feel the impulse, begin engaging, deliberately, in the incompatible substitute.

Keeping this food diary is crucial to the process of losing weight. It is a vital part of what psychologists call "self-monitoring," a way to keep tabs on your progress and performance—not only to see where you need to take corrective action, but also

Personalized Food Diary

Day of Week: _____

Date: _____

Time	Food Eaten	Amount	Compliance	Calories	Place	Circumstances

to highlight the positive changes you're making. People who self-monitor their behavior are more successful at losing weight and keeping it off than those who choose to not self-monitor. So let me encourage you to self-monitor. What you do not acknowledge is only going to get worse until you do.

On the following page is a sample diary. You should make as many photocopies as you need of this page. You don't have to use the diary forever—just long enough for you to see what's working and what's not—and to get the hang of what you need to be correcting on a day-to-day basis so that you can take important and timely coping steps.

Remember, you can use this diary as a meal planner to map out your meals for the next day, and as a log to identify correctable aspects of your behavior that you need to change. To help you fill this out, here are some important instructions:

- In column 1 *(time)*, record the time of day you plan to eat. If you do not know which time you'll be eating, write down "breakfast," "lunch," "dinner," and "snacks."

- In column 2 *(food eaten)*, describe your meal or snack. Write down everything you plan to eat at those meals. If you eat something you have not planned to eat, write that down as soon as possible afterward. (Note the time in the first column, too.) Leave nothing out.

- In column 3 *(amount)*, write down how much you ate (the amount or portion size).

- In column 4 *(compliance)*, note whether your meal or snack complied with your planned menu. Place a check mark in the allotted space if it did.

- In column 5 *(calories)*, write down the calories you consumed for each meal or snack. Add up your calories at the end of each day. (Remember, you do not have to do this forever—just long enough to get a feel for how well you're doing. Just a few days of calculating your calories can pinpoint overlooked sources of calories, plus provide some excellent nutritional self-diagnosis.)

- In column 6 *(place)*, note where you were at the time of the meal or snack—at your dining room table, in the kitchen, watching television, in your car, at your desk, at a social occasion, or at a restaurant, for example.

- In column 7 *(circumstances)*, describe any noteworthy circumstances surrounding the meal or snack, such as your feelings or emotions, whether you felt tired or unusually hungry, or if the meal happened in response to a stressful event.

If you have taken the above steps to putting your weight on project status, you are ready to move on. Using the nutritional strategies that follow, you will be able to reprogram yourself for success rather than failure. Rewards will start rolling in quicker than you think. Your weight control experience will no longer be characterized by wasted moments and frustration, but by a sense of triumph and mastery. It's time to go for it.

Hunger Suppressors

- Lean animal-based proteins such as fish, meat, and poultry
- Fresh fruits
- Fresh vegetables
- Beans and legumes (e.g., kidney beans, pinto beans, or black beans)
- Whole grains and high-fiber cereals
- Soups, broth-based
- Healthy fats (such as olive oil, canola oil, or flaxseed oil)
- Nuts and seeds, unsalted and preferably still in their hulls

Hunger Drivers

- Most fast foods
- Soda and all sweetened beverages
- Alcoholic beverages
- Sugared cereals
- Ice cream and frozen desserts
- Candy and other sweets
- Salty foods such as snack foods (chips, pretzels, salted nuts, snack mixes, etc.)
- Baked goods, including snack cakes, pastries, and doughnuts
- Any food classified as "junk food"

THE 7 KEYS TO WEIGHT LOSS FREEDOM

Key 1—Right Thinking. Lay aside self-defeating, invalid mind-sets that do not work. They have the power to keep you from making different choices or developing new behaviors. Too often, we let these negative notions go unchallenged, and we act as though they were true. You must monitor what you're thinking and challenge whether it is true. If it's not working, replace it with thinking that works.

Key 2—Healing Feelings. Overcome emotional overeating by managing inappropriate reactions to stress; solving problems rather than dwelling on them; changing self-defeating thoughts, since more often than not, feelings follow thoughts; gaining closure on unfinished emotional business; and learning new ways to cope without resorting to food.

Key 3—A No-Fail Environment. Design your world so that you can't help but succeed. This involves removing temptations to eat and rearranging your schedule in order to avoid or minimize triggers to overeat.

Key 4—Mastery over Food and Impulse Eating. There's only one reason why you haven't changed the bad stuff in your life. You're getting something out of it. I'm not saying that you're getting something healthy or positive, but people do not continue in situations, attitudes, or actions that do not give them a payoff. This key helps you identify those payoffs, unplug from them, and replace bad habits with healthy behavior.

Key 5—High-Response Cost, High-Yield Nutrition. To lose weight, you must choose foods that support good behavioral control over your eating, that is, high-response cost, high-yield foods, organized into a moderate, balanced, calorie-controlled plan to ensure weight loss.

Key 6—Intentional Exercise. Prioritize regular exercise into your life most days of the week—walking, jogging, aerobic dance classes, yoga, playing a sport, or lifting weights. Exercise does more than simply burn calories; it changes your self-perception so you stop labeling yourself as a couch potato.

Key 7—Your Circle of Support. Surround yourself with supportive, like-minded people who want you to lose weight and succeed at your health and fitness efforts.

High-Response Cost, High-Yield Nutrition

A THREE-STAGE PLAN TO WEIGHT LOSS FREEDOM

Nutritionally, you need something doable but not drastic that you can do, starting today, to start dropping pounds and inches. This is exactly what this chapter is intended to help you do. What you are about to learn here is a workable, effective three-stage plan for taking weight off and keeping it off—a plan that is built around high-response cost, high-yield foods.

Why are these foods emphasized?

The answer to that is easy: From the perspective of weight management, high-response cost, high-yield foods support behavioral change. They encourage slow eating, they are tremendously satisfying, and they curb cravings and hunger pangs. Because high-response cost foods have not been critically changed during food processing, you do not have to worry about eating added sugar or fat—and suffering the weight-gaining side effects that those additions bring. In short, high-response cost, high-yield foods form the basis of a healthy, nutritious diet because they energize, protect, and build your body.

By contrast, low-response, low-yield foods lead to a considerable amount of mindless, uncontrollable overeating. If you eliminate or cut back on these foods, weight management becomes so much easier and requires far less vigilance over what and how you eat.

This three-stage plan provides total nutrition using everyday foods that are eaten in the real world, allowing you to live normally and at peace with food. It's easy to incorporate into your life, without turning it upside down or driving you nuts. It reestablishes normal patterns of eating behavior so that you don't have to exercise such grit-your-teeth restraint, which is so often the undoing of dieters. This plan is something you can stick to for good, and its effect on your health can be transformative.

Learning, and putting into action, the three stages of my high-response cost, high-yield nutrition plan is at the absolute core of what you must do nutritionally for permanent weight loss. Here is how it works:

STAGE 1:
THE RAPID START PLAN

The Rapid Start Plan is a 14-day, calorie-controlled, carbohydrate-modified plan that helps gear your body for accelerated weight loss. It also initiates the process of *choice shift,* in which your taste preferences for high-sugar, high-fat foods begin to change to a preference for healthier foods. As you replace low-response cost, low-yield foods with healthier alternatives, for example, cookies with apples, oranges, or some other healthy food, your preference for the healthier food becomes stronger and more appetizing. In unison with choice shift, you will also experience diminished cravings for sugar and refined carbohydrates.

When you change your diet with the goal of losing weight, the first initial weeks are absolutely critical. I know through personal experience from working with thousands of people who have been overweight or obese, in addition to valid nutritional research, that losing a significant amount of weight at the very outset of a program can lay constructive groundwork for long-term success. In other words, *initial* weight loss has the chance to lead to *long-term* weight maintenance. If you get a running start on losing weight right away, expect to make it to the finish line as a winner.

The Rapid Start Plan has its genesis in my training as a medical psychologist working with the medical population of patients who were dealing with all of the problems and diseases secondary to obesity. The dietary strategies I designed for these patients enjoyed amazing results, and as a result, I got called on more and more to work with people who were overweight or obese—and so the basics of this nutritional plan were born.

The Rapid Start Plan gives you the freedom to eat a wide variety of food groups: lean proteins, fruits and dairy products (left out of most reducing diets), enough natural starches for energy, unlimited amounts of nonstarchy vegetables, and a variety of healthy fats.

During your 14 days on the Rapid Start Plan:

1. Eat three regular meals a day (breakfast, lunch, and dinner) and two snacks. Try to schedule your meals at fairly regular times, whenever possible. This keeps your blood sugar steady, so that you're less vulnerable to cravings. In addition, it helps you settle into a more disciplined eating pattern.

2. Have a protein serving at each of your three main meals. This breaks down to an egg, two egg whites, or 2 ounces of a lean turkey product (such as turkey bacon or sausage) for breakfast; 4 ounces of protein for lunch; and 4 ounces for dinner. Protein is a hunger suppressor and has a positive effect on metabolic activity.

3. Eat unlimited amounts (but at least four serv-ings) of non-starchy vegetables (salad vegeta-bles, broccoli, cauliflower, green beans, spinach, etc.) daily. These vegetables may be raw, or cooked from fresh or frozen. Eat these foods until you feel satisfied but not stuffed. Learn to tune in to your own hunger and full-ness cues.

4. Modify your intake of starchy carbohydrates (potatoes, rice, whole grains, high-fiber cereal, legumes, etc.) to one serving a day (for women) or two servings a day (for men, since men usually require more calories a day than women do). You'll be temporarily limiting these starchy foods (but not cutting them out alto-gether). Do not eat starchy carbohydrates af-ter your noon meal. Most of your starchy carbohydrates in this stage are natural, unre-fined choices—nothing remotely processed (such as bread or pasta).

5. Eat two servings of fresh fruit daily—but no fruit juice in this stage, because juice does lit-tle to help suppress your appetite.

6. Eat two servings of low-fat dairy foods daily. Often limited or cut out altogether in many di-ets, these foods furnish the bone-building mineral calcium. When calcium supplies dwin-

dle, levels of a hormone called calcitrol go up, with a corresponding negative impact on fat burning. Calcitriol switches off mechanisms that break down fat and activates those that produce it. So: You need dairy foods in your diet, not only for the calcium they provide, but also to support fat metabolism.

7. Choose from healthy fats. Enjoy a tablespoon a day of high-response cost, high-yield fats or oils, or, if the fat is a reduced-calorie product, have two tablespoons a day. Healthy fats are a hunger suppressor. No nuts or seeds are allowed in this stage, since it is too easy to go overboard on these foods.

8. Drink eight to ten glasses of pure water daily. Although you can enjoy a variety of noncaloric beverages, water is your best choice. Drinking too little water leads to dehydration, a state of imbalance that can slow down your metabolism.

9. Eat allowable foods (see below) only from the high-response cost, high-yield food lists. Use the food guide to familiarize yourself with these foods.

10. Do not stay in Stage 1 for more than 14 days, although you may return to this stage if your weight has reached a plateau.

FOODS TO EAT ON THE RAPID START PLAN: HIGH-RESPONSE COST, HIGH-YIELD FOODS

Proteins*

Eggs	Fish	Meat (lean cuts)	Poultry (no skin)	Protein Substitutes**	Shellfish
Hard-boiled	Bass	Beef	Chicken breast	Beans	Clams
Poached	Bluefish	Lamb	Chicken, ground lean	Lentils	Crab
Soft-boiled	Flounder	Pork	Cornish game hen	Soy-based and vegetarian foods	Lobster
Scrambled	Grouper	Veal	Turkey breast	Textured vegetable protein	Mussels
	Haddock		Turkey, ground lean	Tempeh	Oysters
	Halibut		Turkey sausage, lean	Tofu	Scallops
	Ocean perch				Shrimp
	Pollock				
	Salmon				
	Swordfish				
	Trout				
	Tuna				
	Basically any fish				

*For more protein choices, refer to the appropriate sections in the high-response cost, high-yield section of the food guide.

**If you are a vegetarian, these foods can be used as your protein serving at meals.

Carbohydrates

Fruits (Raw)	Non-Starchy Vegetables	Starchy Carbohydrates
Apple	Alfalfa sprouts	*Vegetables:*
Apricot	Arugula	Beans
Banana	Artichokes	Corn
Blackberries	Artichoke hearts	Lentils
Blueberries	Asparagus	Potato
Cherries	Bamboo shoots	Pumpkin
Grapefruit	Beans, green or yellow	Squash, winter
Grapes	Bean Sprouts	Sweet potato
Kiwifruit	Beets	Yams
Lemon	Beet greens	*Whole Grains:*
Lime	Broccoli	Amaranth
Mango	Brussels sprouts	Barley
Melon	Cabbage	Bulgur wheat
Nectarine	Carrots, raw	Corn grits
Orange	Cauliflower	Cream of Wheat
Papaya	Celery, raw	Farina
Peach	Collards	High-fiber cereals*
Pear	Cucumbers	Malt-O-Meal
Pineapple	Eggplant	Millet
Plum	Endive	Oat bran, cooked
Raspberries	Escarole	Oatmeal
Strawberries	Kale	Quinoa
Tangerine	Leeks	Rice, brown or wild
Tangelo	Lettuce	
Watermelon	Mushrooms	

* These include any cold cereal that contains more than 5 grams of fiber per serving. Refer to the section titled "Cereals, cold" on pages 184 to 195 of the guide.

Fruits (Raw)	Non-Starchy Vegetables	Starchy Carbohydrates
	Mustard greens	
	Okra, cooked	
	Onions	
	Parsley	
	Parsnips	
	Peas	
	Peppers, all varieties	
	Rutabaga	
	Shallots	
	Spinach	
	Squash, summer	
	Tomatoes	
	Turnips	
	Turnip greens	
	Watercress	
	Zucchini	

Fats

Flaxseed oil
Margarine, trans-free
Olive oil
Canola oil
Peanut oil
Safflower oil
Salad dressings or mayonnaise, reduced fat
Sesame oil
Sunflower-seed oil
Vegetable oils (nonhydrogenated)

Other Rapid Start Foods

Low-Fat Dairy (Milk and Milk Products)	Noncaloric Liquids and Beverages	Condiments
Cheese, reduced fat	Bouillon or broth, fat-free	Catsup (1 tablespoon)
Cottage cheese, low-fat	Club soda	Gelatin, sugar-free
Milk:	Diet sodas	Herbs and spices
1% low-fat milk	Coffee, brewed or instant	Horseradish
2% reduced-fat milk	Tea	Mustard
Buttermilk, reduced fat	Tea, herbal	Sugar substitutes (aspartame, sucralose)
Nonfat milk, reconstituted from instant with water	Water, bottled or tap	Taco sauce (3 tablespoons)
Skim milk		Vinegar, all varieties
Soy milk		
Yogurt, sugar-free		

How to Build Your Meals from the Rapid Start Lists

Constructing your meal plans from these lists is simple and straightforward, but I've made it easier for you by including two weeks of Rapid Start Menus in the next chapter. So that you get headed in the right direction now, here is an overview of the plan, broken down to the daily level of what to eat and when to eat it.

Breakfast
1 protein serving
1 starchy carbohydrate*

* Men: Add a starchy carbohydrate at lunch.

1 fruit
1 low-fat dairy
1 noncaloric beverage

Lunch

1 protein serving
2 non-starchy vegetables
1 fruit
1 low-fat dairy
1 noncaloric beverage

Dinner

1 protein serving
2 non-starchy vegetables
1 fat
1 noncaloric beverage

Snacks

Fruit (if not eaten with a meal)
Low-fat dairy (if not eaten with a meal)
Raw vegetables

Structured in this manner, your meals might look something like this:

- A sample breakfast might consist of a scrambled egg, high-fiber cereal, low-fat milk, and half a grapefruit.

- A sample lunch might consist of tuna; a generous salad of fresh lettuce and tomatoes with a reduced-fat salad dressing; and a ripe, juicy peach for dessert.

- A sample dinner might consist of roast beef, green beans, and steamed yellow squash, with low-fat, sugar-free fruit yogurt for dessert.

Using the Rapid Start Plan, you have a strategy in place to generate immediate weight loss—and create positive momentum for sustained losses toward your goal and on through to maintaining your weight loss. This is a chance to get things flowing your way so you can make some real progress. Once you have successfully completed 14 days of the Rapid Start Plan, you are now ready to move on to Stage 2.

STAGE 2:
THE HIGH-RESPONSE COST, HIGH-YIELD WEIGHT LOSS PLAN

Nutritionally, you get to switch gears and eat additional amounts of high-response cost, high-yield foods in Stage 2, including extra choices in the categories of vegetables, fruits, starchy carbohydrates, healthy fats, and condiments. In addition to the foods listed in the Rapid Start Plan, the specific foods you may reintroduce in Stage 2 include:

Fruits: fruit juices (unsweetened), frozen fruits (unsweetened), and fruits canned in juice or packed in water.

Nonstarchy vegetables: canned nonstarchy vegetables.

Soups: all soups listed in the high-response cost, high-yield section of the guide (pages 346–359). Soups make an excellent prelude to a meal. If you eat soup, you will feel full, and you will tend to eat less at your meals.

Whole grains: all cereals from the high-response cost, high-yield food lists; whole grain breads, muffins, and crackers; whole wheat and spinach pasta; all starchy carbohydrates listed in the high-response cost, high-yield sections of the food guide (pages 360–441).

Fats: nuts and seeds; reduced-fat peanut butter; any fat listed in the high-response cost, high-yield section of the food guide (pages 246–263).

Condiments: all condiments listed in the high-response cost, high-yield section of the guide. Don't go overboard on condiments; use them sparingly and in the amounts listed in the guide.

Thus, in Stage 2, you can select from any and all of the high-response cost, high-yield foods listed in the guide. This stage gives you more nutritional leeway than the Rapid Start Plan does, and you should stay with it until you reach your get-real weight.

Stage 2 creates greater metabolic control so that your body uses more calories for energy rather than for fat storage. This is because the foods you will eat are low in sugar and refined carbohydrates, as opposed to high-fat, high-sugar foods, which tend to instigate weight gain when eaten in excess. By avoiding the wrong kind of carbohydrates, namely sugary, processed foods, you gain a tremendous edge in managing your weight.

Here are important guidelines for following the High-Response Cost, High-Yield Weight Loss Plan:

1. Continue to eat three regular meals a day (breakfast, lunch, and dinner), as well as two daily snacks.

2. Continue to eat protein at each of your main meals because of its positive effect on metabolism and appetite suppression.

3. Eat unlimited amounts of nonstarchy vegetables (at least four or more servings of these vegetables, including salad vegetables, broccoli, cauliflower, green beans, and spinach) daily. Don't stuff yourself; just eat until you feel satisfied. Choose from raw, or cooked from fresh or frozen, or canned. You may select

from any and all of the non-starchy vegetables listed on pages 360 to 441 of the guide.

4. Increase your intake of starchy carbohydrates to two servings a day if you are a woman; three servings if you are a man.

5. Eat two servings of fruit daily. Remember, you can now choose from fruit juice (unsweetened), frozen fruit (unsweetened), or fruit packed in water or canned in its own juice. For a complete list, refer to pages 282 to 303 of the guide. But remember: For hunger suppression, fiber, and overall nutritional yield, it is preferable to select fresh fruits.

6. Eat two servings of low-fat dairy foods daily.

7. Choose from healthy, high-response cost fats, in the amounts specified: 1 tablespoon of oil, fats, or salad dressing; or 2 tablespoons of reduced-fat fats. Other allowable fats include nuts and seeds; these are listed on pages 246 to 263 of the guide, along with their correct serving size.

8. Drink 8 to 10 glasses of pure water daily.

9. Eat food only from the high-response cost, high-yield food lists. There is a huge variety of these foods, so again, consult the food

guide frequently to familiarize yourself with them.

10. Stay on this plan until you reach your get-real weight. If you reach a plateau or need to restart the food plan, you may go back on the Rapid Start Plan for no more than 14 days.

How to Build Your Meals from the Food Guide Lists

To plan your meals in this stage, follow the template below and use the food lists in the guide:

Breakfast
   1 protein serving
   1 starchy carbohydrate*
   1 serving of fruit juice
   1 low-fat dairy product
   1 noncaloric beverage

Lunch
   1 protein serving
   2 nonstarchy vegetables
   1 starchy carbohydrate
   1 fruit
   1 low-fat dairy product
   1 noncaloric beverage

* Men: Add a starchy carbohydrate at lunch or dinner.

Dinner
1 protein serving
2 or more nonstarchy vegetables
1 fat
1 noncaloric beverage

Snacks
Fruit (if not eaten with a meal)
Low-fat dairy product (if not eaten with a meal)
Raw vegetables

By way of example, your Stage 2 meals might look something like this:

- A sample breakfast might consist of turkey sausage, whole wheat toast, low-fat milk, and orange juice.

- A sample lunch might consist of vegetable soup, whole wheat crackers, baked chicken, and fruit cocktail (water-packed) for dessert.

- A sample dinner might consist of grilled salmon, stewed tomatoes, a large tossed salad with low-fat dressing, and nonfat, sugar-free fruit yogurt for dessert.

Stage 2 is very "livable," and you'll find 21 days of menus in the next chapter. These menus include a variety of foods and nutrients that are normally excluded on typical diets—foods that naturally promote positive changes in eating behavior. These foods are mostly "hunger suppressors" that help control your hunger to avert physiologically based cravings that you normally experience on restrictive diets. By following this plan, you will normalize your eating patterns, so that chaotic, mindless eating will become a thing of the past.

How Much to Eat: Portion Guidelines

The next important question that now must be answered is: Exactly how much should you eat each day of various types of foods?

You should refer to the high-response cost, high-yield food lists beginning on page 150 to determine serving sizes of allowable foods for all three stages of the food plan.

If you do not like the idea of weighing and measuring, however, what I recommend is a system of portion management that frees you from the obsessive need to constantly handle measuring utensils and food scales all day long. All you have to do is picture portions of food relative to the size of your hand, or to other everyday items. For example:

Food	Portion Size
Meat, fish, or poultry	The palm of your hand, your computer mouse, or a deck of cards
Vegetables	
Raw	Your fist
Cooked	Your hand when cupped
Starchy carbohydrates	
Cereal and cooked grains	Your hand when cupped
Serving of bread	1 slice or size of a computer disk
Bagel	½ bagel
English muffin	½ English muffin
Muffin	1 cupcake wrapper
Crackers	Refer to number of crackers listed in the food guide.
Legumes and other starchy vegetables	Your hand when cupped
Fruit	
Raw piece	Tennis ball
Canned (water or juice), or frozen	Your hand when cupped
Berries (raw or frozen), raw chopped fruit	Your fist
Dairy foods	
Milk and yogurt	Your fist
Cottage cheese	Your hand when cupped
Cheese	A pair of dice
Sandwich cheese	1 slice or size of a computer disk
Fats	
1 tablespoon of fats, oils, salad dressings, or nuts and seeds	Your thumb to the first joint, a teabag, or a walnut

STAGE 3:
ULTIMATE MAINTENANCE

When you reach your get-real weight, you have crossed the finish line. But this is not the end of the race. You must continue to manage your weight and place a high priority on keeping it off. Stage 3—Ultimate Maintenance—is about keeping your weight under control for a lifetime. So don't quit until you've gone the distance. If you stop short now, you'll throw out all the hard work you've done so far. Do what it takes to maintain your weight, and you'll keep your momentum going in the direction of permanent weight loss.

When you are nutritionally maintaining and managing your weight, the good news is that you can eat slightly more food, provided you stay active and exercise on a very regular basis.

This plan liberalizes the number of servings you may eat, mainly from the high-response cost, high-yield food lists. As your guide in this regard, simply use the following serving allotments to assist you in your food planning; and post it on your refrigerator door:

- Protein and protein substitutes: 3 servings
- Nonstarchy vegetables: as many as you like (don't skimp here)
- Starchy carbohydrates: 3 to 4 servings
- Fruits: 3 to 4 servings

- Low-fat dairy products: 2 to 3 servings
- Healthy fats: 1 to 2 servings

As a resource to help you, please refer to the sample Ultimate Maintenance menus provided in the next chapter. I've provided you with a week's worth of menus, consisting of 1,800 to 2,000 calories a day. You do not have to eat exactly as these menus specify; simply use them to direct your own food planning. But please take them seriously, along with all the other tools and techniques you are using to create the level of health you want and deserve.

When following the Ultimate Maintenance Plan, you must continue to exercise a degree of self-control over your eating. While no food is really off-limits, you must learn to refuse those foods you don't handle well and choose better ones. Don't eat a food that is a problem for you, because it may trigger a full-blown binge. As you follow this maintenance plan, please stay flexible. If you want to eat cake and ice cream at your child's birthday party, then by all means, have it. But don't obsess over it and feel guilty. Obsessing over what to eat and what not to eat will only sabotage your maintenance efforts, making it more difficult to maintain your weight loss. Your life should allow for some occasional treats, as long as you keep from bingeing or returning to a pattern of free-for-all eating.

Tools for Maintenance

Before leaving this chapter, let me be straight with you: The vast majority of people who eventually reach their target weight do not retain that goal. Did you know that there are just as many people trying to lose weight as there are people who are considered obese? The rate of obesity and the number of "dieters" in America are climbing in parallel!

It's like this: You have a long history of learned and overlearned behaviors—in the way you eat, the way you think, the way you feel, and the way you act—so overlearned, in fact, that they have become second-nature habits to which you instinctually drift when under stress or pressure, or whenever you're not actively managing your weight, your health, and your life with a great degree of awareness and programming. Second-nature habits do not change quickly. That's why there is so much truth in the familiar saying *Old habits die hard.*

But STOP right here: This does not have to be true for you. If you have applied seven keys to your life, you now know something about why you eat and why you are overweight, and what you can do about it. Because knowledge is power, you have the wherewithal to get on the right track and head in a different direction.

When you maintain your weight, there is still a lot of work ahead. It takes effort, action, and commitment to shake free of your past negative programming. There is still a part of you that is comfortable in these old ways of being and doing, and it is that part of you that perhaps doesn't want things to change and will put up a good fight to resist it.

Having reached your goal weight, you may feel that you can handle things now and that you can let down your guard. But as I have often stated, *weight is managed, not cured.* You must never relax your watchfulness over your thoughts, feelings, and actions. Your guiding objective must always be to manage your weight, and indeed, your overall health, with a keen sense of alertness.

As you prepare to go forward into the future, let me encourage you to look back at the considerable work you did in *The Ultimate Weight Solution.* It's perfectly acceptable and, in fact, a good idea to "re-audit" your internal dialogue, emotional eating, stress, environment, nutrition habits, exercise, and support level. Maybe it helps to reexamine yourself in these areas in two, four, six months, or a year or more from now.

For right now, I'd like you to push to express yourself in specific terms: how and why it is important to you to maintain your weight loss. Perhaps because you reduced your intake of low-response cost foods and now eat more wholesome, high-response cost foods *in the amount your body needs for optimum functioning,* you love the physical and mental stamina you now enjoy. Maybe you realize that for you to keep your weight off, you must maintain certain good habits such as eating three structured meals a day, not skipping breakfast, planning ahead for what you will eat, and not eating food right out of its package. Maybe you now see the value of checking the number of calories or the correct serving sizes of food if you are unsure about what or how much to eat. Or possibly you recognize that staying active keeps you fit and makes you feel younger, more energetic, and less tempted to choose foods that would tear down this newfound physical vitality.

All of these sorts of descriptions should be expressed in what I call *Your Maintenance Management Formula.* This can serve as a written reminder of what you have personally learned about losing weight so that if your weight should ever start inching upward again, you have a written, detailed description of what has helped you. This description, or formula, can also help you prepare in advance for various danger zones, or barriers, that lie in wait, so that you know how to handle them and then hang on to what you have worked so hard to achieve.

Let's start writing your maintenance management formula right now. All you have to do is fill out the sheet below by responding to the questions provided. Be detailed and thorough in your answers.

My Personal Maintenance Management Formula

Write five positive statements about why you like being at your get-real weight:

1. _____

2. _____

3. _____

4. _____

5. _____

Write a short paragraph below describing how it feels to have pulled this off:

_____

_____

_____

_____

_____

List five reasons why you do not return to being overweight:

1. _____

2. _____

3. _____

4. _____

5. _____

Make a list of the behaviors that have worked well for you. Use as much space as you need. This is an important opportunity to remind yourself of the programming that has helped you. (These behaviors might include not eating too fast, not eating while watching TV, eating more fruits and vegetables, selecting low-fat foods, or refusing to eat sugary foods; or this list could include habits such as exercising, keeping junk food out of your house, using incompatible substitutes to fight off eating urges and impulses, or practicing positive, rational self-talk. If you need reminding, reread the relevant-to-you parts of *The Ultimate Weight Solution.)*

1. _____

2. _____

3. _____

4. _____

5. _____

6. _____

7. _____

8. _____

9. _____

10. _____

11. _____

12. _____

13. _____

14. _____

15. _____

16. _____

17. _____

18. _____

19. _____

20. _____

Make a list of what you see as your greatest barriers to maintaining your weight. Maybe these are bingeing when you are under stress or feeling fatigued. Perhaps you still think of yourself as overweight and unworthy, which puts you at a very high risk of regaining the fat you never psychologically shed. Or possibly you think you will relax your effort and slide back into some poor eating or exercise habits. Be specific and as concrete as you can when describing what you see as your toughest barriers up ahead.

1. _____

2. _____

3. _____

4. _____

5. _____

6. _____

7. _____

8. _____

9. _____

10. _____

For each barrier you identified and described, write a strategy or strategies for how you will overcome it. (If you want to, skip ahead and read through the next chapter—it contains some very effective strategies for weight loss and for weight maintenance—then come back here when you're finished.) Map out how you will handle this barrier in a rational, manageable fashion, without making foolish choices. Don't let yourself off the hook here. This is an important part of advanced planning so that you will not be hijacked by situations in your life.

1. _____

2. _____

3. _____

4. _____

5. _____

6. _____

7. _____

8. _____

9. _____

10. _____

Describe how you plan to "self-monitor" your weight, and how often, from here on out to make sure that it is not creeping upward again. Failure to self-monitor is one of the top reasons why people allow their weight to pile back on. Will you weigh yourself once a week? Will you measure your waistline? Will you check how your clothes fit, and whether they're getting too snug again in places? In the space below, write down how you will self-monitor, and how often.

Method(s) of self-monitoring:

_____

Frequency of self-monitoring:

_____

You should give yourself an acceptable weight-gain range, say five pounds or so, that you will not let yourself exceed. But if your weight does exceed that range, you must take action. What exactly will you do if your weight gets out of bounds? Get back on your calorie-controlled food plan? Start keeping your personalized food journal again? Reread and apply the seven keys? Work on more effective and meaningful accountability? Ramp up your exercise program? In the space below, describe some specific steps that you will have to take to regain control (draw from what helped you before).

Steps for dealing with weight gain:

_____

_____

_____

_____

_____

By answering the questions above and doing this work, you now have a working formula of exactly what you need to do in order to manage your weight for the long haul. Understand that once you create a proactive plan like this, you take a crucial step toward maintaining your focus and momentum and you pave the way for more success.

The Ultimate Weight Solution Menus

To make meal planning easy and workable for you, I've included several menu plans for all three stages: 14 days of Rapid Start menus; 21 days of High-Response Cost, High-Yield Weight Loss Plan menus; and 7 days of Ultimate Maintenance menus. There is also a sample vegetarian menu at the end of this chapter if you require help in figuring out such a food plan.

Initially, you might be more comfortable following a prescribed menu because it removes so much of the iffyness involved in meal planning and helps ease the transition into new ways of eating. With these menus, remember to refer to the food guide for serving sizes, or rely on the portion management guidelines I discussed in the previous chapter.

STAGE 1:
THE RAPID START PLAN:
14 DAYS OF SAMPLE MENUS

The Rapid Start menus supply an average of 1,100 to 1,200 calories a day, with approximately 30 percent of those calories from protein, 45 percent from carbohydrates, and 25 percent from fat. On average, the menus furnish 30 grams of fiber a day. These menus are also low in sugar, sodium, saturated fat, and cholesterol.

Day 1

Breakfast
1 serving high-fiber cereal (e.g., All-Bran, Bran Buds, Fruit & Fibre, or Fiber One)
1 cup low-fat, skim, or soy milk
1 egg, scrambled (or two egg whites, scrambled)
Strawberries (or other seasonal fruit)
Coffee or tea

Snack
Pear

Lunch
Water-packed tuna with one sliced tomato served on a generous bed of lettuce, chopped

green peppers, radishes, and other salad
vegetables
2 tablespoons low-calorie Italian salad dressing

Snack
1 cup low-fat, sugar free plain yogurt mixed
with 1 tablespoon sugar-free apricot preserves

Dinner
Roasted chicken breast
Asparagus spears, steamed or boiled
Summer squash (crookneck), steamed or boiled

Day 2
Breakfast
Turkey breakfast sausage, 2 links
Oat bran cereal, cooked
½ grapefruit
Coffee or tea

Snack
Banana smoothie: 1 frozen banana blended
with 1 cup low-fat milk or soy milk and
artificial sweetener (optional)

Lunch
Mediterranean salad: ½ cup garbanzo beans on
generous bed of mixed greens and chopped
salad vegetables

1 tablespoon olive oil mixed with balsamic
vinegar to taste

Snack
1 cup low-fat, sugar-free yogurt
(any flavor)

Dinner
Grilled salmon
Broccoli, steamed or boiled
Carrots, cooked

Day 3

Breakfast
Fat-free ham, 2 slices
Low-fat granola mixed with 1 cup low-fat,
sugar-free yogurt (any flavor)
Orange
Coffee or tea

Snack
Apple

Lunch
Chicken Caesar salad: cubed grilled chicken
breast, shredded Romaine lettuce, with an
assortment of other chopped salad
vegetables, 2 tablespoons reduced-fat
Caesar salad dressing

Snack
 ½ cup low-fat cottage cheese, with baby carrots
    and other cut-up raw vegetables

Dinner
 Beef tenderloin
 Green peas, boiled
 Cauliflower, steamed or boiled

Day 4
Breakfast
 1 egg, scrambled
 Oatmeal, cooked
 1 cup low-fat, skim, or soy milk
 Cantaloupe (or other seasonal fruit)
 Coffee or tea

Snack
 Fresh berries

Lunch
 Black bean chili: ½ cup cooked black
    beans, 2 tablespoons salsa, 2 tablespoons
    chopped onions, ½ cup stewed
    tomatoes

Snack
 1 cup low-fat, sugar-free yogurt
    (any flavor)

Dinner

Roasted turkey breast
Brussels sprouts, steamed or boiled
Tossed salad
2 tablespoons low-fat French salad dressing

Day 5

Breakfast

2 egg whites, scrambled
1 serving high-fiber cereal
1 cup low-fat, skim, or soy milk
Raspberries (or other seasonal fruit)
Coffee or tea

Snack

Cut up assorted raw vegetables
1 ounce reduced-fat Swiss cheese

Lunch

Grilled chicken breast
Shredded cabbage tossed with 2 tablespoons
    low-fat cole slaw dressing

Snack

Pear

Dinner

Baked Cornish game hen
Carrots, cooked
Kale, cooked

Day 6

Breakfast
Turkey bacon, 2 slices
Oat bran cereal, cooked
Nectarine or peach
Coffee or tea

Snack
1 cup low-fat, sugar-free yogurt

Lunch
Broiled hamburger patty, extra lean
Tossed salad
2 tablespoons low-fat salad dressing
1 cup raw grapes

Snack
½ cup low-fat cottage cheese with cut-up raw
   vegetables

Dinner
Baked cod or other whitefish
French-style green beans, boiled
Yellow squash, steamed or boiled

Day 7

Breakfast
1 egg, scrambled
Corn grits, cooked

Honeydew melon
Coffee or tea

Snack
Apple

Lunch
Cooked eggplant topped with ½ cup tomato
  sauce, ½ cup cubed tofu, and 1 ounce of
  grated fat-free Mozzarella cheese
Tossed salad with 1 tablespoon olive oil and
  balsamic vinegar

Snack
1 cup plain low-fat, sugar-free yogurt with
  1 tablespoon sugar-free strawberry preserves

Dinner
Roasted pork tenderloin
Cabbage, boiled
Okra slices, boiled

Day 8

Breakfast
Turkey sausage, 2 links
1 serving high-fiber cereal
1 cup low-fat, skim, or soy milk
½ grapefruit
Coffee or tea

Snack
Sliced cucumbers dipped in ½ cup low-fat
cottage cheese

Lunch
Vegetarian lunch: ½cup kidney beans topped
with 2 tablespoons salsa
Artichoke, steamed, leaves dipped in
2 tablespoons low-fat Italian dressing
Raw baby carrots

Snack
Pear

Dinner
Eye of the round
Tomatoes, stewed
Cauliflower, steamed or boiled

Day 9
Breakfast
Turkey bacon, 2 slices
Smoothie: Blend 1 cup low-fat, skim, or soy
milk with berries
Coffee or tea

Snack
Apple

Lunch
Broiled hamburger patty, extra lean
Spinach salad: chopped fresh spinach, ½ cup
  white beans, 2 tablespoons chopped onion,
  2 tablespoons chopped red pepper, and
  1 tablespoon olive oil with balsamic vinegar
  to taste

Snack
1 cup low-fat, sugar-free yogurt (any flavor)

Dinner
Baked chicken breast
Yellow snap beans, boiled
Fresh tomato, sliced

Day 10

Breakfast
2 egg whites, scrambled
Shredded Wheat
1 cup low-fat, skim, or soy milk
Banana, sliced
Coffee or tea

Snack
Plum

Lunch
Three bean salad: ½ cup garbanzo beans,
  ¼ cup kidney beans, ½ cup cooked green

beans, 2 tablespoons chopped onion,
2 tablespoons chopped roasted red peppers,
and 2 tablespoons low-fat Italian dressing—
served on a bed of Romaine lettuce

Snack
1 cup low-fat, sugar-free yogurt (any flavor)

Dinner
Steamed Alaskan king crab
Mixed vegetables, steamed (broccoli, zucchini,
yellow squash)

Day 11

Breakfast
1 egg, poached
Oatmeal, cooked
Orange
Coffee or tea

Snack
Fruit smoothie: 1 cup low-fat, skim, or soy milk
blended with berries, with artificial sweetener
(optional)

Lunch
Ground turkey, lean, broiled or grilled
Grilled portabella mushroom
Fresh tomato, sliced, topped with 1 ounce
reduced-fat feta cheese

Snack
   Cut-up raw vegetables

Dinner
   Grilled salmon
   Broccoli and cauliflower medley,
      steamed
   Tossed salad with 1 tablespoon olive oil

Day 12
Breakfast
   Turkey sausage, 2 links
   1 serving high-fiber cereal
   1 cup low-fat, skim, or soy milk
   Raspberries (or other seasonal fruit)
   Coffee or tea

Snack
   Pear

Lunch
   Spinach and shrimp salad: cooked shrimp,
      2 tablespoons chopped onion, 1 sliced
      tomato, raw spinach, and 2 tablespoons
      low-fat mayonnaise

Snack
   Cut-up raw vegetables dipped in ½ cup low-fat
      cottage cheese

Dinner
Grilled sirloin steak
Broccoli, steamed
Yellow squash, steamed or boiled

Day 13

Breakfast
2 egg whites, scrambled
Cream of Wheat cereal
1 cup melon balls (or other seasonal fruit)
Coffee or tea

Snack
Orange

Lunch
Low-fat chef salad: 2 slices reduced-fat ham,
1 ounce low-fat/low-sodium cheddar cheese,
chopped lettuce and assorted cut-up salad
vegetables, 2 tablespoons low-fat French
dressing

Snack
1 cup low-fat, sugar-free yogurt (any flavor)

Dinner
Grilled tuna steak
Yellow snap beans, steamed or boiled
Asparagus, steamed or boiled

Day 14

Breakfast
Turkey sausage, 2 links
1 serving high-fiber cereal
1 cup low-fat, skim, or soy milk
Sliced peaches
Coffee or tea

Snack
1 cup low-fat, sugar-free yogurt (any flavor)

Lunch
Grilled chicken breast
French-style green beans, boiled
Baked potato, medium

Snack
Banana

Dinner
Roast beef
Stewed tomatoes
Tossed salad with 2 tablespoons low-fat blue
   cheese dressing

STAGE 2: THE HIGH-RESPONSE COST, HIGH-YIELD WEIGHT LOSS PLAN: 21 DAYS OF SAMPLE MENUS

The High-Response Cost, High-Yield Weight Loss menus supply an average of 1,200 calories a day, with approximately 30 percent of those calories from protein, 47 percent from carbohydrates, and 23 percent from fat. On average, the menus furnish 25 to 30 grams of fiber a day and are low in sugar, sodium, saturated fat, and cholesterol.

Day 1
Breakfast
  1 egg, poached
  Oat bran, cooked
  1 cup low-fat, skim, or soy milk
  Banana
  Coffee or tea

Snack
  Apple

Lunch
  Water-packed tuna
  1 cup vegetable soup
  Salad greens and sliced tomato with
    2 tablespoons reduced-fat salad dressing
  Whole wheat roll (medium)

Snack
1 cup low-fat, sugar-free yogurt
   (any flavor)

Dinner
Sirloin steak
Broccoli, steamed or boiled
Green beans, boiled

Day 2

Breakfast
1 egg, poached
1 slice multigrain bread
Raspberries (or other seasonal fresh fruit)
Coffee or tea

Snack
Low-fat, skim, or soy milk or low-fat, sugar-free
   yogurt (any flavor)

Lunch
Steamed shrimp
Tossed salad with 1 tablespoon olive oil
   vinaigrette dressing
½ cup water-packed pineapple

Snack
Cut-up raw vegetables dipped in ½ cup low-fat
   cottage cheese

Dinner
Turkey breast
Stewed tomatoes
Summer squash, steamed
½ cup brown rice

Day 3
Breakfast
Turkey sausage, 2 links
Corn grits, cooked
½ grapefruit
Coffee or tea

Snack
1 cup low-fat, sugar-free yogurt (any flavor)

Lunch
1 cup vegetarian chili
Cut-up raw vegetables dipped in 2 tablespoons
reduced-fat ranch salad dressing

Snack
Smoothie: low-fat, skim, or soy milk blended
with frozen strawberries

Dinner
Grilled chicken breast
Kale, boiled
½ cup mashed sweet potatoes

Day 4

Breakfast
2 egg whites, scrambled
Bran muffin
1 cup orange juice
Coffee or tea

Snack
Low-fat, sugar-free coffee, vanilla, or lemon
yogurt

Lunch
Open-faced turkey sandwich: turkey breast,
1 slice reduced-fat Swiss cheese, 1 slice
whole wheat bread, lettuce and tomato slices,
and 1 tablespoon reduced-fat mayonnaise

Snack
Apple

Dinner
Lean pork roast
Spinach, steamed
Tossed salad with 1 tablespoon reduced-fat
salad dressing

Day 5

Breakfast
Turkey ham (lean), 2 slices
1 serving high-fiber cereal

1 cup low-fat, skim, or soy milk
Blueberries (or other seasonal fruit)
Coffee or tea

Snack
Smoothie: low-fat, skim, or soy milk blended
with frozen unsweetened peaches

Lunch
Pita sandwich: canned salmon, whole wheat
pita bread, chopped celery, sliced tomato, and
1 tablespoon reduced-fat mayonnaise
Raw carrots

Snack
1 cup low-sodium vegetable juice

Dinner
Roasted Cornish game hen
Summer squash, steamed or boiled
Tossed salad with 1 tablespoon reduced-fat
salad dressing

Day 6
Breakfast
2 egg whites, scrambled
1 serving high-fiber cereal
1 cup low-fat, skim, or soy milk
½ grapefruit
Coffee or tea

Snack

Diced mango (or other seasonal fruit)

Lunch

Greek salad: 1 ounce reduced-fat feta cheese,
½ cup garbanzo beans, Romaine lettuce,
2 tablespoons chopped onion, 3 black olives
(pitted), and 2 tablespoons reduced-fat
Caesar salad dressing
Whole wheat bread (optional)

Snack

Raw baby carrots and other raw cut-up
vegetables

Dinner

Grilled swordfish
Turnip greens, boiled
½ cup Acorn squash, mashed

Day 7

Breakfast

2 slices turkey bacon
½ small-diameter (2.5"–3") whole wheat bagel
Cantaloupe
Coffee or tea

Snack

Smoothie: 1 cup low-fat, skim, or soy milk
blended with a frozen banana

Lunch
Steamed shrimp, cole slaw (made with
2 tablespoons reduced-fat cole slaw
dressing), sliced tomato, cocktail sauce

Snack
Cut-up raw vegetables
1 ounce reduced-fat cheddar cheese

Dinner
Lean ground beef
Mixed vegetables
Whole wheat pasta with nonfat spaghetti sauce

Day 8

Breakfast
2 egg whites, scrambled
Multigrain oatmeal, cooked
1 cup low-fat, skim, or soy milk
1 cup sliced fresh peaches
Coffee or tea

Snack
Apple
1 cup low-fat, sugar-free yogurt (any flavor)

Lunch
Canned salmon, served on salad greens with
1 tomato, sliced, and 2 tablespoons reduced-
fat salad dressing

Snack
Fresh cut-up vegetables

Dinner
Roasted pork tenderloin
Baked sweet potato, medium
Broccoli, steamed

Day 9

Breakfast
1 egg, poached
1 slice multigrain bread
Raspberries (or other seasonal fruit)
Coffee or tea

Snack
1 ounce reduced-fat cheese
Whole grain crackers

Lunch
Baked chicken
1 cup vegetable soup
½ cup fruit cocktail, water-packed

Snack
1 cup low-sodium vegetable juice

Dinner
Baked turkey breast
Green peas
Stewed tomatoes

Day 10
Breakfast
Turkey bacon, 2 strips
1 serving high-fiber cereal
1 cup low-fat, skim, or soy milk
½ grapefruit
Coffee or tea

Snack
Pear

Lunch
1 cup vegetarian chili
Broccoli, steamed

Snack
Cut-up raw vegetables with ½ cup low-fat
cottage cheese

Dinner
Chicken breast, grilled
½ cup corn, cooked
Tossed salad with 1 tablespoon olive oil, mixed
with balsamic vinegar

Day 11

Breakfast
Turkey ham (lean), 2 slices
Smoothie: 1 cup low-fat, skim, or soy milk
   blended with 1 cup strawberries
Coffee or tea

Snack
1 cup low-fat, sugar-free coffee, vanilla, or
   lemon yogurt

Lunch
Tuna sandwich: water-packed tuna,
   2 slices whole wheat bread, lettuce,
   2 slices tomato, and 1 tablespoon reduced-fat
   mayonnaise
Raw baby carrots

Snack
Apple

Dinner
Lamb loin roast
Cauliflower, steamed or boiled
Spinach, steamed or boiled
1½ teaspoons trans-free margarine for
   vegetables

Day 12

Breakfast
1 egg, hard-boiled
1 serving high-fiber cereal
1 cup low-fat, skim, or soy milk
Blueberries
Coffee or tea

Snack
Smoothie: soy milk blended with frozen
  banana

Lunch
Pita sandwich: canned salmon, 1 whole wheat
  pita bread, 2 tablespoons chopped celery, and
  1 tablespoon reduced-fat mayonnaise
1 cup tomato soup (condensed), prepared with
  water

Snack
Cut-up raw vegetables

Dinner
Roasted Cornish game hen
Yellow squash, cooked
Tossed salad
1 tablespoon reduced-fat dressing

Day 13
Breakfast
2 egg whites, scrambled
Bran muffin
½ grapefruit
Coffee or tea

Snack
1 cup nonfat, sugar-free yogurt (any flavor)

Lunch
Greek salad: 1 ounce reduced-fat feta cheese,
Romaine lettuce, ½ cup garbanzo beans,
2 tablespoons chopped onion, 3 black olives,
and 2 tablespoons reduced-fat Caesar salad
dressing

Snack
Apple

Dinner
Grilled swordfish
½ cup mashed butternut squash
Turnip greens, steamed or boiled

Day 14
Breakfast
1 egg, poached
½ whole wheat English muffin

Cantaloupe
Coffee or tea

Snack
1 ounce reduced-fat cheese
Ry-krisp crackers

Lunch
Steamed shrimp
Tossed salad, 2 tablespoons reduced-fat salad
 dressing

Snack
Grapes

Dinner
Reduced-carbohydrate "spaghetti": meat
 sauce made with lean ground beef and
 ½ cup nonfat spaghetti sauce served over
 cooked spaghetti squash
Italian vegetables, cooked from frozen

Day 15
Breakfast
2 egg whites, scrambled
Low-fat granola mixed into 1 cup low-fat,
 sugar-free yogurt (any flavor)
1 cup grapefruit juice
Coffee or tea

Snack
Pear

Lunch
Turkey chef salad: reduced-fat turkey ham,
  1 ounce reduced-fat Swiss cheese, chopped
  tomato served over a generous bed of lettuce,
  with 2 tablespoons low-fat French dressing

Snack
1 cup low-sodium vegetable juice

Dinner
Broiled scallops
½ cup corn, cooked
French-style green beans, steamed or boiled

Day 16

Breakfast
1 egg, hard-boiled
Smoothie: 1 cup low-fat, skim, or soy milk
  blended with frozen unsweetened blueberries
Coffee or tea

Snack
1 cup low-fat, sugar-free yogurt (any flavor)

Lunch
Beef patty, extra lean, broiled
1 whole wheat roll

Cut-up raw vegetables
2 tablespoons light ranch salad dressing for
vegetables
Stewed tomatoes

Snack
Banana

Dinner
Roasted turkey breast
½ cup brown rice
Broccoli and cauliflower, steamed or boiled

Day 17
Breakfast
French toast: 1 slice whole wheat bread,
dipped in 1 egg beaten with ¼ cup
low-fat, skim, or soy milk, fried on nonstick
skillet
2 tablespoons sugar-free syrup
1 cup orange juice
Coffee or tea

Snack
Smoothie: ¾ cup low-fat, skim, or soy milk
blended with 1 frozen banana

Lunch
Chicken Caesar salad: grilled chicken breast,
Romaine lettuce, sliced tomato, and

2 tablespoons reduced-fat Caesar salad
dressing

Snack

1 cup low-fat, sugar-free yogurt (any flavor)

Dinner

Baked ham, extra lean
Baked sweet potato, medium
Collard greens, boiled or steamed

Day 18

Breakfast

Turkey sausage, 2 links
1 serving high-fiber cereal
1 cup low-fat, skim, or soy milk
Blueberries
Coffee or tea

Snack

1 cup low-sodium vegetable or tomato juice

Lunch

Reduced-fat burrito: ½ cup black beans,
    1 corn tortilla, 2 tablespoons salsa,
    3 tablespoons chopped onion, and
    1 tablespoon jalapenos
1 large tomato, sliced

Snack
½ cup fruit cocktail, water-packed
1 cup low-fat, sugar-free yogurt (any flavor)

Dinner
Broiled sirloin steak
Tossed salad with 1 tablespoon salad dressing
Mixed vegetables, steamed or boiled

Day 19

Breakfast
1 egg, scrambled
Grits
1 cup grapefruit juice
Coffee or tea

Snack
Cut-up raw vegetables dipped in ½ cup low-fat
cottage cheese

Lunch
Chef salad: reduced-fat ham, 1 ounce reduced-
fat cheddar cheese, salad greens, chopped
red bell pepper, and 1 tablespoon olive oil,
mixed with balsamic vinegar

Snack
Strawberries

Dinner
Grilled salmon
½ cup lima beans, boiled
Summer squash, steamed or boiled

Day 20

Breakfast
1 egg, poached
1 slice whole wheat toast
Banana
Coffee or tea

Snack
1 ounce reduced-fat cheese
Apple

Lunch
1 cup bean soup
Tossed salad
2 tablespoons reduced-fat salad dressing

Snack
1 cup low-fat, sugar-free yogurt (any flavor)

Dinner
Roast beef
½ cup mashed potatoes
Green beans, steamed or boiled
Zucchini, steamed or broiled

Day 21

Breakfast
Turkey sausage, 2 links
Oatmeal, cooked
Blackberries (or other seasonal fruit)
Coffee or tea

Snack
1 cup low-fat, sugar-free yogurt (any flavor)

Lunch
Grilled chicken breast
Brussels sprouts, steamed or boiled
Carrots, boiled
1½ teaspoons trans-free margarine

Snack
½ cup pineapple packed in its own juice with
½ cup low-fat cottage cheese

Dinner
Baked ham, lean
Cabbage, boiled
½ acorn squash, baked
1½ teaspoons trans-free margarine

Stage 3: Ultimate Maintenance Plan: 7 Days of Sample Menus

With the Ultimate Maintenance Plan, you increase your calories to 1,800 to 2,000 calories a day, as well as add more servings of high-response cost, high-yield foods.

Day 1
Breakfast
1 egg, scrambled
1 bagel, with 1 tablespoon nonfat cream cheese
1 baked apple, medium
1 cup low-fat, skim, or soy milk
Coffee or tea

Snack
Pear

Lunch
Sandwich: reduced-fat luncheon meat,
    1 tablespoon reduced-fat mayonnaise, slice
    of tomato and 2 lettuce leaves, and 2 slices
    whole grain bread
½ cup baked beans
½ cup cole slaw

Snack
1 cup low-fat, sugar-free yogurt (any flavor)
Peach (or other seasonal fruit)

Dinner
Sirloin steak
Tossed salad
1 tablespoon nonfat salad dressing
Vegetable medley: broccoli, cauliflower, carrots,
   summer squash—boiled or steamed

Day 2

Breakfast
Turkey sausage, 2 links
Fat-free granola
1 slice raisin bread toast
2 teaspoons low-sugar jelly
Berries
1 cup low-fat, sugar-free, fruit-flavored yogurt
   (any flavor)
Coffee or tea

Snack
Apple

Lunch
Tuna salad: water-packed tuna, one celery
   stalk (chopped), 1 tablespoon sweet
   relish, 1 tablespoon mayonnaise, and
   quartered tomato, served on a large bed
   of lettuce
1 serving of whole grain crackers
Orange

Snack

Smoothie: low-fat, skim, or soy milk blended with 1 cup frozen unsweetened strawberries

Dinner

Baked chicken breast
½ cup brown rice
Broccoli, steamed or boiled
Stewed tomatoes
Fruit cocktail, in natural juice

Day 3

Breakfast

Turkey bacon, 2 strips
Oatmeal or other cooked whole grain cereal
Banana
1 cup low-fat, skim, or soy milk
Coffee or tea

Snack

Nectarine or other seasonal fresh fruit

Lunch

Peanut butter sandwich: 2 tablespoons reduced-fat peanut butter and 2 slices whole grain bread
1 cup vegetable soup
2 cups cut-up raw cauliflower and broccoli with cherry tomatoes
Peach

Snack
1 cup low-fat, sugar-free, fruit-flavored yogurt
   (any flavor)
Orange

Dinner
Grilled salmon
½ cup mashed sweet potatoes
Tossed salad
1 tablespoon nonfat salad dressing

Day 4

Breakfast
1 egg, scrambled (or 2 egg whites, scrambled)
Grits
1 slice whole wheat toast
1 cup orange juice
Coffee or tea

Snack
Smoothie: 1 cup low-fat, skim, or soy milk
   blended with frozen unsweetened fruit

Lunch
Baked chicken on:
1 chopped tomato on a large bed of salad
   greens
2 tablespoons reduced-fat French salad
   dressing
1 serving of whole wheat crackers

Snack

Apple

Dinner

Pork loin roast
Turnip greens, boiled
½ acorn squash, baked
Green beans, boiled
½ cup unsweetened applesauce

Day 5

Breakfast

2 egg whites, scrambled
1 bran muffin
1 serving high-fiber cereal
1 cup lowfat, skim, or soy milk
½ grapefruit
Coffee or tea

Snack

Dried fruit
2 tablespoons dry roasted peanuts

Lunch

Chef salad: reduced-fat ham, 1 tomato
(chopped), salad greens, and 2 tablespoons
reduced-fat French dressing
1 whole wheat dinner roll, medium

Snack
  Cut-up raw vegetables
  3 tablespoons nonfat vegetable dip

Dinner
  Baked turkey
  ½ cup mashed sweet potatoes
  Mixed vegetables, steamed or boiled
  ½ cup frozen low-fat yogurt
  Blueberries

Day 6

Breakfast
  1 egg, poached
  ½ English muffin
  Fresh chopped fruit
  1 cup nonfat, sugar-free, fruit-flavored yogurt
    (any flavor)
  Coffee or tea

Snack
  1 cup low-sodium vegetable juice
  1 slice low-fat cheese

Lunch
  1 cup bean soup
  Tossed salad
  1 tablespoon salad dressing, any flavor

Cornbread muffin, medium
Apple

Snack
3 cups air-popped popcorn
Orange

Dinner
Baked or broiled scallops
½ cup brown rice
Mixed vegetables, steamed or boiled
Sliced cooked beets

Day 7
Breakfast
1 egg, cooked (or 2 egg whites, scrambled)
1 slice raisin bread toast
½ cup pineapple chunks, in natural juice
1 cup low-fat, skim, or soy milk
Coffee or tea

Snack
Orange

Lunch
Broiled hamburger patty, lean
1 whole wheat bun
Garnishes: 1 slice onion, 1 slice tomato, 1 leaf
  lettuce

2 teaspoons mustard, 2 teaspoons catsup
Cabbage, boiled

Dinner
Baked ham
½ cup mashed potatoes
Asparagus, steamed

SAMPLE VEGETARIAN MENU

If you are a vegetarian, servings of meat can be replaced with any of the following: ½ cup beans/
legumes (such as kidney beans); ½ cup tofu (great in
pasta recipes); veggie burgers or soy burgers (available
as frozen); meatless or soy hot dogs; or foods such as
soy bacon, soy ham, soy sausage, and texturized soy
protein, which resembles ground beef (this can be
used to replace ground beef in various recipes). To replace dairy, use soy milk and soy cheeses. Thus, a
good weight-management menu for a strict vegetarian
would look something like this:

Breakfast
Soy bacon, 2 strips
1 serving high-fiber cereal
1 cup soy milk
1 fresh fruit

Snack
Pieces of celery filled with 2 tablespoons reduced-
fat peanut butter

Lunch
Large vegetarian chef salad made with a variety of mixed greens and salad vegetables, 2 slices of soy ham (diced), 1 ounce of soy cheese (diced), and tossed with 2 tablespoons of fat-free dressing

Snack
Soy smoothie: blend one cup soy milk with 1 frozen banana, ¼ teaspoon vanilla, and some artificial sweetener

Dinner
Tofu pasta dish: ½ cup cooked whole wheat pasta, ½ cup nonfat, sugar-free spaghetti sauce, with seasonings, and ½ cup tofu (crumbled over pasta)
1 cup of cooked mixed vegetables, Italian style

For more menus, please log on to www. drphil.com, where you'll have an opportunity to participate in online support communities and learn valuable guidelines on weight loss and weight maintenance.

FOUR

No-Fail Solutions: Food Strategies for Success

For successful weight management, you must have in place particular plans for dealing with what you know will be the weakest spots in your efforts. Your particular weakness could be poor behavioral control, eating away from home, poor eating habits in general, splurging on vacations or during holidays, or overeating in response to stress. For example, do you typically drop in front of the TV with a bag of chips when you get home from work? In social situations, do you eat and drink far more than what is in keeping with your weight management goals? At restaurants, or on vacations, do you eat to your heart's content, without thinking about what this might do to your waistline?

Whatever your trouble spot is—and I'm sure you already know it—you need some strategies, skills, and solutions that will allow you to stop sabotaging yourself and your weight. This chapter is designed to give you those skills, and help you consider ways in which you can begin to make each of them more of a daily element in your life. The more you try to apply these things, the more successful your weight management efforts will be. So start now. Here are more than a hundred different ways you can change what is going on in your day-to-day life, and change your weight in the process.

BEHAVIORAL STRATEGIES

You may get tired of hearing it, but I'll never get tired of repeating it. When you choose the behavior, you choose the consequences.

Much of your excess weight can be traced directly to specific behaviors that are driving your results. Before you get defensive and retreat into denial, make no mistake about the following. Whatever your weight, you set it up that way. This does not mean that you did it on purpose. Nevertheless, you are the responsible party. Until you reckon with this fact, you will have a difficult time getting your weight management efforts under control.

To bring this point into sharper focus, please take a good look at my "hit list" of weight-gaining behaviors on pages 94 and 95. I want you to see that the things you do really stack up, calorie-wise and pound-wise. Also, note in the fourth column how much weight you can gain over the course of one year unless you stop these eating behaviors. When you realize how you've been sabotaging yourself, you can learn from your mistakes and begin to remove these behaviors as barriers to your success.

The good news is that you can choose differently from now on. You can behave your way to success. The following are positive steps you can take to help eliminate negative eating behaviors:

- Replace bad habits with incompatible actions. When you examine your own eating habits, and you get real about the fact that they are perpetuating your weight problem, then you need to eliminate them; you need to break those bad habits. "Break" is actually a misnomer, because we don't actually "break" habits. In order to eliminate one habitual behavior, you must replace it with a new behavior that is *incompatible* with the one you want to eliminate. When you make a new habit incompatible with the old one, the bad one will gradually lose its grip over you, since the two habits cannot coexist at the same time. For example, it is virtually impossible to spoon ice cream out of the carton if you are taking a shower. Taking a shower is incompatible with gorging on ice cream.

  One reason this plan of attack works so powerfully is that substituting an incompatible behavior for a bad habit takes your mind off the habit you want to weaken. When you are at work on activities such as gardening, play-

HIT LIST OF WEIGHT-GAINING BEHAVIORS

(3,500 extra calories = 1 pound) Eating Behavior	Weekly Caloric Cost	Annual Caloric Cost	Potential Weight Gain Per Year
Eating second helpings (200 calories per helping) three times a week	600 extra calories a week	31,200 extra calories a year	9 pounds
Habitual overeating, every day, 380 extra calories a day	2,660 extra calories a week	138,320 extra calories a year	40 pounds
Eating a super-sized bagel (4.5" diameter, 323 calories) three times a week, rather than having a small bagel (3" diameter, 156 calories)	500 extra calories a week	26,000 extra calories a year	8 pounds
Eating Big Macs (or equivalent, 570 calories) twice a week, rather than choosing a small-sized hamburger (260 calories)	620 extra calories a week	32,240 extra calories a year	9 pounds
Eating one glazed doughnut (290 calories every day at work during your coffee break	1,450 extra calories a week	75,400 extra calories a year	22 pounds
Drinking a cup of whole milk (150 calories) twice a day, rather than having skim milk (86 calories)	896 extra calories a week	46,600 extra calories a year	13 pounds
Drinking one regular soda a day (144 calories), rather than having a calorie-free soda	1,008 extra calories a week	52,400 extra calories a year	15 pounds

Behavior	Extra calories a week	Extra calories a year	Weight gain
Snacking on 15 to 20 potato chips a day (150 calories)	1,050 extra calories a week	54,600 extra calories a year	16 pounds
Eating a bowl of regular ice cream (280 calories) five times a week, rather than having a bowl of nonfat frozen yogurt (160 calories)	600 extra calories a week	31,200 extra calories a year	9 pounds
Bingeing twice a week (1,000 to 3,000 calories per binge)	2,000 to 6,000 extra calories a week	104,000 to 312,000 extra calories a year	30 to 89 pounds
Eating out at a fast-food restaurant five times a week (56 extra calories per fast-food meal), compared to having a healthy meal prepared at home	280 extra calories a week	14,560 extra calories a year	4 pounds
Snacking while watching television, five hours a week (136 extra calories per snack)	680 extra calories a week	35,360 extra calories a year	10 pounds
Nighttime eating, five episodes a week (270 calories per episode)	1,350 extra calories a week	70,200 extra calories a year	20 pounds
Drinking three beers at Happy Hour once a week (146 calories per beer)	438 extra calories a week	22,776 extra calories a year	7 pounds

The information in this chart is based on typical caloric counts of foods and beverages, as well as on scientific studies of the caloric cost of specific eating behaviors. Results may vary from person to person. Annual weight gain is based on calculating the estimated yearly caloric cost of each behavior, then dividing by 3,500 calories (the number of additional calories it takes to gain one pound).

ing with your kids, meditating, or journaling, your mind is usually not on food.

So the trick is to enact one or more incompatible substitutes when you feel like overeating, or otherwise going off your food plan. These activities form a new cadre of coping tools that you can substitute for overeating. The more tools and activities you can plug into your day as coping strategies, the more likely you are to get the results you want.

The chart below lists numerous activities that compete with eating and can be used as incompatible substitutes. Use this list or create one of your own to push yourself into action when the urge to overeat hits you.

INCOMPATIBLE SUBSTITUTES FOR OVEREATING

Activities for Fun and Enjoyment
Pursue a favorite hobby, or take up something new you'd like to learn.
Work on a craft.
Work in your garden.
Play a game with your kids or your friends.
Learn a new sport or game.
Visit your neighbors, or talk to a friend.
Write letters or send e-mails to friends or family.
Write in your journal.
Give yourself a manicure.

Go to a good movie, or rent a video.
Read your favorite magazine.
Read a good book.
Plan your next vacation.
Watch a sunrise or sunset.
Spend time with your children.

Activities for Relaxation

Do relaxation exercises such as deep breathing
   or yoga.
Go for a walk, jog, swim, or bike ride.
Head to the gym and work out.
Exercise to an exercise video.
Dance to some upbeat music.
Take a shower or a leisurely bath.
Have a massage.
Pamper yourself with a day of beauty at a day
   spa or salon.
Listen to music.
Sing along with your favorite music.
Engage in prayer or meditation.
Write a poem.
Take a short nap.
Take the day off and go on a day trip.

Activities You Must Do

Do housework.
Work on a home improvement project.
Pay your bills.
Balance your checkbook.
Rearrange the furniture in a room or two.
Wash your car.
Clean out your closets or your drawers.

Run errands.
Do all the things your dentist wants you to do—
  brush, floss, rinse with mouthwash.
Volunteer for a project, then follow through on
  your commitments.
Take your dog for a walk.

- Change your eating style. Certain eating behaviors can lead to weight gain. These include eating too fast, snacking while watching television, sampling food while cooking, and eating in several rooms in your home, among other habits. These and other habits are examples of *mindless eating,* in which you shovel in an enormous amount of calories in a very short period of time without even realizing it. What you must do is replace mindless eating with its incompatible substitute, *mindful eating,* in which you concentrate on what and how you are eating. Mindful eating helps prevent overeating and leads to constructive behavioral change. What follows are some specific strategies you can use to counter mindless eating with mindful eating.

If you are a fast eater who needs to slow down:
- After your food is placed in front of you, wait five minutes before you eat it.

- Place small mouthfuls of food on your fork or in your spoon.
- Completely swallow food from each mouthful before you add any more to your fork or spoon.
- Put your utensils down between bites.
- Use smaller utensils (try a cocktail fork, for example)—no soup spoons, ladles, or otherwise oversize tableware for shoveling in food.
- Consciously take time to taste, chew, and savor the food you eat.
- Stretch out your meals, making them last thirty minutes instead of five or ten minutes, to allow for a reduction in hunger. One way to do this is to take a five-minute break at about ten minutes into your meal.
- Take sips of water or other noncaloric beverages between bites.
- Introduce a one- or two-minute delay between courses.

If you have trouble patrolling your portions:
- Measure your food if you're afraid of overeating.
- If you don't have the patience to measure out your food, use plates, glasses, and bowls in the serving sizes you need.
- Use a smaller plate for your meals.
- Purchase single-serving foods.
- Try the divided plate method of portion

control. Fill half your plate with non-starchy vegetables, one fourth of your plate with a starchy carbohydrate, and the remaining fourth with a lean protein.

If you have a habit of eating leftovers:
- Put away all the food involved in preparing a meal.
- Have the table cleared of serving plates.
- Leave the table after you've finished eating.
- Have someone else clean leftovers off the plates after meals.
- Ask your family to scrape their plates directly into the garbage disposal after meals so that you won't be tempted to gorge on the leftovers.
- Leave some food on your plate.
- Purchase food in smaller packages or quantities so that you rarely have leftovers.

If you tend to eat while standing or while on the move:
- Localize your eating: Select one area of your home—your dining room, breakfast nook, or some other area reserved only for eating—and eat *all* of your food at a designated table in that area. That includes regular meals, snacks, and beverages.
- Vow to not eat while driving in your car; standing in front of your open refrigerator;

reading a book, magazine, or newspaper; sitting in your bed; or talking on the phone. In other words, do not pair other behaviors with eating. Doing so only distracts your attention from your eating behavior, and you will lose all sense and awareness of how much you are consuming. If you are engaging in any of these behaviors while eating, you're not focused on your eating. This means you are not in control.

* Stop eating foods right out of their bags or packages.

If you sample food while cooking:
* Place a small portion of the food on a plate; sit down and taste it.
* Chew sugar-free gum while cooking.
* Minimize your time in the kitchen.
* Ask someone else in your family to occasionally prepare meals.

If your eating is chaotic and largely unplanned:
* Keep your personalized food diary. It is an effective tool for meal planning as well as a self-diagnostic tool for pinpointing small slips in your behavior before they become big ones. It lets you review and learn from your behaviors.
* Change your routine so that your drive to and from work doesn't take you by bak-

eries, fast-food restaurants, or other tempting eateries.

- Make food choices mindfully by asking yourself a simple question: "Does this food or meal, in this amount, contribute to my health and to effective weight control?" If the answer is no, if you are choosing to eat something, or too much of something, that does not support your goal of health and weight management, then you need to rethink your decision.

If you overeat at night:

- Brush your teeth in the evening after dinner to signal that you've finished eating for the night.
- Read a book or magazine prior to going to bed; or substitute any activity you can think of that is incompatible with eating.

If you watch television while snacking:

- Eat only in your designated eating place— at your kitchen or dining room table.
- Eliminate all distractions while eating—including television (turn it off).
- Continue to keep problem foods out of your house, or else you'll indulge when an impulse to eat seizes you.

Mastering even one or two of the preceding bad behaviors will liberate you from counterproductive eating and dramatically reduce your weight. So if you want your weight to be lower than it has been in the past, get to work on these actions and disciplines. They will give you success.

NUTRITIONAL STRATEGIES

Other areas for improvement may involve making some day-to-day tweaks in your nutrition and meal planning. Do you skip meals because you think you don't have enough time to eat? Do you go grocery shopping without a list and end up filling your pantry with foods you don't need? When you choose healthy foods, are you eating the same boring rabbit food, day after day, and now you're deep in a food rut that is causing you to rebel? You are about to find some extremely useful ways to help you create results that are better aligned with reaching your get-real weight. So let's put some more verbs in your sentences and some more action into your life with the following.

- Do not—I repeat, do not skip breakfast. Your body requires refueling after going eight to twelve hours without food. Not eating breakfast leads to cravings later and is a factor in overweight and obesity. If time is a problem in the morning: fix a breakfast shake or smoothie, made by blending fruit and low-fat milk; eat a bowl of packaged high-fiber cereal; or have a meal replacement bar or beverage, along with some fresh fruit.

- Expand your nutritional repertoire and try something new. Each week, introduce into your diet at least one fruit or vegetable you've never touched in the past.

- Cook "in bulk" on the weekends. Have cut-up vegetables ready for salads; mashed sweet potatoes ready for reheating; chili that can be microwaved; or chicken breasts that can be warmed up.

- Shop for "healthy" convenience foods, such as salad in a bag, so that you don't have to spend time chopping up salad vegetables.

- If you are in a hurry or too tired to cook and you must pop a packaged food into the microwave for a meal, at least serve it with a salad and fruit for dessert.

- Purchase more low-fat cooking gadgets—nonstick pots and pans, vegetable steamer, or rice cooker—to help you prepare more dishes that do not require the addition of fat.

- If you must help yourself to seconds, help yourself to vegetables.

- Cut the cocktails. Alcohol provides a triple whammy: It increases your appetite, lowers your inhibitions so you eat more, plus research shows that drinking alcohol will cause your body to store more calories as fat.

- Plan in advance when you will snack and what you will eat for that snack. This is far better—and safer—than unplanned snacking, for example, having a bag of chips or a bowl of candy that you mindlessly grab while watching TV or reading.

- Choose snacks from high-response cost, high-yield foods that supply good nutrition, rather than from nutritionally weak foods: a small bran muffin instead of a pastry, an apple instead of vending machine crackers, a glass of low-fat milk or soy milk instead of a soft drink.

- Take the same healthful snacks to work so that you won't be tempted by vending machine selections or fattening food brought in by your coworkers.

- Never eat any snack from its original container or package. Place it on a plate and eat your snack in a designated place.

- When grocery shopping:
  - Shop from a grocery list, prepared when you are not hungry or stressed out.
  - Determine exactly what you need for a particular period of time, and don't overbuy.
  - Stick to the outer aisles where the fresh, additive-free foods are located. There's a logical reason for this placement: Fresh foods require more frequent restocking and therefore must be situated as close to the outside shipping docks and stockrooms as possible.
  - Never go grocery shopping when you're hungry. The entire store, from the food aisles to the checkout line, can tempt you to buy foods that you neither want nor need.
  - Assign someone else in your family the job of grocery shopping on occasion in order to limit your exposure to food.

- Try not to use food as a reward when you've reached mile markers on the way to your get-real weight. This undoes any good you've done to yourself and shifts into reverse any progress you've made toward your weight loss goals. Instead, reward yourself with a new outfit, a new pair of walking shoes, a trip to a day spa, a new CD or DVD, or a special book.

What you have just read about are small, manageable changes you can easily make in activities you do every day. If you get practical about making these changes, you will begin the process of reprogramming yourself to get in the shape you want to be in.

RESTAURANT STRATEGIES

For many of you, eating away from home, particularly at restaurants, is problematic. The key is to take some time to preplan for those situations and identify those things that could and should be the focus of your management efforts. When you decide to dine out:

- Select a restaurant that offers a variety of foods so that you can choose healthier menu items.

- Obtain a copy of the menu before going to a designated restaurant in order to decide ahead of time what you will order.

- Take control over the choice of restaurant. Go where you know you can order food that supports your weight control goals.

- Call the restaurant in question to determine whether they serve low-fat or low-calorie foods.

- Be assertive with the waitstaff; tell your server you want your food prepared without fats, oils, or sauces.

- Avoid all-you-can-eat and buffet-style restaurants or cafeterias, at least until you are less vulnerable to the sight of food. If you must go to a buffet-style restaurant, survey the entire buffet before you jump in line so that you can decide which selections are the healthiest and will support your weight control efforts. Use a smaller plate at buffet-style restaurants—either a salad plate or a dessert plate. Visit the food line only once; don't give in to the lure of the all-you-can-eat deal. Opt to order from the menu (if available), rather than choose from the buffet.

- Avoid ordering complete dinners, which often include unneeded portions, and opt instead for à la carte selections, since they give you more control over what you eat.

- If you know you are going to eat out for dinner, plan to have a lighter lunch to help balance and control calories.

- Say "no" to cocktails when dining out. Alcohol is high in sugar and calories, with the potential to contribute to weight gain. In addition, alcohol overstimulates your appetite and lowers your inhibitions about overeating.

- Ask the server to remove the bread basket after you've been served (hopefully your dinner companions will support you on this request). Removing the bread removes a huge temptation and source of extra calories.

- Curb your appetite by ordering a cup or bowl of broth-based soup, or a salad, prior to your meal.

- Stop sabotaging yourself with appetizers (other than a light soup or salad). The calorie counts of some of the most popular appetizers are through the roof. For example, fried onion rings = 2,000 calories; buffalo wings = 1,000 calories; cheese fries = 3,000 calories (eat those once a week and you can put on nearly a pound a week, or roughly 50 pounds a year!).

- Order high-response cost entrées—those that take time and effort to eat. Some suggestions: peel-and-eat steamed shrimp, steamed crab legs, artichokes, or a large dinner salad with dressing on the side.

- Get fluent in restaurant lingo. Sauces like béchamel, béarnaise, gratin, and hollandaise are synonyms for high fat and high choles-terol. *Sautéed* usually means cooked in but-ter. *Fried* is a red flag, since all fried food is loaded with fat and calories. So are gravy and cream sauces, since these are high in fat, cholesterol, and calories.

- Be clear, specific, and *polite* when making requests of your server. Simply state: "I'd like my chicken grilled dry, without butter, oil, or margarine."

- If you're feeling that your resolve is weak, have someone order for you. Make sure that someone is in your circle of support and will order a healthy, low-calorie entrée for you.

- When ordering a salad, ask for dressing on the side, order half the dressing, or request no dressing at all (opt for lemon or vinegar in-stead).

- Consider sharing an entrée with your dining companion, particularly if the restaurant is known for over-sizing or supersizing its por-tions.

- When ordering beef, stick to lower-fat cuts. These include London broil, sirloin, flank steak, and tenderloin. Lower-fat pork and veal selections include pork chops, pork loin, veal chops, and roast veal. (High-fat meats include prime rib, chopped steak made from chuck, ground lamb or pork, spareribs, and pork sausages.)

- Trim all visible fat from your meat.

- For poultry, order skinless chicken or turkey, while generally staying away from goose or duck (which tend to be higher in fat).

- Stick to entrées that are cooked by simple methods, such as broiling, baking, steaming, roasting, or braising. Fancier dishes such as casseroles are very likely to contain elevated levels of fat, calories, cholesterol, and sodium.

- Your best bets for breakfast at restaurants include hot and cold cereals (unsugared), fresh fruit, unsweetened fruit juices (small size), skim milk, artificially sweetened low-fat yogurt, or eggs, scrambled egg whites, or scrambled egg substitutes. Avoid large or jumbo muffins (they're loaded with fat, sugar, and calories); and pancakes, waffles, or French toast (which are usually prepared on a greased griddle).

- For lunch, avoid the urge to choose quick-to-eat low-response cost foods when time is at a premium (as it usually is during the lunch hour). Stick to salads with dressing on the side, while staying away from potato salad, macaroni salad, and coleslaw, which are usually made with a ton of mayonnaise. Sandwiches made with whole wheat bread or pita bread and white-meat poultry or lean roast beef are preferable to cheeseburgers or sandwiches prepared with high-fat lunch meats like salami, corned beef, or pastrami.

- Practice salad bar smarts. Stick to leafy greens and lettuces, fresh vegetables, and reduced-fat dressing. Don't spoon dressing over your salad; instead, pour it into a small bowl so that you can use a small, designated amount on your salad.

- Be aware of fattening additives lurking in certain salad bar items. Three-bean salad, for example, is high in sugar. Cottage cheese at some salad bars is of the whole-milk variety and therefore high in fat. So are prepared salads (again—potato salad, macaroni salad, and coleslaw), as well as shredded cheese. Bacon bits, pickles, and olives are high in sodium.

- A lot of restaurants will make up a vegetable plate for you if you ask them.

- Practice your behavioral eating–style skills not just at home, but also at restaurants: After your food is placed in front of you, wait five minutes before you eat it. Place small mouthfuls of food on your fork or in your spoon. Pause between bites and put your utensils down. Completely swallow food from each mouthful before you add any more to your fork or spoon. Consciously take time to taste, chew, and savor the food you eat. Take sips of water or other noncaloric beverages between bites.

- For dessert, choose fresh fruit, fruit salad, or sorbet (which is usually fat-free but higher in sugar).

- Don't feel guilty about leaving food on your plate. Do it!

- Ask the server to not bring the dessert cart to your table.

- Do an audit of your "dining out frequency." Count up how many times a week you eat out at restaurants. If your frequency is excessive—such as seven or more times—then you need to rethink your dining-out habits. People generally tend to eat more food when dining out. Plus, there is a lot of hidden fat and sugar in menu items you'd think were low-cal, so you may be sabotaging yourself unnecessarily here. Make a commitment to eat out no more than once or twice a week (such as on Friday evenings to celebrate the end of the workweek), or on special occasions such as a birthday or anniversary. Make eating out an event, not an everyday occurrence.

TRAVEL AND VACATION STRATEGIES

Traveling and taking vacations can be difficult too, but try to exert the same control in your choice making that you would do at home or when eating out. If you're having difficulty in these areas, here are some strategies worth enacting:

- If you are flying, you don't have to settle for the typical airline food. If traveling by air, call the airline ahead of time (usually twenty-four hours) to request a special meal. Airlines can usually accommodate diabetic, vegetarian, low-fat, low-calorie, and low-sodium meals. You can make such requests practically anywhere, even on cruises, as long as you give the food preparation personnel plenty of notice.

- If the circumstances are such that you simply cannot control your choices, take it easy and eat smaller portions.

- If possible, take your own food to guarantee some control over what you eat while traveling or on vacation.

- Never travel on an empty stomach. This makes you less likely to cave in to food cues, such as fast-food vendors at airports. Eat a healthy, filling meal before you start your trip. If feasible, consider packing light and healthful snack foods, such as fresh or dried fruits, or cut-up vegetables.

- Self-monitor your food intake while away from home, using your personalized food diary and this food guide to help you stay the course. Pack both of these items.

- If your alcohol consumption tends to increase while on vacation, devise strategies to compensate, such as ordering club soda, diet drinks, or other nonalcoholic but low-calorie beverages.

- Do not take a vacation from your workouts. Stay with your regular exercise program by walking, using hotel exercise facilities, or purchasing a week's membership at a local gym. During layovers, walk briskly around the airport for exercise. Exercising will burn off extra calories, plus help relieve the stress that is so often associated with traveling.

SOCIAL STRATEGIES

Staying the course during special occasions such as holidays, parties, or celebrations can be a challenge unless you have plans in place to deal with the circumstances. Make a deal with yourself that you will try at least one or two of these the next time you are confronted with a social situation that makes it tempting to overeat or disregard your food plan:

- Plan ahead. On days when you'll be attend-ing parties or get-togethers, consume fewer calories by eating a light breakfast and lunch. "Bank," or save, most of your calories for later on.

- Continue to self-monitor during the holidays by writing down what you eat and how many calories you consume in your personalized food diary. Research suggests that people who self-monitor their food intake can and will lose weight during the holidays.

- Consider a "prediet." Try losing two or three pounds prior to the holidays to give yourself some room to move up the scales.

- Eat something light before you go to a party in order to avoid arriving too hungry. If you let yourself get too hungry, your stomach and your eyes will make your food choices for you, instead of your brain.

- Concentrate more on people and conversation at parties, and less on the food or drinks.

- Make the most nutritious choices possible at parties or gatherings: fresh fruits, raw vegetables, whole grain crackers, or lean proteins.

- If you are the host or hostess, there is no rule of hospitality that says you must serve fattening food for your guests. Try concocting lower-fat foods by altering recipes and using low-fat substitutes for high-fat ingredients. For example, you can replace all or part of the sour cream in dip recipes with plain low-fat yogurt. High-fat cheeses can be replaced by lower-fat products. You can also use reduced quantities of salt, sugar, and other sweeteners in recipes.

- Deal effectively with saboteurs. Your friends and family may present the biggest challenges to changes you want to make, especially at family get-togethers and celebrations. Sometimes friends and family won't take no for an answer and want to push food at you. In cases like this, try replies like, "No thanks, I just ate." "Can't have that. Doctor's orders." "Can you wrap it for me?" (Then toss it once you get home.) "Better not. An extra helping means an extra workout this week." "I'd love to, but I've got that class reunion coming up."

  Guard against feeling guilty for focusing attention on yourself and standing up for yourself. It's okay to make time for yourself so that you can make your goals. You must take care of yourself before you can take care of others, and now is the time to do that.

- Take control of the social situation. If you're invited to an event where mostly low-response cost, low-yield foods will be served, graciously ask the host or hostess if you can bring some of your own food. Or be direct. Explain why you are not eating certain foods. You may be surprised at how some people may start supporting you when you stand up for yourself like this.

If, after all your planning and good intentions, you do overindulge, don't go on a guilt trip. Guilt is a useless emotion that only weakens your resolve to successfully manage your weight. Get over it and move on.

STRESS-EATING STRATEGIES

Never in your life will you be without stress—problems, challenges, and difficult moments that are simply a part of living. You know that if things are going well at work, for example, you can count on conflict at home, or vice versa. There is rarely a time in your life when all is at peace and balanced. That's not good or bad; it is simply the ebb and flow of how life works. To be alive means to experience stress.

With stressful situations comes the potential for overeating as a way to escape anxiety and pressure. If you're someone who struggles with your weight, then I'm willing to bet that you medicate with food as a stress reliever a good deal of the time, abusing food because it provides comfort and consolation when you are worried, irritated, annoyed, lonely, bored, or depressed.

Stress—particularly when it is prolonged and unresolved—provokes weight-sustaining physiological changes in your body. When you are under stress, your body releases stress hormones that automatically stimulate your appetite and set off cravings, prompting you to eat huge quantities of fattening food. These stress hormones trigger other bodily changes that may result in greater fat distribution around your waist. Overeating as a way to cope with stress may prove fatal to your weight-management efforts. You've got to step up and out of this behavior. Take a moment now to consider some of the following strategies:

- Be accountable for how you react to stress. One of my life laws states that *there is no reality; only perception.* What this means is that you are accountable for how you respond to everything in your life. Whether it's an infuriating phone call, a lost opportunity, or a person who has treated you poorly, your response to that event creates your experience.

  But behind that response is a perception— the way you interpret or assign meaning to what you are experiencing. If your response (your interpretation) to a stressor is typically negative, pessimistic, or gloom-and-doom, you are creating an experience for yourself that is self-defeating and infinitely more stress provoking. On the other hand, if you interpret the situation more positively, or realistically, you won't be so likely to become unglued, fall apart, or go into a panic mode.

  When it comes to how you see things, you do have choices. You choose the reactions that create your level of stress. You have the power to choose your own perceptions and your own reactions; start choosing differently, with more clarity, more confidence, and more self-control. If you shake up your belief system and test your typical perceptions and reactions to events, rather than blindly or habitually holding on to them, the freshness of your new perspective can be startling. The freshness of your perspective can keep you from falling apart and resorting to food when the going gets tough. (Reading key 2, Healing Feelings, in *The Ultimate Weight Solution* will give you additional insights for managing the stress in your life and the emotions it produces.)

• Take a problem-solving approach to stress. Confront head-on whatever is wrong in your life and do something about it. If you don't, if you let these problems go unchallenged, you will pay the price and set yourself up for further physical and mental breakdown. The push to resolve the stress-provoking situation must come from you. You can either sit around and stew about the stressful situation or you can make the choice to be self-directed, take action, and adopt a solution-side approach to your life.

• Nourish your body with healthy alternatives. There are nutritious foods that will induce the same calming effect as high-sugar comfort foods, but without the unpleasant side effects. Among the most effective anxiety-management foods are fresh fruits, vegetables, and whole grains. Specifically, these foods are natural carbohydrates, which release serotonin, a brain chemical that lifts and improves your mood. Green leafy vegetables such as spinach and Romaine lettuce are bursting with a vitamin called folic acid, a mood-balancing nutrient. Other good-mood foods include fish and unprocessed turkey. Fish, in particular, is a food that has been linked to a lower incidence of depression because of the brain-healthy fats it contains.

The point is, for emotional comfort from food, you have to build certain foods into your food plan to help you normalize your mood for the day. This is nutritional knowledge that you can put to use on a day-to-day basis. Rather than sabotage your body's true needs, you can support them with high-nourishment foods.

• Practice relaxation. If you're stressed out and treat yourself to a plate of cookies or a bag of candy because you "deserve it," get real. There are other ways to treat yourself and restore calm without resorting to a food binge. That's why you must carve out time in your life for tension-reducing activities. I suspect that if you habitually overeat in reaction to stress, then you have no clue as to how to relax without a food binge. You are more accustomed to putting something fattening in your mouth to get relief rather than using nonfood activities to calm yourself down.

These alternatives include, but are not limited to, exercising (a powerful stress reliever!), performing relaxation exercises, and listening to music. According to most research, these activities work directly on your nervous system by releasing endorphins, the brain's natural tranquilizers, to produce a state of reduced anxiety and a feeling of calm. These activities are natural, nonchemical, and inexpensive relaxants.

There's no good reason for you to experience any nutritional backsliding when you have strategies in place to handle it. When these situations arise, as you know they will, you won't panic and start eating everything in sight. You will simply say to yourself, "This is the very thing I knew would happen, and I know how to deal with it. I won't panic, and I won't give in just because I am encountering normal challenges of day-to-day life. I am in control."

As you manage your weight, never lose sight of the stakes involved. Your stakes are your health, your emotional well-being, your hopes and dreams, and the quality of your entire life. If you choose to bail out on managing your weight, be prepared to be another casualty of poor lifestyle decisions and choices.

Each day of progress you make, each action you take, has a positive effect. Trust in your ability to do it, and never forget that small and subtle changes in what you do are moving you in the right direction.

How to Use the Food Guide

We all have room to improve the quality of our health in general and our diets in particular. So often, we need the right tools and the right knowledge to guide us. Now you've come to the part of this book where you will find valuable reference material on food that relates primarily to its effect on your weight and to your ability to manage it. This section provides information on the nutritional content of high-response, high-yield foods—the type of food you should eat—and low-response, low-yield foods, the type of food you should limit or avoid.

If you are familiar with *The Ultimate Weight Solution: The 7 Keys to Weight Loss Freedom,* you know that I am not a fan of counting calories, calculating carbohydrate or fat grams, or multiplying nutrient percentages. What I do advocate, however, in any change or improvement, is accountability—a way to check yourself to make sure that you are progressing steadily toward your get-real weight. Accountability can come in the form of a person in your circle of support to whom you commit to make periodic reports on what you plan to do, and it can come in the form of an informational tool like this book. This guide provides a measure of accountability by furnishing information to help you choose which foods are best for healthy weight management.

Without the accountability that this fundamental information provides, you are apt to con yourself about certain foods, thinking that they may not be so fattening after all. Then you're left wondering why you're not shedding weight as steadily as you wish or meeting your get-real weight goal. So consider this information carefully. The more you learn about the nutritional content of these foods, the better equipped you will be to make positive changes and increase your chances of living vigorously throughout your entire life.

ACCESSING FOODS IN THE GUIDE

I have organized *The Ultimate Weight Solution Food Guide* in such a way as to make it as convenient as possible for you to locate, look up, and access foods you want to include in your meal planning. In the pages that follow, the guide is organized into my two broad classifications of foods: *High-Response Cost, High-Yield Foods* and *Low-Response Cost, Low-Yield Foods,* each with a huge listing of individual foods. Under each classification, foods are alphabetized into categories such as Beef, Beverages, Cheese, Cereals, and so forth. Within those categories, individual foods in their many variations and options are listed for you in alphabetical order, as well. This breakdown of foods is intended to make it easy to find the foods you want to look up.

Let's say, for example, that you want information on apples, a high-response cost, high-yield fruit. Check the table of contents, where you'll find an alphabetized listing of food categories, and go to "fruits" under the high-response cost, high-yield listing. Turn to the page where the fruit listings begin and go to the "a's." Fruits appear alphabetically, so it is easy to locate "apples." Under "apples," you will find nutrient information for various types of apples, including raw, and peeled or unpeeled.

Now let's move on to talking about the nutrient information in my food guide. Each food entry lists the following information in this order: food name, serving size, calories, and the amount of each of the following (in grams or milligrams): protein, carbohydrate, total fat, saturated fat, cholesterol, fiber, sugar, and sodium. The information targeted in this guide is relevant for lifetime weight control. Keeping an eye on these nutrients can have a hugely significant impact on your weight and on the overall health of your body. Here is an explanation of each piece of nutrient information and why it is important.

Serving Size

The Ultimate Weight Solution Food Guide defines for you exactly what healthy, sensible portions should be, so you should use this information to determine the size and amount of your portions at meals.

Unfortunately, the world of food has changed—and changed drastically. Over the past twenty years, the portion sizes of foods we normally eat, both at home and at restaurants, have been increasing exponentially. You know I'm right, but as proof, a number of nutritional studies published in scientific journals in recent years have turned the rock over on this trend, only to reveal some rather alarming findings. Consider:

- Hamburgers have "grown" from 5.7 ounces to 7 ounces (an increase of 97 calories).
- Mexican-style foods such as burritos and tacos have increased from 6.3 ounces to 8 ounces (an additional 133 calories).
- The classic recipe for Toll House chocolate chip cookies from a 1949 cookbook yields 100 cookies; today, the same recipe in an updated, revised cookbook yields 60 cookies. This means the cookies are almost twice as big if you follow the recipe in the modern edition of the cookbook.
- A 16-ounce Coke is today considered "small," yet supplies 202 calories—a huge amount for a beverage.

- One convenience store sells a 64-ounce soft drink called a "Double Gulp"—and the *800 calories* that come with it.
- Car makers now install larger cup holders in new models in order to accommodate these super-sized drinks.

I could go on, but here is the problem with all of this as I see it: The food and restaurant industries, in particular, have so oversized food and meals that, as a food-consuming society, we have been conditioned over time to think that "large," "giant," and "monster" sizes are the norm. What is astonishing is that we no longer recognize which amounts of food are correct and appropriate for our weight and our level of physical activity. We have let ourselves get brainwashed!

You may think that the jumbo bran muffin you eat for breakfast every morning is a healthy choice. But consider this: It may supply upward of 600 calories, compared to a normal-sized bran muffin at 100 calories, meaning that you are packing away an extra 500 calories every morning—which could easily translate into a weight gain of 1 pound a week, or 52 pounds a year! Most people can no longer differentiate between a normal-sized serving and a super-sized one. We've started to look at a cheeseburger as a cheeseburger, never mind that it is giant or gargantuan-sized.

Supersized starts to look right-sized, often with terrible health consequences, one of which is obesity in children and adults. It is simply no coincidence that the supersizing of food portions has paralleled the supersizing of Americans, that is, the alarming rise in obesity.

The larger the portion, the more calories it has in it. Furthermore, it has been proven, time and time again in research, that large portions encourage people to eat more. It is simply a fact of eating behavior that people will eat what is put in front of them. If more food is there, you will eat more food.

As consumers, we value a greater quantity of food and drink for a lower price—a value that the food industry is more than willing to provide. We also buy on impulse, and the food industry capitalizes on this behavior. So when a server asks you, "Do you want to supersize that?", go on alert. One survey of fast-food restaurants discovered that upgrading, or super-sizing, a meal at a burger eatery provided 1,380 more calories for only 58 cents more. That's a great value—until you realize what it is doing to your waistline.

You and your family are being reeled in by these billion-bucks industries. I'm calling on you to stop taking the bait. Don't be lured by these deals. Know the costs to your weight and to your health. If you continue to cave in to impulse buying and the lure of the meal deal, then you're setting yourself up for more years of being overweight. It's about you deciding whether you are going to be baited for the rest of your life, waiting to get hooked. You control what you buy or don't buy;

you control where you eat and what you eat when you get there. Like it or not, a lot of cause and effect is in your hands. The more knowledge you have about what's going on in the world around you, the more power you have to control the outcomes in your life.

If this guide is to be of any value to you, you must commit to referencing its serving sizes when you plan meals or go out to eat. You won't have to do this forever, just long enough to relearn what "sensible" means in relation to "supersized."

If you understand that portion sizes can doom your weight control efforts, then you've got the battle half won. You'll stop eating more than you need and more than you want because you have figured it out. In short, you get it.

Calories

As I have already emphasized, I am not in favor of counting or memorizing calories, because for many people trying to lose weight, this fuels obsessions with food and dieting. What's more, most people have neither the time nor the patience to count calories. Managing your portion sizes is a better way to go, because it automatically curbs your caloric intake.

Even so, I feel that it is important to at least be aware of the caloric content of certain foods—particularly low-response, low-yield foods, since many of these foods contain a rather shocking level of calories. (Did you know, for example, that 16 ounces of a flavored coffee may contain nearly 400 calories?) You may think you know the calorie count of every food, but then again, you may not. Most people still need a refresher course in calories, mainly because of supersizing and the fact that servings today are larger and contain far more calories than most people think.

What is well known, though, is that eating a certain number of calories each day will help you lose or maintain your weight. When you eat more calories than your body requires metabolically or can burn off in activity, you will store the surplus as fat. Eat fewer calories than your body needs, and your body will start burning fat for energy.

The magic number in weight management is 3,500—the number of calories to create one pound of fat. For perspective, 3,500 calories of food equals about fifteen 1.5-ounce chocolate candy bars or fifty-seven slices of white bread. Eat that many candy bars or that many slices of bread, in addition to your normal three squares a day, and you will gain a pound of fat.

Reducing calories is the chief determinant of weight loss. You can do this by decreasing the number of calories you consume and/or by increasing the amount of exercise you do. For most people, a balanced plan of 1,200 to 1,500 calories a day, without the wholesale restriction of entire food groups, is effective for shedding excess pounds. If you are unsure of the calorie count of some foods, or how many calories you consume on a day-to-day basis, you can use this food guide to look them up and keep yourself accountable.

Protein

Protein is the nutritional equivalent of a handyman, absolutely essential for the repair and maintenance of your body, fixing up and renewing it on a day-to-day basis. You need protein to make hormones, disease-fighting antibodies, and muscle tissue—and to some extent, to provide your body with energy. Protein is typically found in fish, poultry, meat, and dairy products. Grain products and vegetables (particularly beans and legumes) supply some protein, too.

In this food guide, most of the serving sizes for animal proteins such as meat, fish, and poultry are given in 4-ounce servings to deliver a slightly higher amount of protein in your diet. Protein has important metabolic effects on weight loss and thus plays a critically important, yet sometimes uncredited, role in healthy weight management. When provided at slightly higher levels in your diet, protein helps step up metabolic activity for greater fat-loss potential. As a hunger suppressor, protein is also filling; having some at each meal keeps your appetite in check. Further, you will regain less weight during maintenance if you continue to eat higher-protein meals after you have lost weight. Because of its metabolic benefits, sufficient protein in your diet improves your ability to maintain your weight loss.

For effective weight loss, protein should comprise approximately one-fourth to one-third of your total daily calories, or 25 to 33 percent. On a 1,200-calorie diet, that translates to 300 to 400 protein calories a day, or 75 to 100 grams; on a 1,500-calorie diet, 375 to 500 calories a day, or 94 to 125 grams.

Carbohydrates

These energy foods have been much maligned, accused of being excess calories from the major fat promoters. In truth, though, it is largely excess calories from the processed and refined variety of carbohydrates (like those found in white bread, cake, and snack foods) that is causing so much of the trouble. Loaded with added sugar and fat, processed carbohydrates tend to jack up your blood sugar, and since what goes up must come down, there is a corresponding drop in blood sugar after a couple of hours. This state of low blood sugar results in food cravings. So when you eat refined, processed carbohydrates, your hunger returns rapidly—which is why such foods are hunger drivers. Plus, in response to that surge in blood sugar, your body releases the hormone insulin, which encourages the storage of calories as fat. By avoiding these foods in favor of natural, higher-fiber carbohydrates (fruits, vegetables, and whole grains), you gain a tremendous edge in managing your weight.

Ideally, a diet in which 40 to 45 percent of your daily calories come from healthy, high-fiber sources of carbohydrates will produce a good rate of weight loss. (That equates to 480 to 540 calories, or 120 to 135 grams, on a 1,200-calorie diet; 600 to 675 calories, or 150 to 169 grams, on a 1,500-calorie diet.)

The optimal number of grams of carbohydrates per day to drive weight loss has not yet been nailed down conclusively; however, you can lose weight efficiently with 120 to 175 grams a day, without dipping below 100 grams and sacrificing your physical and mental energy as a result.

The grams of carbohydrates represented in the food guide are the total grams of carbohydrates. Although listed separately in the guide, the grams of sugar and fiber are counted as part of total carbohydrates.

Total Fat

You need some fat in your diet, largely because fat supplies nutrients called "fatty acids." These vital components of fat drive a number of important chemical activities in your body, including the production of energy, the protection of cell membranes, and the absorption of vitamins A, D, E, and K (collectively known as the fat-soluble vitamins).

From a weight-control standpoint, fat has some

very specific advantages. As a hunger suppressor, it is slow to break down and thus makes you feel full even after protein and carbohydrates have left your stomach. Fat also prompts your intestinal walls to release a special hormone that curbs the appetite and may help prevent overeating.

Clearly, fat is good for your body—but not in excess. The surplus calories you eat from fat are more likely to be stored as body fat than calories from either protein or carbohydrates, and nutritional research bears this out. Okay, so what about all those diets that let you slather butter and mayonnaise all over your food? Please understand something about such diets: They still reduce calories, and calorie reduction is the number one factor, the common denominator, that drives weight loss. When calories are over and above your metabolic needs, you'll get fat, and when those extra calories are mostly from fat, you'll probably get fatter. Of course, there is no question that a lower-fat diet helps normalize total cholesterol: LDL cholesterol, HDL cholesterol, and triglycerides—all the various blood fats that figure into the health of your cardiovascular system.

Generally, the recommendation for good health is to curtail your fat intake to 30 percent or less of your total daily calories. Using the chart below, find the average number of calories you eat daily, then look to see how many grams of fat should comprise your maximum intake in order to keep your daily fat calories at around 30 percent.

Average Daily Calories	Fat
1,200	40 grams
1,500	50 grams
1,800	60 grams
2,000	67 grams
2,200	73 grams
2,400	80 grams

In the food guide, you will find the total fat content (in grams) of high-response, high-yield foods, as well as of low-response, low-yield foods. If you wish, use this information to add up the number of grams of fat you eat throughout the day. It is good planning to choose foods lower in total fat. By government labeling standards, a food product considered "low-fat" contains less than 3 grams of fat per serving.

You do not have to become an obsessive fat gram counter, however. Populating your diet with enough vegetables and some fruits and some whole grains automatically ensures a lower-fat diet, eliminating the need to fixate on fat grams.

Saturated Fats

Part of the total fat in foods is saturated fat, found mostly in animal products. It is smart, and indeed a good idea, to pay attention to the amount of saturated fat in certain foods because of its health implications. Saturated fats raise total cholesterol and levels of LDL cholesterol by interfering with the liver's ability to remove cholesterol from your blood. In addition, saturated fats make your cells insensitive to the hormone insulin (technically termed "insulin resistance"), whose job it is to clear excess sugar from your bloodstream. As a consequence, cells have trouble removing excess sugar from your blood.

As a general rule, foods that are high in saturated fats also tend to be high in a dangerous type of fat known as trans fats, found mostly in stick margarine, vegetable shortening, and many processed foods. If a food label reads "hydrogenated" or "partially hydrogenated oil," this indicates the presence of trans fats. Trans fats push cholesterol levels up and have other detrimental effects on your health.

Saturated fats should make up no more than 10 percent of your total daily calories. Your saturated fat gram maximum, based on your daily average calories, is listed in the chart below.

Average Daily Calories	Saturated Fat
1,200	13 grams
1,500	17 grams
1,800	20 grams
2,000	22 grams
2,200	24 grams
2,400	27 grams

If you'd rather not have to tally up saturated fat grams, the following list provides guidelines on how to automatically lower your saturated fat intake.

How to Slash Fat and Saturated Fat

- Scrap the fatty meat and replace it with leaner cuts, fish, poultry, or vegetable-based proteins such as beans or lentils.

- Trim the fat off meat prior to cooking it.

- Cook meat or poultry on a rack so that the fat will drain off.

- Remove the skin from chicken, turkey, or other poultry prior to cooking (poultry skin is very high in fat).

- Avoid buying prebasted turkey, which is sometimes injected with coconut oil (very high in saturated fat).

- Do not add oil to water while cooking pasta. (The addition of oil only prevents boilovers; the pasta doesn't need it.)

- Do not add butter, milk, or cream when making mashed potatoes. Try low-fat milk, fat-free evaporated skim milk, or buttermilk instead.

- Be familiar with high saturated fat foods and avoid or limit them in your diet (refer to the chart below).

- Continue to use only low-fat or nonfat dairy products.

- Get friendly with trans-free margarines and spreads. Many of these are listed in the high-response cost, high-yield section of this guide.

- Avoid nondairy creamers and nondairy toppings. These are high in saturated fat from coconut or palm oils.

- Replace whole milk in recipes with its less fatty counterparts: skim milk, low-fat milk, soy milk, evaporated skim or low-fat milk, or buttermilk.

- Sauté vegetables in broth or bouillon rather than in butter or margarine.

- Use "yogurt cheese" in place of sour cream and high-fat dips. Spoon two cups of nonfat plain yogurt into a coffee filter; place the filter in a strainer that fits over a bowl, cover, and place in the refrigerator overnight. In the morning, you will have yogurt cheese, which can be mixed with herbs and used for dipping raw vegetables.

- Cut back on whole eggs, and instead use egg whites, which contain virtually no fat.

- For cooking, use a cooking spray rather than adding butter, margarine, or oil.

- An olive oil spray can add flavor to salads, vegetables, and chicken and fish dishes, but without the fat calories. The spray distributes a tiny bit of fat over a lot of food and can save you nearly 100 calories of fat.

- At the grocery store, look for low-fat alternatives to yogurt, cottage cheese, salad dressings, and mayonnaise.

- Slash the fat or oil in recipes by a third, or replace part of the fat with applesauce. You will not sacrifice flavor or texture.

Foods High in Saturated Fat
Bacon
Beef fat
Bologna, salami, and other lunch meats
Butter
Cheese
Chocolate

Cocoa butter
Coconut oil
Commercially baked goods
Cream
Cream cheese
Egg yolks
Fatty meats and poultry
Fried foods
Hydrogenated vegetable oil
Ice cream
Lard
Milk, whole
Palm and palm kernel oil
Shortening
Sour cream
Stick margarine
Suet

When you're cutting back on saturated fats and trans fats, don't eliminate fats that are good for you. These include unsaturated fats, found in fish and vegetable oils. They can trigger healthy drops in triglycerides and bad cholesterol (LDL) in your blood, plus help your body handle blood sugar more efficiently. Other top-drawer fats that exert strong protection include olive oil, canola oil, and flaxseed oil; all are useful and healthy additions to good nutrition.

In the food guide, you will find that fat content per serving is expressed as total fat/saturated fat. For example: for 4 ounces of roasted chicken

---

WHEN A DOSE OF FAT IS DANGEROUS

High-fat meals can be inherently harmful. They step up the rate at which blood clots, and abnormal clotting is the instigator of most heart attacks. What's more, high-fat meals make your arteries less elastic, and this impedes blood flow through them.

If you want to protect yourself against this danger, try to make sure that your meals are mostly low-fat ones. What exactly constitutes a "low-fat meal"? For women, this generally means a meal with 15 grams of fat or less (4 grams of saturated fat or less). This is based on a daily limit of 45 grams of total fat and 12 grams of saturated fat.

For men, this generally means a meal with 20 grams of fat or less (6 grams of saturated fat or less). This is based on a daily limit of 65 grams of total fat and 18 grams of saturated fat.

---

breast, the entry is 4 grams/1 gram. Foods considered low in saturated fat contain less than 1 gram of this type of fat per serving.

Cholesterol

Cholesterol is a fatlike substance manufactured by your liver and provided in your diet through animal products such as eggs, meat, poultry, fish, dairy products, and lard. Only foods of animal origin contain cholesterol.

Eating foods with cholesterol can raise the cholesterol in your blood, but only to a small extent. As a general rule, about 15 percent of the cholesterol in your blood comes from the food you eat, and the rest—85 percent—is manufactured by your body. In most people, the body maintains an equilibrium in response to dietary cholesterol. If you eat a lot of high-cholesterol foods, then your body will make less cholesterol, for example. What really hikes up your blood cholesterol, particularly LDL cholesterol, is eating too much saturated fat. So to reduce cholesterol in your blood, it is vital to slash the saturated fat in your diet.

There is a percentage of Americans—about 20 to 30 percent—who are sensitive to dietary cholesterol, however. These people, along with anyone at risk for heart disease (if you're overweight, or have high blood pressure or elevated blood fats, you're at risk), should monitor their dietary cholesterol. The American Heart Association recommends 200 milligrams a day of dietary cholesterol for those with heart disease or its risk factors (overweight and obesity are risk factors), and 300 milligrams a day for the general population.

The food guide can make you accountable to yourself in this regard, since it lists the cholesterol content in food. A "low cholesterol" food is one that contains 20 milligrams or less of cholesterol per serving.

TOP 30 FOODS FOR
CURBING CHOLESTEROL

These foods all contain a type of fiber known as soluble fiber, which has a cholesterol-lowering effect in the body, andy may be good dietary choices for improving your blood cholesterol profile.

Nonstarchy Vegetables
Artichoke
Turnips
Brussels sprouts
Cabbage
Broccoli

Starchy Vegetables
Sweet potato
Acorn squash
Potato with skin

Legumes
Kidney beans
Cranberry beans
Butter beans
Black beans
Navy beans
Lentils
Pinto beans

Great Northern
beans
Garbanzo beans
Soy-based foods

Fruits
Mango
Figs, dried
Kiwifruit
Orange
Plum

Cereals and Grains
Oat bran
Oatmeal
Bran Buds
Raisin Bran
All-Bran
Bran flakes
Pearl barley

Fiber

Fiber is the indigestible portion of plant foods that keeps our digestive system running smoothly. It also keeps you trim by promoting feelings of fullness, stabilizing your blood sugar, and keeping your hunger at bay. You're less likely to overeat at a single sitting if your meal is a high-fiber one.

Certain types of fiber, namely fiber from fruits and vegetables, have a modest calorie-curbing effect, too. Fiber pushes food through your digestive tract more rapidly. As a result, your body may not have enough time to absorb all the calories and fat that pass through and so they are excreted. Fewer calories are left to be stored as body fat. Scientific evidence suggests that if you follow a high-fiber, low-fat diet, as this plan suggests, you can lose three times more weight than if you followed a low-fat diet only.

Legumes (beans and lentils), fruits, vegetables, and whole grains are among the foods most plentiful in fiber. You need between 25 and 35 grams a day of fiber for good health. Foods considered high in fiber contain at least 2.5 to 3 grams or more per serving. Fiber is one nutrient definitely worth counting.

Sugar

So many of you have failed to lose weight and keep it off because of sugar and sweets. If a hunk

---

COUNTING FIBER

Here are some easy-to-remember ways for calculating fiber so that you reach at least 25 grams:

Foods with 6 grams or more
½ cup canned kidney beans, garbanzo beans, lima beans, or black beans
1 serving of All-Bran, All-Bran with Extra Fiber, or Fiber One cereal

Foods with 4 to 5 grams
1 cup fresh berries (strawberries, blueberries, or raspberries)
1 pear with skin
1 serving dried fruit
1 serving bran flakes or Raisin Bran
1 cup cooked broccoli
1 medium sweet potato (baked with skin)

Foods with 2 to 3 grams
1 apple with skin
1 banana
1 orange
1 cup raw chopped vegetables
1 slice high-fiber bread
½ cup cooked grains (brown rice, wild rice, barley)
½ cup whole grain pasta

---

of your calories comes from sweet, sugar-laden food, it is likely that your natural chemistry is almost constantly in a state of metabolic turmoil. Refined sugar (also called "added sugar") and foods that contain it are digested quickly and they dump sugar into the bloodstream quite rapidly. In many people, this makes insulin levels spike upward, causing calories to be converted into sustainable body fat rather than being burned for energy. It's not uncommon to experience more hunger and more cravings in the aftermath of this insulin response—all of which can lead to overeating.

Sugar and sweets can also be, for many people, as addictive as cigarettes, drugs, or alcohol, summoning up a loss of control that resembles the behavior of addiction, and they can be just as difficult to give up. Physiologically, these foods excite the same circuits in your brain that are stimulated by pleasure-inducing drugs, delivering a mild and short-lived high.

If sugar is a problem for you, you have to acknowledge this fact and go about changing it. You cannot achieve a trim, fit body if you keep caving in to sugar cravings. Your body will just not cooperate. Failure to give up added sugar will create more trouble than you can ever imagine.

But the good news is that once you kick the sugar habit, your desire for sweets will probably diminish. If you avoid sweets, for even a few weeks, your taste buds will become deprogrammed from loving the taste of sugar, and you'll experience fewer cravings.

You need to recognize what the sabotaging effects of eating too much sugar are on your body

APPROXIMATE SUGAR CONTENT
OF POPULAR FOODS*

Food	Teaspoons
Fortune cookie	1 teaspoon
Sugar cookie, fat-free	2 teaspoons
Oatmeal cookie, fat-free	3 teaspoons
Vanilla ice cream, ½ cup	3 teaspoons
Angel food cake, 1 piece	4 teaspoons
Toaster pastry, low-fat	5 teaspoons
Chocolate candy bar	5 teaspoons
Cranberry sauce, 1 slice	5½ teaspoons
Frozen meal, Salisbury steak with potatoes and corn, low-fat	6 teaspoons
French toast sticks, 5 pieces	6½ teaspoons
Lemonade mix, prepared with water, 1 cup	7 teaspoons
Yogurt, fruit-flavored, low-fat, 8 ounces	7 teaspoons
Soft drink, cola, 12 ounces	10 teaspoons
Vanilla shake, fast-food, 20 ounces	12 teaspoons
Bottled fruit drink, 20 ounces	17 teaspoons

* Estimates were tabulated from USDA data and from food labels.

and the role it plays in your weight. You also need to be aware of how much sugar there is in foods—which is why this food guide includes grams of sugar per serving in many of the foods listed. That way, you can start cutting back on sugar-added foods in order to get better control of your weight.

But what limits should you place on sugar consumption? There is no easy answer to that question, since recommended levels for sugar intake have not been established. One prevailing recommendation is that you cap your intake of added sugar at 10 percent or less of your total daily calories. For example:

Average Daily Calories	Added Sugar Maximum
1,200	30 grams
1,500	38 grams
1,800	45 grams
2,000	50 grams
2,200	55 grams
2,400	60 grams

Generally, each gram of sugar in a food comes from 4 teaspoons of sugar, although some of that sugar may come from natural sources if the food is a fruit, vegetable, or dairy product. "Sugar-free" foods provide less than 0.5 gram of sugars per serving. (Sugar-free does not mean carbohydrate-free.) If a food label says "no sugar added," this means that no form of sugar has been put into the food during processing or packaging.

Be aware, too, that sugar in foods often comes disguised under other names on labels (see page 171 for an explanation of hidden sugars in foods), so you may be eating more added sugars than you think you are. For tips on reducing sugar in your diet, see the box on page 165.

You do not need to worry about the natural sugar in fruits, vegetables, and dairy products, however.

DE-SUGAR YOUR DIET

- Use the food guide to track the sugar you consume during the day, since it can really mount up. Eating a bowl of frosted cold cereal, a can of cola, and a candy bar, for example, can add nearly 70 grams of sugar to your diet.
- Drink water, diet sodas, or herbal teas in place of sweetened soft drinks.
- Avoid sugary low-response cost, low-yield foods, such as candy, cookies, cakes, pies, pastries, and other sugary baked goods—even fat-free versions, which often contain as much sugar as their counterparts.
- Choose canned fruits that are packed in water or in their own juice.
- Get in the habit of having fresh fruit for dessert and snacks instead of having candy or sweets. Eventually, your choice will shift from sweets to natural foods that will satisfy you in a big way.
- Avoid fruit drinks, beverages, and "ades"; these products contain only 5 to 10 percent real juice and are loaded with added sugar.
- Prepare your own fruit-flavored yogurt by adding fresh or canned fruit to plain yogurt, or blend in sugar-free preserves or jam.
- Use artificial sweeteners, but use them in moderation.

This type of sugar comes wrapped up in vitamins, minerals, fiber, and antioxidants and is not the source of your excess pounds.

Sodium

Another food additive that is a potential health liability for some people is sodium. Foods in their natural state contain some sodium, a mineral that helps maintain normal water balance in the body and helps regulate the rhythm of your heart. Most sodium in our diets, however, comes in the form of sodium chloride, better known as "table salt," that is added to food during processing. Many low-response cost, low-yield foods, such as lunch meats, fast foods, snack foods, cheeses, baked goods, and cereals, are loaded with sodium. So are canned foods and pickles. Carbonated soft drinks also contain sodium.

Salty foods also tend to be high in fat—a combination that is addictive in its taste appeal and compels you to devour greasy foods like potato chips in ever-increasing amounts. (Sodium comes in many forms; see the table on page 171 for examples.)

If you are overweight, you absolutely must watch your sodium intake. In a twenty-year study of nearly ten thousand people, for each additional 1¼ teaspoons of salt eaten by people who were overweight, the risk of dying from heart disease increased 61 percent and the risk of dying from a stroke increased 89 percent. Among people who were of normal weight, extra salt did not confer an extra risk. The reason for this effect is most likely because a high-sodium diet can promote high blood pressure—an established risk factor for

SHAKE THE SALT HABIT

- Use the food guide to check the sodium content of the foods you eat each day to get some idea of how much salt you may be eating. Make adjustments if necessary.
- Read food labels more often to check the amount of sodium in servings.
- Cut back on fast food and other low-response cost, low-yield foods known to be high in sodium.
- Use salt sparingly—at the table and in cooking.
- Steer clear of salty foods, such as lunch meats (unless they are the low-sodium variety), pickled foods, salted nuts, chips, and snack foods.
- Choose low-sodium foods more often, such as low-sodium vegetable juice, crackers, cheeses, pickles, and soups.
- Select no-salt or low-sodium condiments such as catsup, mayonnaise, chili sauce, mustard, and soy sauce.
- Eat more fresh fruits and vegetables (which are low in sodium).
- Flavor your foods with salt-free herbs, spices, lemon juice, and extracts.
- Use salt substitutes.

heart disease—or aggravate it, particularly in people who are salt sensitive (meaning that even a small amount of salt can trigger a rise in blood pressure).

Whether you are salt sensitive or not, regardless of your blood pressure, cutting back on salt is still

LABEL LINGO—SODIUM

If you monitor sodium, learn how to interpret food labels to understand labeling that refers to sodium content. For example:

Sodium free: Fewer than 5 milligrams per serving.
Very low sodium: 35 milligrams or less per serving.
Low sodium: 140 milligrams or less per serving.
Reduced sodium: The food contains 25 percent less sodium than usual.
Lite/light: The food contains 50 percent of the usual amount of sodium.
Unsalted: No salt was added during the processing.

a wise move. Most of us eat too much salt anyway, when in reality we require a minimum of 500 milligrams (about a tenth of a teaspoon) and no more than 2,400 milligrams a day (that's about a teaspoon). Your preference for salt may weaken the less you use it in your diet, so start reducing your sodium by controlling the saltshaker and choosing a greater variety of low-sodium foods. I've listed tips for restricting salt in your diet in the box on page 167.

Abbreviations and Symbols

As you begin to look up the foods in which you're interested, keep in mind the following abbreviations:

carb	carbohydrate
chol	cholesterol
dia	diameter
fl. oz.	fluid ounce
g	gram
mg	milligram
oz.	ounce
pkt	packet
prep	prepared according to recipe or package directions
prot	protein
sat	saturated
serving	serving size identified on a food label
t	trace
tbsp.	tablespoon
tsp.	teaspoon
w/	with
w/o	without
na	information not available
0	zero (no nutrient value)

(Note: A designation of "na" does not mean an absence of a particular nutrient, only that analysis of that food for that nutrient is lacking.)

All of the nutrient data in *The Ultimate Weight Solution Food Guide* is based on information from the United States government, from producers of brand-name foods, and from fast-food restaurant chains. Also consulted were scientific journal articles that analyzed nutrient content of various foods.

We all do better when we know that there are certain consequences to what we choose. This is specific information that will help you better evaluate your foods and stop sabotaging your health and your weight. Choose better foods this time, and you will choose a different outcome—weight loss freedom! Use this guide as part of your accountability system. I suggest that you keep it close by, taking it wherever you go—from the supermarket to restaurants. It will help you make commonsense food choices that let you achieve and remain at your get-real weight.

HIDDEN SOURCES OF SUGARS AND SODIUM IN FOODS

Sugars
Beet sugar
Brown sugar
Cane sugar
Corn sweetener
Corn syrup
Dextrin
Dextrose
Fructose
Galactose
Glucose
High fructose corn syrup
Honey
Lactose
Levulose
Maltodextrin
Maltose
Mannitol*
Maple syrup
Molasses
Raw sugar
Sorbitol*
Sucrose
Turbinado sugar
White grape juice
Xylitol*

Sodium
Baking powder
Baking soda (sodium
    bicarbonate)
Brine (salt and water)
Disodium inosinate
Disodium phosphate
Monosodium glutamate
    (MSG)
Salt (sodium chloride)
Sodium alginate
Sodium ascorbate
Sodium benzoate
Sodium caseinate
Sodium citrate
Sodium hydroxide
Sodium nitrate
Sodium proprionate
Sodium saccharin

* These are sugar alcohols, produced from fruit or dextrose. All three contain the same number of calories as sugar. One of the main differences is that they are absorbed more slowly in the body than sugar is, and therefore are believed to be better for people with diabetes, who must maintain good blood sugar control. Sugar alcohols do not lead to tooth decay, unlike other sugars.

The Ultimate Weight Solution Food Guide

HIGH-RESPONSE COST, HIGH-YIELD FOODS: BEEF

Food	Serving	Calories	Prot (g)	Carb (g)
Ground, Lean				
Hamburger, 85% lean, pan-browned	3 oz.	218	24	0
Hamburger, 85% lean, broiled	3 oz.	197	21	0
Hamburger, 90% lean, pan-browned	3 oz.	196	24	0
Hamburger, 90% lean, broiled	3 oz.	173	21	0
Hamburger, 95% lean, pan-browned	3 oz.	164	25	0
Hamburger, 95% lean, broiled	3 oz.	139	22	0
Beef, Lean Cuts				
Bottom round, lean only, trimmed to 0" fat, all grades, roasted	4 oz.	207	33	0
Bottom round, lean only, trimmed to 0" fat, choice, roasted	4 oz.	219	33	0

Fat/Sat Fat (g)	Chol (mg)	Fiber (g)	Sugars (g)	Sodium (mg)
13/5	77	0	0	76
12/5	73	0	0	67
10/4	76	0	0	74
9/4	70	0	0	64
6/3	76	0	0	72
5/2	65	0	0	60

8/2.5	88	0	0	75
9/3	88	0	0	75

Beef (cont.)	Serving	Calories	Prot (g)	Carb (g)
Bottom round, lean only, trimmed to 0" fat, select, roasted	4 oz.	194	33	0
Bottom round, lean only, trimmed to ¼" fat, all grades, roasted	4 oz.	214	33	0
Bottom round, lean only, trimmed to ¼" fat, choice, roasted	4 oz.	224	33	0
Bottom round, lean only, trimmed to ¼" fat, select, roasted	4 oz.	203	33	0
Bottom round, lean and fat, trimmed to ⅛" fat, all grades, roasted	4 oz.	260	31	0
Bottom round, lean and fat, trimmed to ⅛" fat, select, roasted	4 oz.	248	31	0
Eye of the round, lean only, trimmed to 0" fat, all grades, roasted	4 oz.	188	33	0

Fat/Sat Fat (g)	Chol (mg)	Fiber (g)	Sugars (g)	Sodium (mg)
6/2	88	0	0	75
8/3	88	0	0	75
9/3	88	0	0	75
7/2	88	0	0	75
14/5	90	0	0	73
13/5	90	0	0	73
5/2	78	0	0	70

Beef (cont.)	Serving	Calories	Prot (g)	Carb (g)
Eye of the round, lean only, trimmed to 0" fat, choice, roasted	4 oz.	198	33	0
Eye of the round, lean only, trimmed to 0" fat, select, roasted	4 oz.	176	33	0
Eye of the round, lean only, trimmed to ¼" fat, select, roasted	4 oz.	181	33	0
Eye of the round, lean and fat, trimmed to 0" fat, select, roasted	4 oz.	182	33	0
Flank steak, lean only, trimmed to 0" fat, choice, broiled	4 oz.	235	31	0
Flank steak, lean and fat, trimmed to 0" fat, choice, broiled	4 oz.	256	30	0
Porterhouse steak, lean only, trimmed to 0" fat, all grades, broiled	4 oz.	240	30	0

Fat/Sat Fat (g)	Chol (mg)	Fiber (g)	Sugars (g)	Sodium (mg)
6/2	78	0	0	70
4/1	78	0	0	70
5/2	78	0	0	70
5/2	78	0	0	70
11.5/5	76	0	0	94
14/6	77	0	0	92
13/4	70	0	0	78

Beef (cont.)	Serving	Calories	Prot (g)	Carb (g)
Porterhouse steak, lean only, trimmed to 0" fat, choice, broiled	4 oz.	254	29	0
Porterhouse steak, lean only, trimmed to 0" fat, select, broiled	4 oz.	220	30	0
Porterhouse steak, lean only, trimmed to ¼" fat, choice, broiled	4 oz.	244	30	0
Porterhouse steak, lean only, trimmed to ¼" fat, select, broiled	4 oz.	230	31	0
Round, tip round, lean only, trimmed to 0" fat, all grades, roasted	4 oz.	199	33	0
Round, tip round, lean only, trimmed to 0" fat, choice, roasted	4 oz.	204	33	0
Round, tip round, lean only, trimmed to 0" fat, select, roasted	4 oz.	193	32.5	0

Fat/Sat Fat (g)	Chol (mg)	Fiber (g)	Sugars (g)	Sodium (mg)
14.5/5	74	0	0	78
10/4	66	0	0	78
13/4	78	0	0	78
11/4	66	0	0	78
7/2	92	0	0	74
7/2.5	92	0	0	74
6/2	92	0	0	74

Beef (cont.)	Serving	Calories	Prot (g)	Carb (g)
Round, tip round, lean only, trimmed to ¼" fat, all grades, roasted	4 oz.	210	32.5	0
Round, tip round, lean only, trimmed to ¼" fat, choice, roasted	4 oz.	213	32.5	0
Round, tip round, lean only, trimmed to ¼" fat, select, roasted	4 oz.	204	32.5	0
Round, tip round, lean and fat, trimmed to 0" fat all grades, roasted	4 oz.	216	32	0
Round, tip round, lean and fat, trimmed to 0" fat, choice, roasted	4 oz.	227	32	0
Round, tip round, lean and fat, trimmed to 0" fat, select, roasted	4 oz.	211	32	0
Round, tip round, lean and fat, trimmed to ⅛" fat, all grades, roasted	4 oz.	248	31	0

Fat/Sat Fat (g)	Chol (mg)	Fiber (g)	Sugars (g)	Sodium (mg)
8/3	92	0	0	74
8/3	92	0	0	74
7/2.5	92	0	0	74
9/3	92	0	0	73
10/4	93	0	0	73
8/3	92	0	0	73
13/5	93	0	0	71

Beef (cont.)	Serving	Calories	Prot (g)	Carb (g)
Round, tip round, lean and fat, trimmed to ⅛" fat, choice, roasted	4 oz.	258	31	0
Round, tip round, lean and fat, trimmed to ⅛" fat, select, roasted	4 oz.	238	31	0
T-bone steak, lean only, trimmed to 0" fat, all grades, broiled	4 oz.	214	29	0
T-bone steak, lean only, trimmed to 0" fat, choice, broiled	4 oz.	224	29	0
T-bone steak, lean only, trimmed to 0" fat, select, broiled	4 oz.	201	29	0
T-bone steak, lean only, trimmed to ¼" fat, all grades, broiled	4 oz.	229	31	0
T-bone steak, lean only, trimmed to ¼" fat, choice, broiled	4 oz.	232	30	0

Fat/Sat Fat (g)	Chol (mg)	Fiber (g)	Sugars (g)	Sodium (mg)
14/5	93	0	0	71
12/4	93	0	0	73
10/3.5	62	0	0	80
11/4	63	0	0	80
8/3	61	0	0	80
11/4	65	0	0	85
11/4	67	0	0	87

Beef (cont.)	Serving	Calories	Prot (g)	Carb (g)
T-bone steak, lean only, trimmed to ¼" fat, select, broiled	4 oz.	224	31	0
Tenderloin, lean only, trimmed to 0" fat, choice, broiled (filet mignon, beef medallions)	4 oz.	240	32	0
Top round, lean only, trimmed to 0" fat, all grades, braised (London broil)	4 oz.	226	41	0
Top round, lean and fat, trimmed to 0" fat, choice, braised (London broil)	4 oz.	245	40	0
Top round, lean only, trimmed to 0" fat, select, braised (London broil)	4 oz.	215	41	0
Top round, lean and fat, trimmed to 0" fat, select, braised (London broil)	4 oz.	227	40	0

Fat/Sat Fat (g)	Chol (mg)	Fiber (g)	Sugars (g)	Sodium (mg)
10/4	60	0	0	80
11/4	95	0	0	71
6/2	102	0	0	51
8/3	102	0	0	51
5/1.5	102	0	0	51
6/2	102	0	0	51

Beef (cont.)	Serving	Calories	Prot (g)	Carb (g)
Top round, lean only, trimmed to ¼" fat, all grades, braised (London broil)	4 oz.	232	41	0
Top round, lean only, trimmed to ¼" fat, all grades, broiled (London broil)	4 oz.	204	36	0
Top round, lean and fat only, trimmed to ⅛" fat, select, broiled (London broil)	4 oz.	222	35	0
Top sirloin, lean only, trimmed to 0" fat, all grades, broiled	4 oz.	216	34	0
Top sirloin, lean only, trimmed to 0" fat, choice, broiled	4 oz.	227	34	0
Top sirloin, lean only, trimmed to 0" fat, select, broiled	4 oz.	204	34	0

Fat/Sat Fat (g)	Chol (mg)	Fiber (g)	Sugars (g)	Sodium (mg)
6/2	102	0	0	51
5.5/2	95	0	0	69
8/3	96	0	0	68
8/3	101	0	0	75
9/3.5	101	0	0	75
6/2.5	101	0	0	75

Beef (cont.)	Serving	Calories	Prot (g)	Carb (g)
Top sirloin, lean only, trimmed to ¼" fat, all grades, broiled	4 oz.	221	34	0
Top sirloin, lean only, trimmed to ¼" fat, choice, broiled	4 oz.	229	34	0
Top sirloin, lean only, trimmed to ¼" fat, select, broiled	4 oz.	211	34	0
Top sirloin, lean and fat, trimmed to 0" fat, all grades, broiled	4 oz.	244	33	0
Top sirloin, lean and fat, trimmed to 0" fat, choice, broiled	4 oz.	260	33	0
Top sirloin, lean and fat, trimmed to 0" fat, select, broiled	4 oz.	221	34	0

Fat/Sat Fat (g)	Chol (mg)	Fiber (g)	Sugars (g)	Sodium (mg)
8/3	101	0	0	75
9/3.5	101	0	0	75
7/3	101	0	0	75
11/4.5	101	0	0	74
13/5	101	0	0	73
8.5/3	101	0	0	74

Beef (cont.)	Serving	Calories	Prot (g)	Carb (g)
Variety Meats,* Lean				
Beef heart, simmered	4 oz.	198	33	0
Beef kidneys, simmered	4 oz.	163	29	1
Beef liver, braised	4 oz.	182	28	4

* Although relatively low in fat, organ meats are high in dietary cholesterol.

Fat/Sat Fat (g)	Chol (mg)	Fiber (g)	Sugars (g)	Sodium (mg)
6/2	219	0	0	71
4/1	439	0	0	152
6/2	441	0	0	79

HIGH-RESPONSE COST, HIGH-YIELD FOODS: BEVERAGES

Food	Serving	Calories	Prot (g)	Carb (g)
Coffee				
Brewed	I cup	5	t	I
Brewed, decaf	I cup	5	t	I
Chicory added, instant	I cup	10	t	2
Espresso, restaurant prepared	100 grams	9	t	1.5
French vanilla flavor, sugar-free, fat-free, instant, prepared	I cup	25	t	5
French mocha flavor, sugar-free, fat-free, instant, prepared	I cup	24	t	5
Instant	I cup	5	t	I
Instant, decaf	I cup	4	t	t
Sugar-Free				
Carbonated/mineral water	I cup	0	0	0
Club soda	I can (12 fl. oz.)	0	0	0

Fat/Sat Fat (g)	Chol (mg)	Fiber (g)	Sugars (g)	Sodium (mg)
0/0	0	0	0	5
0/0	0	0	0	5
0/0	0	0	0	14
t/t	0	0	0	14
t/t	0	t	t	65
t/t	0	1	t	36
0/0	0	0	0	7
0/0	0	0	0	0

0/0	0	0	0	2
0/0	0	0	0	75

Beverages (cont.)	Serving	Calories	Prot (g)	Carb (g)
Diet soft drinks	I can (I2 fl. oz.)	0	t	t
Lemonade, low-calorie, w/ aspartame, prepared	I cup	5	0	I
Municipal water	I cup	0	0	0
Soft drink mix, tropical flavor, unsweetened, powder	I serving	I	0	t

Beverages/Tea

	Serving	Calories	Prot (g)	Carb (g)
Brewed	I cup	2	0	t
Brewed, decaf	I cup	2	0	I
Chamomile, brewed	I cup	2	0	t
Herbal, brewed	I cup	2	0	t
Instant, unsweetened	I cup	2	0	t
Instant, unsweetened, lemon-flavored	I cup	5	0	I
Sugar-free, low-calorie, w/ aspartame	I cup	3	t	t

Fat/Sat Fat (g)	Chol (mg)	Fiber (g)	Sugars (g)	Sodium (mg)
0/0	0	0	t	21
0/0	0	0	0	7
0	0	0	0	5
0/0	0	0	t	15

0/0	0	0	0	7
0/0	0	0	0	na
0/0	0	0	0	2
0/0	0	0	0	2
0/0	0	0	0	7
0/0	0	0	0	14
0/0	0	0	t	2

Beverages (cont.)	Serving	Calories	Prot (g)	Carb (g)
Sugar-free, low-calorie, lemon-flavored w/ saccharin	1 cup	5	0	1

Fat/Sat Fat (g)	Chol (mg)	Fiber (g)	Sugars (g)	Sodium (mg)
0/0	0	0	0	24

HIGH-RESPONSE COST, HIGH-YIELD FOODS: BREADS, BREAD PRODUCTS, AND CRACKERS

Food	Serving	Calories	Prot (g)	Carb (g)
Breads and Bread Products				
Bagel, oat bran	3" dia	176	7	37
Bagel, plain, enriched	3" dia	190	7	37
Cracked wheat bread	1 slice	65	2	12
Egg bread	1 slice	115	4	19
Mixed grain bread	1 slice	65	3	12
Oat bran bread	1 slice	71	3	12
Oat bran bread, reduced-calorie	1 slice	46	2	10
Oatmeal bread	1 slice	73	2	13
Oatmeal bread, reduced-calorie	1 slice	48	2	10
Pita bread, whole wheat	4" dia	74	3	15
Protein bread	1 slice	47	2	8
Pumpernickel bread	1 slice	65	2	12
Raisin bread	1 slice	71	2	14

Fat/Sat Fat (g)	Chol (mg)	Fiber (g)	Sugars (g)	Sodium (mg)
l/t	0	2.5	na	350
l/t	0	2	na	368
l/t	0	1.4	na	135
2/t	20	1	na	197
l/t	0	2	na	127
l/t	0	1	na	122
l/t	0	3	na	81
l/t	0	1	na	162
t/t	0	na	na	89
l/t	0	2	na	149
t/t	0	1	na	104
t/t	0	2	na	174
l/t	0	1	na	101

Breads (cont.)	Serving	Calories	Prot (g)	Carb (g)
Rice bran bread	I slice	66	2	12
Rye bread	I slice	83	3	15
Rye bread, reduced calorie	I slice	47	2	9
Tortilla, corn (not fried)	I medium (6" dia)	42	I	9
Tortilla, whole wheat	I medium (7" dia)	84	3	23
Wheatberry bread	I slice	65	2	12
Wheat bran bread	I slice	89	3	17
Wheat bread, reduced-calorie	I slice	46	2	10
Wheat germ bread	I slice	73	3	13.5
Whole wheat bread	I slice	69	3	13

Muffins

	Serving	Calories	Prot (g)	Carb (g)
English muffin, wheat	I muffin	127	5	26
English muffin, whole-wheat	I muffin	134	6	27
English muffin, whole-wheat, toasted	I muffin	135	6	27

Fat/Sat Fat (g)	Chol (mg)	Fiber (g)	Sugars (g)	Sodium (mg)
1/t	0	1	na	119
1/2	0	2	na	211
t/t	0	3	na	93
.5/t	na	1	na	31
.5/t	na	2	na	196
1/t	0	1	na	132
1/t	0	1.5	na	175
t/t	0	3	na	118
t/t	0	t	na	155
1/t	0	2	na	148

1/t	0	3	na	218
1/t	0	4	na	420
1/t	0	5	na	422

Breads (cont.)	Serving	Calories	Prot (g)	Carb (g)
Mixed grain, includes granola	1 muffin	155	6	31
Oat bran	1 small	178	5	32
Oat bran	1 mini	46	1	8
Oat bran, prepared from recipe, made w/reduced fat milk (2%)	1 muffin	169	4	24
Wheat bran, toaster-type w/raisins	1 muffin	106	2	19
Wheat bran, toaster-type w/raisins, toasted	1 muffin	106	2	19

Crackers

	Serving	Calories	Prot (g)	Carb (g)
Crispbread, rye (including Wasa crispbread)	2 crackers	74	2	16
Crispbread, rye, large (triple cracker)	1 cracker	92	2	21
Flatbread, Norwegian	3 crackers	63	1	14
Matzo, whole wheat	1 matzo	98	4	22

Fat/Sat Fat (g)	Chol (mg)	Fiber (g)	Sugars (g)	Sodium (mg)
1/t	0	2	na	275
5/1	0	3	na	259
1/t	0	1	na	67
7/1	22	2	na	266
3/t	6	3	na	178
3/1	3	3	na	179

t/t	0	3	na	52
t/t	0	4	na	66
t/t	0	3	na	45
t/t	0	3	na	1

Breads (cont.)	Serving	Calories	Prot (g)	Carb (g)
Melba toast, rye	4 toasts	76	2	15
Melba toast, wheat	4 toasts	76	3	15
Rye wafers, plain	2 wafers	74	2	18
Rye wafers, seasoned, large (triple cracker)	1 wafer	84	2	16
Whole wheat crackers	4 crackers	72	1	10
Whole wheat crackers, low salt	4 crackers	72	1	11

Fat/Sat Fat (g)	Chol (mg)	Fiber (g)	Sugars (g)	Sodium (mg)
1/t	0	2	na	180
t/t	0	2	na	168
t/t	0	5	na	174
2/t	0	5	na	195
3/t	0	2	na	104
3/t	0	2	na	40

HIGH-RESPONSE COST, HIGH-YIELD FOODS: CEREALS

Food	Serving	Calories	Prot (g)	Carb (g)
Cereals, Cold*				
100% Bran Cereal (Post)	⅓ cup	82	4	22
All-Bran (Kellogg)	½ cup	81	4	23
All-Bran with Extra Fiber (Kellogg)	½ cup	50	3	20
All-Bran Bran Buds (Kellogg)	⅓ cup	74	2	24
Banana Nut Crunch (Post)	I cup	249	5	44
Basic 4 (General Mills)	I cup	202	4	42
Bran Flakes (Post)	¾ cup	96	3	24
Cheerios, multi-grain (General Mills)	I cup	108	2	24
Complete Oat Bran Flakes (Kellogg)	¾ cup	105	3	23
Complete Wheat Bran Flakes (Kellogg)	¾ cup	92	3	23

* Some of these cereals may contain added sugar; however, many are high in beneficial fiber.

Fat/Sat Fat (g)	Chol (mg)	Fiber (g)	Sugars (g)	Sodium (mg)
t/t	0	8	7	120
1/t	0	10	6	80
1/t	0	13	t	124
t/t	0	13	8	201
6/t	0	4	12	253
3/t	0	3	14	316
1/0	0	5	6	220
1/t	0	3	6	201
1/t	0	4	6	210
t/t	0	5	5	207

Cereals (cont.)	Serving	Calories	Prot (g)	Carb (g)
Cracklin' Oat Bran (Kellogg)	¾ cup	225	5	39
Crunchy Bran (Quaker)	¾ cup	90	1	23
Fiber One (General Mills)	½ cup	59	2	24
Fruit & Fibre (Post)	1 cup	212	4	42
Granola w/ raisins, lowfat (Kellogg)	⅔ cup	231	5	48
Granola w/o raisins, lowfat (Kellogg)	½ cup	186	4	39
Granola w/ raisins, lowfat (Quaker)	½ cup	195	4	40.5
Grape-Nuts (Post)	½ cup	208	6	47
Grape-Nuts Flakes (Post)	¾ cup	106	3	24
Great Grains (Post)	⅔ cup	204	4	40
Kashi GoLean (Kellogg)	50 grams	157	10.5	35
Kashi GoLean Crunch (Kellogg)	50 grams	188	8	34
Kashi Good Friends (Kellogg)	50 grams	154	5	40

Fat/Sat Fat (g)	Chol (mg)	Fiber (g)	Sugars (g)	Sodium (mg)
8/2	0	6	17	157
1/0	0	5	6	232
t/t	0	14	0	129
3/t	0	5	16	280
3/1	0	3	17	148
2/t	0	3	14	120
3/t	1	17	3	119
1/t	0	5	7	354
t/t	0	2.5	5	140
5/t	0	4	13	156
1.5/0	0	12.5	8	44
3/0	0	7.5	12.5	90
2/0	0	13.5	10	116

Cereals (cont.)	Serving	Calories	Prot (g)	Carb (g)
Kashi Heart to Heart (Kellogg)	50 grams	178	6	38
Life (Quaker)	¾ cup	120	3	25
Multi-Bran Chex (General Mills)	1 cup	166	3	41
Mueslix (Kellogg)	⅔ cup	198	5	40
Raisin Bran (Kellogg)	1 cup	188	5	45
Raisin Bran (Post)	1 cup	187	5	46
Raisin Nut Bran (General Mills)	1 cup	209	5	41
Rice Chex (General Mills)	1¼ cup	117	2	27
Shredded Wheat (Post)	2 biscuits	156	5	38
Shredded Wheat, spoon-sized (Post)	1 cup	167	5	41
Shredded Wheat 'N Bran (Post)	1¼ cup	197	7	47
Smart Start (Kellogg)	1 cup	182	3	43
Special K (Kellogg)	1 cup	117	7	22

Fat/Sat Fat (g)	Chol (mg)	Fiber (g)	Sugars (g)	Sodium (mg)
2.5/0	0	10	7.5	136
1/t	0	2	6	164
1/t	0	6	11	322
3/t	0	4	17	171
1/t	0	7	19	350
1/t	0	8	20	360
4/t	0	5	16	250
t/t	0	t	2.5	292
t/t	0	5	t	3
t/t	0	6	t	3
1/t	0	8	t	3
t/t	0	2	15.5	281
t/t	0	t	4	224

Cereals (cont.)	Serving	Calories	Prot (g)	Carb (g)
Total, Corn Flakes (General Mills)	1⅓ cup	112	2	26
Total, Raisin Bran (General Mills)	1 cup	171	4	41
Total, whole grain (General Mills)	¾ cup	97	2	22.5
Uncle Sam	1 cup	237	9	36
Wheaties (General Mills)	1 cup	107	3	24

Cereals/Hot

	Serving	Calories	Prot (g)	Carb (g)
Corn grits, white, w/o salt	½ cup	73	2	16
Corn grits, yellow, w/o salt	½ cup	73	2	16
Corn grits, instant, butter flavor (Quaker)	1 pkt	101	2	21
Corn grits, instant, cheddar cheese flavor (Quaker)	1 pkt	99	2	20
Corn grits, instant, plain (Quaker)	1 pkt	89	2	21
Cream of Rice, w/o salt	½ cup	63	1	14

Fat/Sat Fat (g)	Chol (mg)	Fiber (g)	Sugars (g)	Sodium (mg)
t/t	0	t	3	209
l/t	0	5	20	239
t/t	0	2	5	192
6/l	0	11	1	113
l/t	0	3	4	218

Fat/Sat Fat (g)	Chol (mg)	Fiber (g)	Sugars (g)	Sodium (mg)
t/t	0	t	na	0
t/t	0	t	na	0
l/t	0	1	t	323
2/t	0	1	na	510
t/t	0	1	na	289
t/t	0	t	na	1

Cereals (cont.)	Serving	Calories	Prot (g)	Carb (g)
Cream of Wheat, instant, w/o salt	½ cup	77	2	16
Cream of Wheat, mix 'n eat, plain	1 pkt	102	3	21
Cream of Wheat, quick, w/o salt	½ cup	64	2	13
Cream of Wheat, regular, w/o salt	½ cup	66	2	14
Farina, w/o salt	½ cup	58	2	12
Malt-O-Meal, plain, w/o salt	½ cup	61	2	13
Maypo, w/o salt	¾ cup	128	4	24
Multi-grain oatmeal, dry	½ cup	133	4.5	29
Nestum	½ cup	95	3	17
Oats, instant, plain	½ cup	69	3	12
Oats, instant, w/ bran and raisins	1 pkt	158	5	30
Oats, old-fashioned, w/o salt	⅔ cup	150	5	27
Oat bran	½ cup	146	7	25

Fat/Sat Fat (g)	Chol (mg)	Fiber (g)	Sugars (g)	Sodium (mg)
t/t	0	1	na	4
t/t	0	t	na	241
t/t	0	1	na	69
t/t	0	1	na	1
t/t	0	2	na	0
t/t	0	t	na	1
2/t	0	4	na	7
1/t	0	5	na	1
t/0	0	3.5	0	5
1/t	0	2	na	188
2/t	0	5.5	na	248
3/t	0	4	0	0
3/t	0	6	na	2

Cereals (cont.)	Serving	Calories	Prot (g)	Carb (g)
Oatmeal, instant, w/ apples and cinnamon	1 pkt	125	3	26
Oatmeal, Quick 'n Hearty, honey bran (Quaker)	1 pkt	151	4	31
Oatmeal, Quick 'n Hearty, regular flavor (Quaker)	1 pkt	106	4	19
Ralston, w/o salt	½ cup	67	3	14
Roman Meal, plain, cooked, w/ salt	½ cup	74	3.5	16.5
Roman Meal, plain, cooked, w/o salt	½ cup	74	3.5	16.5
Roman Meal with Oats, w/ salt	½ cup	85	3.5	17
Roman Meal with Oats, w/o salt	½ cup	85	3.5	17
Wheatena	½ cup	68	2	14
Whole wheat, hot natural cereal, w/ salt	½ cup	75	2.5	17
Whole wheat, hot natural cereal, w/o salt	½ cup	75	2.5	17

Fat/Sat Fat (g)	Chol (mg)	Fiber (g)	Sugars (g)	Sodium (mg)
1/t	0	2.5	na	121
2/t	0	3	11	253
2/t	0	2	na	153
t/t	0	3	na	3
t/0	0	4	na	99
t/0	0	4	na	1
1/0	0	4	na	270
1/0	0	4	na	5
t/t	0	3	na	289
t/t	0	2	na	282
t/t	0	2	na	0

HIGH-RESPONSE COST,
HIGH-YIELD FOODS: CHEESES

Food	Serving	Calories	Prot (g)	Carb (g)
Reduced Fat				
Cheddar, lowfat	1 oz.	98	14	1
Colby, lowfat	1 oz.	98	14	1
Cottage, lowfat, 1% milkfat	½ cup	81	14	3
Cottage, lowfat, 2% milkfat	½ cup	102	16	4
Cottage, nonfat	½ cup	62	13	1
Mozzarella, part skim milk	1 oz.	72	7	1
Mozzarella, part skim milk, low moisture	1 oz.	79	8	1
Ricotta, part skim	½ cup	170	14	6

Fat/Sat Fat (g)	Chol (mg)	Fiber (g)	Sugars (g)	Sodium (mg)
4/2	12	0	0	347
4/2	12	0	0	347
1/t	5	0	0	459
2/1	9	0	0	459
t/t	5	0	0	9
5/3	16	0	0	132
5/3	15	0	0	150
10/6	38	0	0	154

HIGH-RESPONSE COST, HIGH-YIELD FOODS: CONDIMENTS

Food	Serving	Calories	Prot (g)	Carb (g)
Condiments				
A-1 Steak Sauce	1 tbsp	15	0	3
Barbecue sauce	2 tbsp	23	t	4
Catsup	1 tbsp	16	t	4
Catsup, green (Heinz)	1 tbsp	20	0	5
Catsup, low sodium	1 tbsp	16	t	4
Chili sauce (Chef Mate hot dog, Nestlé)	1 tbsp	17	t	2
Cocktail sauce (Del Monte)	2 tbsp	50	t	12
Enchilada sauce (Ortega)	2 tbsp	15	t	2
Horseradish	1 tbsp	7	t	2
Hot pepper sauce	¼ tsp	0	t	t
Mustard (Grey Poupon)	1 tbsp	15	0	0
Mustard, yellow	1 tbsp	10	t	1

Fat/Sat Fat (g)	Chol (mg)	Fiber (g)	Sugars (g)	Sodium (mg)
0/0	0	na	2	280
t	0	t	na	255
t/t	0	t	na	178
0/0	0	0	4	190
t/t	0	t	na	3
t/t	1	t	t	100
0/0	0	na	11	455
t/t	0	.5	t	77
t/t	0	t	na	47
0/0	0	0	na	32
0/0	0	na	na	360
t/t	0	.5	na	168

Condiments (cont.)	Serving	Calories	Prot (g)	Carb (g)
Picante sauce (Ortega)	2 tbsp	10	t	2
Picante sauce, medium (La Victoria)	2 tbsp	8	t	1
Picante sauce, mild (La Victoria)	2 tbsp	8	t	1
Salsa	2 tbsp	9	t	2
Salsa, black bean and corn	2 tbsp	16	1	3
Salsa, Chunky Chili Dip (La Victoria)	2 tbsp	9	t	2
Salsa, green chili, mild (La Victoria)	2 tbsp	8	t	1
Salsa, green jalapena (La Victoria)	2 tbsp	10	t	1
Salsa Ranchero, hot (La Victoria)	2 tbsp	9	t	2
Salsa, red jalapena (La Victoria)	2 tbsp	12	t	2
Salsa, Thick 'N Chunky, hot (La Victoria)	2 tbsp	8	t	1

Fat/Sat Fat (g)	Chol (mg)	Fiber (g)	Sugars (g)	Sodium (mg)
t/t	0	0	t	252
t/na	0	t	1	150
t/na	0	t	1	179
t/t	0	.5	na	139
0/0	0	.5	1	125
t/na	na	t	na	148
t/na	na	t	t	172
t/na	0	t	.6	180
t/na	0	t	1	169
t/na	0	t	1	146
t/na	0	t	1	131

Condiments (cont.)	Serving	Calories	Prot (g)	Carb (g)
Salsa, Thick 'N Chunky, medium (La Victoria)	2 tbsp	8	t	1
Salsa, Thick 'N Chunky, mild (La Victoria)	2 tbsp	8	t	1
Soy sauce, low sodium	1 tbsp	9	1	1.5
Spaghetti/marinara sauce	½ cup	71	2	10
Tabasco sauce	1 tsp	1	t	t
Taco sauce, green, mild (La Victoria)	2 tbsp	9	t	2
Taco sauce, green, medium (La Victoria)	2 tbsp	9	t	2
Taco sauce, red, mild (La Victoria)	2 tbsp	13	t	3
Taco sauce, red, medium (La Victoria)	2 tbsp	13	t	3
Tartar sauce, low calorie	1 tbsp	31	t	2
Teriyaki sauce, generic	2 tbsp	30	2	6

Fat/Sat Fat (g)	Chol (mg)	Fiber (g)	Sugars (g)	Sodium (mg)
t/t	0	t	1	158
t/na	0	t	1	156
t/t	0	t	na	600
3/t	0	2	na	515
t/t	0	0	na	30
t/na	0	t	1	190
t/na	0	t	1	190
t/na	0	t	2	210
t/na	0	t	2	210
2.5/t	3	na	na	82
0/0	0	0	na	1380

Condiments (cont.)	Serving	Calories	Prot (g)	Carb (g)
Teriyaki sauce (Kikkoman)	2 tbsp	30	2	4
Teriyaki sauce (Nestlé)	2 tbsp	42	t	7
Vinegar	1 tbsp	2	0	t
Worcestershire sauce	1 tsp	0	0	0

Pickles and Olives*

Dill pickle	1 spear	5	t	1
Dill pickle, chopped	½ cup	13	t	3
Dill pickle, large (4" long)	1 pickle	24	1	6
Dill pickle, medium (3¾" long)	1 pickle	12	t	3
Dill pickle, small	1 pickle	7	t	2
Sour pickle	1 spear	3	t	1
Sour pickle, chopped	½ cup	36	t	2

* While generally low in calories, these foods tend to be high in sodium and should probably be avoided if your physician has advised you to follow a sodium-restricted diet.

Fat/Sat Fat (g)	Chol (mg)	Fiber (g)	Sugars (g)	Sodium (mg)
0/0	0	0	4	1220
1/t	0	0	6	319
0/0	0	0	na	0
0	0	0	0	60

t/t	0	t	na	385
t/t	0	1	na	917
t/t	0	2	na	1731
t/t	0	1	na	833
t/t	0	t	na	474
t/t	0	t	na	362
t/t	0	1	na	936

Condiments (cont.)	Serving	Calories	Prot (g)	Carb (g)
Sour pickle, large (4" long)	1 pickle	15	t	3
Sour pickle, medium (3¾" long)	1 pickle	7	t	1
Sour pickle, small	1 pickle	4	t	1
Sweet pickle (Gherkin)	1 spear	23	t	6
Sweet pickle (Gherkin), large (3" long)	1 pickle	41	t	11
Sweet pickle (Gherkin), medium (2¾" long)	1 pickle	29	t	8
Sweet pickle (Gherkin), midget (2⅛" long)	1 pickle	7	t	2
Sweet pickle (Gherkin), small (2½" long)	1 pickle	18	t	5
Olive, green	5 olives	23	0	t
Olives, ripe, canned, colossal	1 olive	12	t	1

Fat/Sat Fat (g)	Chol (mg)	Fiber (g)	Sugars (g)	Sodium (mg)
t/t	0	2	na	1631
t/t	0	1	na	785
t/t	0	t	na	447
t/t	0	t	na	188
t/t	0	t	na	329
t/t	0	t	na	235
t/t	0	t	na	56
t/t	0	t	na	141
2.5/t	0	na	na	na
1/t	0	t	na	135

Condiments (cont.)	Serving	Calories	Prot (g)	Carb (g)
Olives, ripe, canned, jumbo	1 olive	7	t	t
Olives, ripe, canned, large	1 olive	5	t	t
Olives, ripe, canned, small	1 olive	4	t	t

Fat/Sat Fat (g)	Chol (mg)	Fiber (g)	Sugars (g)	Sodium (mg)
l/t	0	t	na	75
t/t	0	t	na	38
t/t	0	t	na	28

HIGH-RESPONSE COST,
HIGH-YIELD FOODS: EGGS

Food	Serving	Calories	Prot (g)	Carb (g)
Eggs				
Egg substitute, liquid	¼ cup	53	8	t
Egg white	2 large	33	7	t
Egg white, dried powder	I tbsp	53	12	I
Egg, whole, fresh	I extra large	86	7	I
Egg, whole, fresh	I jumbo	97	8	I
Egg, whole, fresh	I large	75	6	I
Egg, whole, fresh	I medium	66	5.5	.5
Egg, whole, fresh	I small	55	5	t
Egg, whole, hard-boiled	I large	78	6	t
Egg, whole, poached	I large	75	6	t

Fat/Sat Fat (g)	Chol (mg)	Fiber (g)	Sugars (g)	Sodium (mg)
2/t	1	0	0	111
0/0	0	0	0	108
t/0	0	0	0	173
6/2	246	0	0	73
6.5/2	276	0	0	82
5/1.5	213	0	0	63
4/1	187	0	0	55
4/1	157	0	0	47
5/2	212	0	0	62
5/2	212	0	0	140

HIGH-RESPONSE COST, HIGH-YIELD FOODS: FAST FOODS, ALLOWABLE

Food	Serving	Calories	Prot (g)	Carb (g)
Fast Foods/Salads*				
Arby's:				
Caesar Salad	I serving	90	7	8
Caesar Side Salad	I serving	45	4	4
Grilled Chicken Caesar Salad	I serving	230	33	8
Chick-Fil-A:				
Chargrilled Chicken Garden Salad	I serving	180	22	9
Southwest Chargrilled Salad	I serving	240	25	17
Dairy Queen:				
Grilled Chicken Salad w/ fat-free Italian dressing	I serving	230	26	13
Jack in the Box:				
Asian Chicken Salad	I serving	140	15	18
Southwest Chicken Salad	I serving	320	28	28

* Dressing not included

Fat/Sat Fat (g)	Chol (mg)	Fiber (g)	Sugars (g)	Sodium (mg)
4/2.5	10	3	na	170
2/1	5	2	na	95
8/3.5	80	3	na	920

6/3	70	3	5	660
8/3.5	60	5	6	770

9/4	75	3	7	1290

1.5/0	25	6	11	470
13/6	60	8	6	920

Fast Foods (cont.)	Serving	Calories	Prot (g)	Carb (g)
Side Salad	I serving	50	3	4

McDonalds:

	Serving	Calories	Prot (g)	Carb (g)
California Cobb, w/o chicken	I serving	160	11	7
Caesar Salad, w/o chicken	I serving	90	7	7
Grilled Chicken Caesar Salad	I serving	210	26	11
Grilled Chicken California Cobb Salad	I serving	280	30	11

Subway (6 grams of fat or less):

	Serving	Calories	Prot (g)	Carb (g)
Ham	I serving	110	11	11
Roast Beef	I serving	120	12	10
Roasted Chicken Breast	I serving	140	16	12
Subway Club	I serving	150	17	12
Turkey Breast	I serving	100	11	11
Turkey Breast & Ham	I serving	120	13	11
Veggie Delite	I serving	50	2	9

Fat/Sat Fat (g)	Chol (mg)	Fiber (g)	Sugars (g)	Sodium (mg)
3/1.5	10	2	2	65

Fat/Sat Fat (g)	Chol (mg)	Fiber (g)	Sugars (g)	Sodium (mg)
11/4.5	85	3	4	450
4/3	10	3	3	170
7/3	60	3	3	680
14/6	130	3	4	960

Fat/Sat Fat (g)	Chol (mg)	Fiber (g)	Sugars (g)	Sodium (mg)
3/1	25	3	3	1070
3/1.5	20	3	3	720
3/1	45	3	4	800
3.5/1.5	35	3	4	1110
2/0	20	3	3	820
3/.5	25	3	3	1030
1/0	0	3	2	310

Fast Foods (cont.)	Serving	Calories	Prot (g)	Carb (g)
Wendy's:				
Caesar Side Salad	I serving	70	7	2
Mandarin Chicken Salad	I serving	150	20	17
Side Salad	I serving	35	2	7
Spring Mix Salad	I serving	180	11	12

Fast Foods/Sandwiches/Poultry

Burger King:

	Serving	Calories	Prot (g)	Carb (g)
BK Veggie Burger, w/o mayo	I serving	310	15	46
Chicken WHOPPER Jr, w/o mayo	I serving	270	25	30

Chick-Fil-A:

	Serving	Calories	Prot (g)	Carb (g)
Chargrilled Chicken Sandwich, w/o butter	I serving	250	26	28
Chargrilled Chicken Deluxe Sandwich, w/o butter	I serving	290	27	31

Dairy Queen:

	Serving	Calories	Prot (g)	Carb (g)
Grilled Chicken Sandwich	I serving	310	24	30

Fat/Sat Fat (g)	Chol (mg)	Fiber (g)	Sugars (g)	Sodium (mg)
4/2	15	1	1	250
1.5/0	10	3	11	650
0/0	0	3	4	20
11/6	30	5	5	230

7/1	0	4	7	890
6/2	40	2	4	840

3/1	70	1	5	980
7/1.5	70	2	5	990

10/2.5	50	3	5	1040

Fast Foods (cont.)	Serving	Calories	Prot (g)	Carb (g)
Jack in the Box:				
Chicken Fajita Pita	1 serving	330	24	35
Kentucky Fried Chicken:				
Honey BBQ Flavored Sandwich	1 serving	310	28	37
Taco Bell:				
Soft taco—chicken	1 serving	190	14	19
Wendy's:				
Grilled Chicken Sandwich	1 serving	300	24	36
Fast Foods/Soups				
Chick-Fil-A:				
Hearty Breast of Chicken Soup	1 cup	140	8	18
Subway:				
Brown and Wild Rice w/ Chicken	1 cup	190	6	17
Chili con Carne	1 cup	310	17	28
Minestrone	1 cup	70	3	11

Fat/Sat Fat (g)	Chol (mg)	Fiber (g)	Sugars (g)	Sodium (mg)
11/4.5	55	3	4	910
6/2	125	2	7	560
6/2.5	30	t	2	550
7/1.5	55	2	6	740
3.5/1	25	1	2	900
11/4.5	20	2	3	990
14/5	35	9	5	900
1/0	15	2	0	1080

Fast Foods (cont.)	Serving	Calories	Prot (g)	Carb (g)
Roasted Chicken Noodle	I cup	90	7	7
Vegetarian Vegetable	I cup	80	2	17

Wendy's:

Chili, small	8 oz.	227	17	21

Fast Foods/Subs

Subway (6 grams of fat or less):

Ham	I 6" sub	290	18	46
Roast Beef	I 6" sub	290	19	45
Roasted Chicken Breast	I 6" sub	320	23	47
Subway Club	I 6" sub	320	24	46
Turkey Breast	I 6" sub	280	18	46
Turkey Breast & Ham	I 6" sub	290	20	46
Veggie Delite	I 6" sub	230	9	44

Fat/Sat Fat (g)	Chol (mg)	Fiber (g)	Sugars (g)	Sodium (mg)
4/1	20	1	1	1180
t/0	0	3	0	1130

6/2.5	35	5	5	870

5/1.5	25	4	7	1270
5/2	20	4	7	910
5/2	45	5	8	1000
6/2	35	4	7	1300
4.5/1.5	20	4	6	1010
5/1.5	25	4	7	1220
3/1	0	4	6	510

HIGH-RESPONSE COST, HIGH-YIELD FOODS: FATS, OILS, AND SALAD DRESSINGS

Food	Serving	Calories	Prot (g)	Carb (g)
Margarines and Spreads*				
Sticks				
Fleischmann's Light Margarine	1 tbsp	50	0	0
Parkay Light Stick	1 tbsp	50	0	0
Promise Buttery Light	1 tbsp	50	0	0
Promise Spread	1 tbsp	90	0	0
Sprays and Pumps				
I Can't Believe It's Not Butter Spray	5 sprays	0	0	0
Pam and similar vegetable sprays	1 spray	7	na	0
Tubs and Squeeze Bottles				
Benecol Spread	1 tbsp	80	0	0
Benecol Light Spread	1 tbsp	45	0	0
Blue Bonnet Home Style Spread	1 tbsp	60	0	0

* The margarine products listed here contain no more than 3 grams of saturated plus trans fat.

Fat/Sat Fat (g)	Chol (mg)	Fiber (g)	Sugars (g)	Sodium (mg)
5/1	0	na	0	na
5/1	0	na	na	75
6/1.5	0	na	na	na
10/2.5	na	na	na	na

0	0	0	0	0
1/t	na	na	na	na

9/1	0	na	na	110
5/.5	0	na	na	110
7/2	0	na	na	110

Fats & Oils (cont.)	Serving	Calories	Prot (g)	Carb (g)
Brummel & Brown Spread with Yogurt	1 tbsp	45	0	0
Canoleo Margarine	1 tbsp	100	0	0
Earth Balance Natural Buttery Spread	1 tbsp	100	0	0
Fleischmann's Light Margarine	1 tbsp	40	0	0
Fleischmann's Original Spread	1 tbsp	80	0	0
Fleischmann's Premium Spread with Olive Oil	1 tbsp	70	0	0
Fleischmann's Unsalted Spread	1 tbsp	80	0	0
I Can't Believe It's Not Butter, Easy Squeeze	1 tbsp	80	0	0
I Can't Believe It's Not Butter Fat Free Spread	1 tbsp	5	0	0
I Can't Believe It's Not Butter Light Spread	1 tbsp	50	0	0

Fat/Sat Fat (g)	Chol (mg)	Fiber (g)	Sugars (g)	Sodium (mg)
5/1	0	0	0	0
11/1	0	0	0	120
11/na	0	na	na	120
4.5/0	0	na	na	na
9/na	na	na	na	na
8/1.5	0	na	0	na
9/1.5	0	na	0	0
8/1.5	0	0	0	95
0/0	0	0	0	90
5/1	0	0	0	90

Fats & Oils (cont.)	Serving	Calories	Prot (g)	Carb (g)
I Can't Believe It's Not Butter Sweet Cream & Calcium Spread	I tbsp	50	0	0
Olivio Premium Spread with Olive Oil	I tbsp	80	0	0
Parkay Calcium Plus Spread	I tbsp	45	0	0
Parkay Light Spread	I tbsp	50	0	0
Parkay Spread	I tbsp	80	0	0
Parkay Squeeze Spread	I tbsp	70	0	0
Promise Buttery Light Spread	I tbsp	50	0	0
Promise Fat Free Spread	I tbsp	5	0	0
Promise Spread	I tbsp	80	0	0
Promise Ultra	I tbsp	40	0	0
Smart Balance Buttery Spread	I tbsp	80	0	0

Fat/Sat Fat (g)	Chol (mg)	Fiber (g)	Sugars (g)	Sodium (mg)
6/1	0	0	0	85
8/1	0	na	na	95
5/1	0	na	na	115
5/1	0	na	na	130
8/2	na	na	na	na
8/1.5	0	na	na	110
5/1	0	0	0	na
0/0	0	0	0	na
8/2	0	0	0	na
4/1	0	0	0	na
9/2.5	0	0	0	na

Fats & Oils (cont.)	Serving	Calories	Prot (g)	Carb (g)
Smart Balance Light Spread	1 tbsp	50	0	0
Smart Beat Fat Free Squeeze Margarine	1 tbsp	5	0	0
Smart Beat Trans Free Super Light Margarine	1 tbsp	20	0	0
Smart Beat Unsalted Light Margarine	1 tbsp	30	0	0
Shedd's Spread Churn Style Country Crock	1 tbsp	60	0	0
Shedd's Spread Country Crock Easy Squeeze	1 tbsp	60	0	0
Shedd's Spread Country Crock Plus Calcium and Vitamins	1 tbsp	50	0	0
Shedd's Spread Light Country Crock	1 tbsp	50	0	0
Take Control Spread	1 tbsp	80	0	0
Take Control Light Spread	1 tbsp	40	0	0

Fat/Sat Fat (g)	Chol (mg)	Fiber (g)	Sugars (g)	Sodium (mg)
5/1.5	0	0	0	na
0/0	0	0	0	na
2/0	0	0	0	105
3/0	0	0	0	na
7/1.5	0	0	0	90
7/1	0	0	0	85
5/1	0	0	0	na
5/1	0	0	0	1
8/1	t	0	0	1
5/.5	t	0	0	85

Fats & Oils (cont.)	Serving	Calories	Prot (g)	Carb (g)
Mayonnaise				
Mayonnaise, regular	1 tbsp	57	t	4
Mayonnaise, regular, soybean-base	1 tbsp	99	t	t
Mayonnaise, fat-free (Kraft)	2 tbsp	22	t	4
Mayonnaise, made w/ tofu	2 tbsp	96	2	2
Mayonnaise, imitation, milk cream	2 tbsp	30	0	4
Mayonnaise, imitation, soybean-base	2 tbsp	70	t	5
Mayonnaise, imitation, soybean-base, w/o cholesterol	1 tbsp	68	t	2
Mayonnaise, light (Kraft)	2 tbsp	100	t	3
Miracle Whip, light (Kraft)	2 tbsp	74	t	5
Miracle Whip Free, nonfat (Kraft)	2 tbsp	27	t	5

Fat/Sat Fat (g)	Chol (mg)	Fiber (g)	Sugars (g)	Sodium (mg)
5/1	4	0	na	105
11/2	8	0	na	78
t/t	3	t	2	240
10/0	0	0	0	232
2/0	12	0	na	152
6/1	7	0	na	149
7/1	0	0	na	50
10/2	11	0	1	239
6/1	8	0	3	263
t/t	3	t	3	252

Fats & Oils (cont.)	Serving	Calories	Prot (g)	Carb (g)
Oils				
Almond oil	1 tbsp	119	0	0
Apricot kernel oil	1 tbsp	119	0	0
Avocado oil	1 tbsp	124	0	0
Butter replacement, w/o fat, powder	1 tsp	6	0	1
Canola oil	1 tbsp	124	0	0
Corn oil, salad or cooking	1 tbsp	120	0	0
Flaxseed oil	1 tbsp	119	0	0
Grapeseed oil	1 tbsp	120	0	0
Hazelnut oil	1 tbsp	119	0	0
Olive oil, salad or cooking	1 tbsp	119	0	0
Peanut oil, salad or cooking	1 tbsp	119	0	0
Sesame oil, salad or cooking	1 tbsp	120	0	0
Safflower oil (70% linoleic), salad or cooking	1 tbsp	120	0	0

Fat/Sat Fat (g)	Chol (mg)	Fiber (g)	Sugars (g)	Sodium (mg)
14/1	0	0	0	0
14/1	0	0	0	0
14/2	na	0	0	0
0/0	0	0	0	20
14/1	0	0	0	0
14/2	0	0	0	0
14/1	0	0	0	0
14/1	0	0	0	0
14/1	0	0	0	0
14/2	0	0	0	0
14/3	0	0	0	0
14/2	0	0	0	0
14/1	0	0	0	0

Fats & Oils (cont.)	Serving	Calories	Prot (g)	Carb (g)
Safflower oil (over 70% safflower) salad or cooking	1 tbsp	120	0	0
Soybean oil, salad or cooking	1 tbsp	120	0	0
Sunflower oil (less than 60% linoleic)	1 tbsp	120	0	0
Sunflower oil (more than 60% linoleic)	1 tbsp	120	0	0
Sunflower oil (more than 70% oleic)	1 tbsp	124	0	0
Walnut oil	1 tbsp	120	0	0
Wheat germ oil	1 tbsp	120	0	0

Salad Dressings

Blue cheese, regular	1 tbsp	76	1	1
Blue cheese lowfat	2 tbsp	60	0	4
Caesar salad dressing, low calorie	2 tbsp	32	0	6
Coleslaw dressing, reduced fat	2 tbsp	112	0	14
French, regular	1 tbsp	69	t	3

Fat/Sat Fat (g)	Chol (mg)	Fiber (g)	Sugars (g)	Sodium (mg)
14/1	0	0	0	0
14/2	0	0	0	0
14/1	0	0	0	0
14/1	0	0	0	0
14/1	0	0	0	0
14/1	0	0	0	0
14/2	0	0	0	0

Fat/Sat Fat (g)	Chol (mg)	Fiber (g)	Sugars (g)	Sodium (mg)
8/1	3	0	na	5
4/2	10	0	na	480
2/0	0	0	4	324
6/2	8	0	14	544
7/2	0	0	na	219

Fats & Oils (cont.)	Serving	Calories	Prot (g)	Carb (g)
French, diet, lowfat	2 tbsp	43	t	7
Italian, regular	1 tbsp	69	t	2
Italian, diet	2 tbsp	32	t	1
Italian, fat-free (Kraft)	2 tbsp	20	t	4
Italian, Light Done Right (Kraft)	2 tbsp	53	t	2
Italian, zesty, (Kraft)	1 tbsp	54	t	1
Ranch, regular (Kraft)	1 tbsp	74	t	t
Ranch, fat-free (Kraft)	2 tbsp	48	t	11
Ranch, Light Done Right, (Kraft)	2 tbsp	77	t	3
Russian, regular	1 tbsp	74	t	2
Russian, low-calorie	2 tbsp	45	t	9
Sesame seed dressing	1 tbsp	66	t	1
Thousand Island, regular	1 tbsp	60	t	2
Thousand Island, low-calorie, diet	2 tbsp	48	t	5

Fat/Sat Fat (g)	Chol (mg)	Fiber (g)	Sugars (g)	Sodium (mg)
2/t	0	0	na	252
7/1	0	0	na	116
3/t	2	0	na	236
t/t	1	t	2	430
4/t	0	t	1.5	228
6/1	0	t	1	253
8/1	4	0	t	144
t/t	0	t	2	354
7/t	8	t	1	303
8/1	3	3	na	130
1/t	2	t	na	278
7/1	0	t	na	150
6/1	4	0	na	112
3/t	5	t	na	300

Fats & Oils (cont.)	Serving	Calories	Prot (g)	Carb (g)
Vinaigrette, balsamic	1 tbsp	50	0	2
Vinaigrette, red wine	1 tbsp	45	t	1

Fat/Sat Fat (g)	Chol (mg)	Fiber (g)	Sugars (g)	Sodium (mg)
4.5/1	0	0	2	165
4.5/na	na	na	na	na

HIGH-RESPONSE COST, HIGH-YIELD FOODS: FISH AND SHELLFISH

Food	Serving	Calories	Prot (g)	Carb (g)
Fish				
Bass, freshwater, mixed species, cooked	4 oz.	165	27	0
Bass, striped, cooked	4 oz.	141	26	0
Bluefish, cooked	4 oz.	180	29	0
Burbot, cooked	4 oz.	130	28	0
Butterfish, cooked	4 oz.	212	25	0
Carp, cooked	4 oz.	184	26	0
Catfish, channel, farmed, cooked	4 oz.	172	21	0
Catfish, channel, wild, cooked	4 oz.	119	21	0
Caviar, black and red, granular	3 tbsp	121	12	2
Cod, Atlantic, canned	4 oz.	119	26	0
Cod, Atlantic, cooked	4 oz.	119	26	0
Cod, Pacific, cooked	4 oz.	119	26	0
Dolphinfish, cooked (mahi mahi)	4 oz.	124	27	0

Fat/Sat Fat (g)	Chol (mg)	Fiber (g)	Sugars (g)	Sodium (mg)
5/1	99	0	0	102
3/1	117	0	0	100
6/1	86	0	0	87
1/t	87	0	0	141
12/na	94	0	0	129
8/2	95	0	0	71
9/2	73	0	0	91
3/1	82	0	0	57
9/2	282	0	0	720
1/t	62	0	0	247
1/t	62	0	0	88
1/t	53	0	0	103
1/t	107	0	0	128

Fish (cont.)	Serving	Calories	Prot (g)	Carb (g)
Drum, freshwater, cooked	4 oz.	173	26	0
Flounder, cooked	4 oz.	133	27	0
Grouper, mixed species, cooked	4 oz.	134	28	0
Haddock, cooked	4 oz.	127	27	0
Halibut, Atlantic and Pacific, cooked	4 oz.	159	30	0
Halibut, Greenland, cooked	4 oz.	271	21	0
Herring, Atlantic, cooked	4 oz.	230	26	0
Herring, Atlantic, kippered, large (7" x 2¼"x ¼")	1 fillet	141	16	0
Herring, Atlantic, pickled, (1¾" x ⅞" x ½")	3 pieces	118	6	4
Herring, Pacific, cooked	4 oz.	283	24	0
Mackerel, Atlantic, cooked	4 oz.	297	27	0
Mackerel, Jack, canned, boneless	4 oz.	177	26	0

Fat/Sat Fat (g)	Chol (mg)	Fiber (g)	Sugars (g)	Sodium (mg)
7/2	93	0	0	109
2/t	77	0	0	119
1/t	53	0	0	60
1/t	84	0	0	99
3/t	46	0	0	78
20/4	67	0	0	117
13/3	87	0	0	130
8/2	53	0	0	597
8/1	6	0	0	391
20/5	112	0	0	108
20/5	85	0	0	94
7/2	90	0	0	430

Fish (cont.)	Serving	Calories	Prot (g)	Carb (g)
Mackerel, King, cooked	4 oz.	152	29	0
Mackerel, Pacific and Jack, mixed species, cooked, boneless	4 oz.	228	29	0
Mackerel, Spanish, cooked	4 oz.	179	27	0
Monkfish, cooked	4 oz.	110	21	0
Mullet, striped, cooked	4 oz.	170	28	0
Ocean perch, Atlantic, cooked	4 oz.	137	27	0
Orange roughy, cooked	4 oz.	101	21	0
Perch, mixed species, cooked	4 oz.	133	28	0
Pike, Northern, cooked	4 oz.	128	28	0
Pike, Walleye, cooked	4 oz.	135	28	0
Pollock, Atlantic, cooked	4 oz.	134	28	0

Fat/Sat Fat (g)	Chol (mg)	Fiber (g)	Sugars (g)	Sodium (mg)
3/1	77	0	0	230
11/3	68	0	0	125
7/2	83	0	0	75
2/na	36	0	0	26
6/2	71	0	0	80
2/t	61	0	0	109
1/t	29	0	0	92
1/t	130	0	0	90
1/t	57	0	0	56
2/t	125	0	0	74
1/t	103	0	0	125

Fish (cont.)	Serving	Calories	Prot (g)	Carb (g)
Pollock, Walleye, cooked	4 oz.	128	27	0
Pompano, Florida, cooked	4 oz.	239	27	0
Rockfish, Pacific, mixed species, cooked	4 oz.	137	27	0
Roe, mixed species, cooked	4 oz.	231	32	2
Salmon, Atlantic, farmed, cooked	4 oz.	233	25	0
Salmon, Atlantic, wild, cooked	4 oz.	206	29	0
Salmon, Chinook, cooked	4 oz.	262	29	0
Salmon, Chinook, smoked (lox), cooked	4 oz.	133	21	0
Salmon, Chum, cooked	4 oz.	175	29	0
Salmon, Chum, drained solids, with bone	4 oz.	160	24	0
Salmon, Coho, farmed, cooked	4 oz.	202	28	0

Fat/Sat Fat (g)	Chol (mg)	Fiber (g)	Sugars (g)	Sodium (mg)
1/t	109	0	0	131
14/5	73	0	0	86
2/1	50	0	0	87
9/2	543	0	0	133
14/3	71	0	0	69
9/1	80	0	0	63
15/4	96	0	0	68
5/1	26	0	0	2267
5/1	108	0	0	73
6/2	44	0	0	552
9/2	71	0	0	59

Fish (cont.)	Serving	Calories	Prot (g)	Carb (g)
Salmon, Coho, wild, cooked	4 oz.	158	27	0
Salmon, pink, canned, solids with bone and liquid	4 oz.	158	22	0
Salmon, pink, cooked	4 oz.	169	29	0
Salmon, Sockeye, canned, drained solids with bone	4 oz.	173	23	0
Salmon, Sockeye, cooked	4 oz.	245	31	0
Sardines, Pacific, canned in tomato sauce, drained solids w/ bone	3 pieces	203	19	0
Sea bass, mixed species, cooked	4 oz.	141	27	0
Sea trout, mixed species, cooked	4 oz.	151	24	0
Shad, American, cooked	4 oz.	286	25	0
Shark	4 oz.	147	24	0
Smelt, Rainbow, cooked	4. oz.	141	26	0

Fat/Sat Fat (g)	Chol (mg)	Fiber (g)	Sugars (g)	Sodium (mg)
5/1	62	0	0	66
7/2	62	0	0	628
5/1	76	0	0	97
8/2	50	0	0	610
12/2	99	0	0	75
14/4	70	0	0	472
3/1	60	0	0	99
5/1	120	0	0	84
20/na	109	0	0	74
5/1	58	0	0	90
4/1	102	0	0	87

Fish (cont.)	Serving	Calories	Prot (g)	Carb (g)
Snapper, mixed species, cooked	4 oz.	145	30	0
Spot, cooked	4 oz.	179	27	0
Sturgeon, mixed species, cooked, boneless	4 oz.	153	23	0
Sunfish, pumpkin seed, cooked	4 oz.	129	28	0
Surimi	4 oz.	112	17	8
Swordfish, cooked	4 oz.	176	29	0
Tilefish, cooked	4 oz.	167	28	0
Trout, mixed species, cooked	4 oz.	215	30	0
Trout, Rainbow, farmed, cooked	4 oz.	192	28	0
Trout, Rainbow, wild, cooked	4 oz.	170	26	0
Tuna, bluefin, fresh, cooked	4 oz.	209	34	0
Tuna, light, canned in water, drained solids	4 oz.	132	29	0

Fat/Sat Fat (g)	Chol (mg)	Fiber (g)	Sugars (g)	Sodium (mg)
2/t	53	0	0	65
7/2	87	0	0	42
6/1	87	0	0	78
1/t	97	0	0	117
1/t	34	0	0	162
6/2	57	0	0	130
5/1	73	0	0	67
10/2	84	0	0	76
8/2	77	0	0	48
7/2	78	0	0	63
7/2	56	0	0	57
1/t	34	0	0	383

Fish (cont.)	Serving	Calories	Prot (g)	Carb (g)
Tuna, white, canned in water, drained solids	4 oz.	145	27	0
Tuna, yellow-fin, fresh, cooked	4 oz.	158	34	0
Turbot, European, cooked	4 oz.	138	23	0
Whitefish, mixed species, cooked	4 oz.	195	28	0
Whiting, mixed species, cooked	4 oz.	131	27	0
Yellowtail, mixed species, cooked	4 oz.	212	34	0

Shellfish

	Serving	Calories	Prot (g)	Carb (g)
Clams, mixed species, canned, drained solids	4 oz.	168	29	6
Clams, mixed species, cooked	4 oz.	168	29	6
Crab, Alaska King, cooked	4 oz.	110	22	0
Crab, Alaska King, imitation, made from surimi	4 oz.	116	14	12

Fat/Sat Fat (g)	Chol (mg)	Fiber (g)	Sugars (g)	Sodium (mg)
3/1	48	0	0	427
1/t	66	0	0	53
4/na	70	0	0	218
9/1	87	0	0	74
2/t	95	0	0	150
8/na	80	0	0	57

2/t	76	0	0	127
2/t	76	0	0	127
2/t	60	0	0	1215
1/t	23	0	0	953

Fish (cont.)	Serving	Calories	Prot (g)	Carb (g)
Crab, Blue, cooked	4 oz.	116	23	0
Crab, Dungeness, cooked	4 oz.	125	25	1
Crab, Queen, cooked	4 oz.	130	27	0
Lobster, Northern, cooked	4 oz.	111	23	1
Lobster, spiny, mixed species, cooked	4 oz.	162	30	4
Oyster, Eastern, canned, drained	4 oz.	63	7	4
Oyster, Eastern, farmed, cooked, dry heat	4 oz.	90	8	8
Oyster, Eastern, wild, cooked, dry heat	4 oz.	82	9	5
Oyster, Eastern, wild, cooked, moist heat	4 oz.	155	16	9
Oyster, Pacific, cooked, moist heat	4 oz.	185	21	11
Scallop, mixed species, imitation, made from surimi	4 oz.	112	14	12

Fat/Sat Fat (g)	Chol (mg)	Fiber (g)	Sugars (g)	Sodium (mg)
2/t	113	0	0	316
1/t	86	0	0	428
2/t	80	0	0	783
1/t	82	0	0	431
2/t	102	0	0	257
2/1	51	0	0	103
2/1	43	0	0	185
2/1	56	0	0	277
6/2	119	0	0	478
5/1	113	0	0	240
t/t	25	0	0	901

Fish (cont.)	Serving	Calories	Prot (g)	Carb (g)
Shrimp, mixed species, canned	4 oz.	136	28	1
Shrimp, mixed species, cooked, moist heat	4 oz.	112	24	0
Shrimp, mixed species, imitation, made from surimi	4 oz.	114	14	10

Fat/Sat Fat (g)	Chol (mg)	Fiber (g)	Sugars (g)	Sodium (mg)
2/t	196	0	0	192
1/t	221	0	0	254
2/t	41	0	0	799

HIGH-RESPONSE COST,
HIGH-YIELD FOODS: FRUITS AND FRUIT JUICES

Food	Serving	Calories	Prot (g)	Carb (g)
Fruits				
Acerola (west Indian cherry), raw	I cup	31	t	8
Apple, dehydrated, sulfured, uncooked	½ cup	104	t	28
Apple, dried, sulfured, uncooked	5 rings	78	t	21
Apple, raw (2¾" diameter), with skin	I fruit	81	t	21
Apple, raw (2¾" diameter), without skin	I fruit	73	t	19
Apple, raw, with skin, sliced	I cup	65	t	17
Apple, raw, without skin, sliced	I cup	63	t	16
Applesauce, unsweetened	½ cup	52	t	14
Apricot, canned, water pack, without skin	½ cup	25	I	6

Fat/Sat Fat (g)	Chol (mg)	Fiber (g)	Sugars (g)	Sodium (mg)
t/t	0	1	na	7
t/t	0	4	na	37
t/t	0	3	na	28
t/t	0	4	na	0
t/t	0	2	na	0
t/t	0	3	na	0
t/t	0	2	na	0
t/t	0	1.5	na	2
t/t	0	1	na	12.5

Fruits (cont.)	Serving	Calories	Prot (g)	Carb (g)
Apricot, canned, water pack, with skin	½ cup	33	I	8
Apricot, dried, sulfured, uncooked	10 halves	84	I	22
Apricot, raw	2	34	I	8
Apricot, raw, sliced	I cup	79	2	18
Avocado, raw, all varieties	¼ fruit	81	I	4
Avocado, raw, without skin and seeds, California	¼ fruit	77	I	3
Avocado, raw, without skin and seeds, Florida	¼ fruit	77	I	3
Banana (7" to 7⅞" long), raw	I fruit	109	I	28
Blackberries, frozen, unsweetened, unthawed	I cup	97	2	24
Blackberries, raw	I cup	75	I	18
Blueberries, frozen, unsweetened, unthawed	I cup	79	I	19
Blueberries, raw	I cup	81	I	20

Fat/Sat Fat (g)	Chol (mg)	Fiber (g)	Sugars (g)	Sodium (mg)
t/t	0	2	na	3.5
t/t	0	2.5	na	4
t/t	0	2	na	0
t/t	0	4	na	2
8/1	0	2.5	na	5
8/1	0	2	na	5
7/1	0	4	na	4
1/t	0	3	na	1
1/t	0	7.5	na	2
1/t	0	8	na	0
1/t	0	4	na	2
t/t	0	4	na	9

Fruits (cont.)	Serving	Calories	Prot (g)	Carb (g)
Cherries, sour, red, canned, water pack	1 cup	88	2	22
Cherries, sour, red, frozen, unsweetened, unthawed	1 cup	71	1	17
Cherries, sour, red, raw, without pits	1 cup	78	2	19
Cherries, sour, red, raw, with pits	1 cup	52	1	12.5
Cherries, sweet, canned, juice pack, pitted	1 cup	135	2	35
Cherries, sweet, canned, water pack, pitted	1 cup	114	2	29
Cherries, sweet, raw without pits	1 cup	104	2	24
Cherries, sweet, raw, with pits	1 cup	84	1	19
Cranberries, raw, chopped	1 cup	54	t	14
Cranberries, raw, whole	1 cup	47	t	12
Currants, black, raw	1 cup	71	1.5	17

Fat/Sat Fat (g)	Chol (mg)	Fiber (g)	Sugars (g)	Sodium (mg)
t/t	0	3	na	17
t/t	0	2.5	na	2
t/t	0	2.5	na	5
t/t	0	1.5	na	3
t/t	0	4	na	8
t/t	0	4	na	2
l/t	0	3	na	0
l/t	0	3	na	0
t/t	0	4.5	na	1
t/t	0	4	na	1
t/t	0	na	na	2

Fruits (cont.)	Serving	Calories	Prot (g)	Carb (g)
Currants, red and white, raw	1 cup	63	2	15
Dates, domestic, natural and dry	5 dates	114	1	31
Figs, canned, water pack	½ cup	66	t	17
Figs, dried, stewed	½ cup	140	2	36
Figs, dried, uncooked	2 figs	97	1	25
Figs, raw, large (2½" dia)	2 figs	95	1	24.5
Fruit cocktail, canned, juice pack	½ cup	55	t	14
Fruit cocktail, canned, water pack	½ cup	38	t	10
Grapefruit, pink, raw, red, and white (4" dia)	½ fruit	41	1	10
Grapefruit, canned sections, juice pack	½ cup	46	1	11
Grapefruit, canned sections, water pack	½ cup	44	1	11
Grapes, American, slip skin, raw	1 cup	62	t	16

Fat/Sat Fat (g)	Chol (mg)	Fiber (g)	Sugars (g)	Sodium (mg)
t/t	0	5	na	1
t/t	0	3	na	1
t/t	0	3	na	1
l/t	0	7	na	6
t/t	0	5	na	4
t/t	0	4	na	1
t/t	0	1	na	5
t/t	0	1	na	5
t/t	0	1	na	0
t/t	0	t	na	9
t/t	0	t	na	2
t/t	0	1	na	2

Fruits (cont.)	Serving	Calories	Prot (g)	Carb (g)
Grapes, European, red or green, Thompson seedless, raw	1 cup	114	1	28
Grapes, canned, Thompson, seedless, water pack	½ cup	49	t	12.5
Guava, common, raw, without refuse	1 fruit	46	1	11
Kiwi fruit, fresh, raw, without skin, large	1 fruit	56	1	13.5
Lemon, raw, without peel (2⅜" dia)	1 fruit	24	1	8
Lemon, raw, with peel (2⅜" dia)	1 fruit	22	1	11.5
Lime, raw (2" dia)	1 fruit	20	t	7
Mango, raw, sliced	1 cup	107	1	28
Melon balls, frozen, unthawed	1 cup	57	1	14
Melon, cantaloupe, raw, wedge (⅛ of large melon)	1 wedge	36	1	8.5
Melon, casaba, raw, wedge (⅛ of melon)	1 wedge	53	2	13

Fat/Sat Fat (g)	Chol (mg)	Fiber (g)	Sugars (g)	Sodium (mg)
l/t	0	1.5	na	3
t/t	0	1	na	7
t/t	0	5	na	3
t/t	0	3	na	5
t/t	0	2.5	na	2
t/t	0	5	na	3
t/t	0	2	na	1
t/t	0	3	na	3
t/t	0	1	na	54
t/t	0	1	na	9
t/t	0	2	na	25

Fruits (cont.)	Serving	Calories	Prot (g)	Carb (g)
Melon, honeydew, raw, wedge (⅛ of 6"–7" dia melon)	1 wedge	56	1	15
Nectarine, raw (2½" dia)	1 fruit	67	1	16
Orange, raw, California, navel (2⅞" dia)	1 fruit	64	1	16
Orange, raw, California, valencia (2⅝" dia)	1 fruit	59	1	14
Orange, raw, Florida (2⅝" dia)	1 fruit	65	1	16
Papaya, raw, cubes	1 cup	55	1	14
Papaya, raw, small (4½" lg x 2¾" dia)	1 fruit	59	1	15
Peaches, canned, juice pack, halves or slices	½ cup	55	1	14
Peaches, canned, water pack, halves or slices	½ cup	29	t	7
Peaches, dried, sulfured, stewed, without added sugar	½ cup	99	1.5	25

Fat/Sat Fat (g)	Chol (mg)	Fiber (g)	Sugars (g)	Sodium (mg)
t/t	0	1	na	16
t/t	0	2	na	0
t/t	0	3.5	na	1
t/t	0	3	na	0
t/t	0	3.5	na	0
t/t	0	2.5	na	4
t/t	0	3	na	5
t/t	0	1.5	na	5
t/t	0	1.5	na	4
t/t	0	3.5	na	3

Fruits (cont.)	Serving	Calories	Prot (g)	Carb (g)
Peaches, dried, sulfured, uncooked, halves	3	93	1	24
Peaches, raw, large (2¾" dia)	1 fruit	68	1	17
Peaches, raw, slices	1 cup	73	1	19
Pears, Asian, raw (2¼" long x 2½" dia)	1 fruit	51	1	13
Pears, canned, juice pack, halves	½ cup	62	t	16
Pears, canned, water pack, halves	½ cup	35	t	9.5
Pear, raw, medium (approx. 2½ per pound)	1 fruit	98	1	25
Persimmons, Japanese, raw (2½" dia)	1 fruit	118	1	31
Persimmons, native, raw, without refuse	1 fruit	32	0	8
Pineapple, canned, juice pack, chunks, crushed, slices	½ cup	75	t	19.5

Fat/Sat Fat (g)	Chol (mg)	Fiber (g)	Sugars (g)	Sodium (mg)
t/t	0	3	na	3
t/t	0	3	na	0
t/t	0	3	na	0
t/t	0	4	na	0
t/t	0	2	na	5
t/t	0	2	na	2
l/t	0	4	na	0
t/t	0	6	na	2
t/t	0	na	na	0
t/t	0	l	na	l

Fruits (cont.)	Serving	Calories	Prot (g)	Carb (g)
Pineapple, canned, water pack, chunks, crushed, slices	½ cup	39	t	10
Pineapple, raw, diced	1 cup	76	1	19
Plantains, cooked, slices	½ cup	89	1	24
Plantains, raw, medium	½ fruit	109	1	28.5
Plums, canned, purple, juice pack, pitted	½ cup	73	t	19
Plums, canned, purple, water pack, pitted	½ cup	51	t	14
Plum, raw (2⅛" dia)	2 fruits	72	1	17
Pomegranate, raw (3⅜" dia)	1 fruit	105	1.5	26
Prunes, dried, stewed, without added sugar, pitted	½ cup	133	1.5	35
Prunes, dried, uncooked	5 fruits	100	1	26
Raisins, golden seedless, not packed	¼ cup	109	1	29

Fat/Sat Fat (g)	Chol (mg)	Fiber (g)	Sugars (g)	Sodium (mg)
t/t	0	1	na	1
1/t	0	2	na	2
t/t	0	2	na	4
t/t	0	2	na	4
t/t	0	1	na	1
t/t	0	1	na	1
1/t	0	2	na	0
t/t	0	1	na	5
t/t	0	8	na	2
t/t	0	3	na	2
t/t	0	1.5	na	4

Fruits (cont.)	Serving	Calories	Prot (g)	Carb (g)
Raisins, seedless, not packed	¼ cup	109	1	29
Raisins, seedless, 5 oz, miniature box	1 box	42	t	11
Raspberries, raw	1 cup	60	1	14
Rhubarb, frozen, uncooked, diced	1 cup	29	1	7
Rhubarb, raw, diced	1 cup	26	1	5.5
Strawberries, frozen, unsweetened, thawed	1 cup	77	1	20
Strawberries, raw, sliced	1 cup	50	1	12
Tangerine (mandarin), canned, juice pack	½ cup	46	1	12
Tangerine (mandarin), raw, large (2½" dia)	1 fruit	43	1	11
Watermelon, raw, diced	1 cup	49	1	11
Watermelon, raw, wedge (¹⁄₁₆ of melon)	1 wedge	92	2	20.5

Fat/Sat Fat (g)	Chol (mg)	Fiber (g)	Sugars (g)	Sodium (mg)
t/t	0	1.5	na	4
t/t	0	t	na	2
l/t	0	8.4	na	0
t/t	0	2.5	na	3
t/t	0	2	na	5
t/t	0	5	na	4
l/t	0	4	na	2
t/t	0	1	na	6
t/t	0	2	na	1
l/t	0	1	na	3
l/t	0	1.5	na	6

Fruits (cont.)	Serving	Calories	Prot (g)	Carb (g)
Fruit Juices/Unsweetened				
Acerola cherry juice	I cup	56	I	I2
Apple juice, canned or bottled	I cup	II7	t	29
Apple juice, from concentrate	I cup	II2	t	28
Cranberry juice, cocktail, low-calorie	I cup	45	0	II
Grape juice, canned or bottled	I cup	I54	I	38
Grapefruit juice, canned	I cup	94	I	22
Grapefruit juice, from concentrate	I cup	I0I	I	24
Grapefruit juice, pink, fresh	I cup	96	I	23
Grapefruit juice, white, fresh	I cup	96	I	23
Lemon juice, bottled	I tbsp	3	0	I
Lemon juice, raw	Yield from I lemon	I2	0	4

Fat/Sat Fat (g)	Chol (mg)	Fiber (g)	Sugars (g)	Sodium (mg)
l/t	0	l	na	7
t/t	0	t	na	7
t/t	0	t	na	17
0/0	0	0	na	7
t/t	0	t	na	8
t/t	0	t	na	2
t/t	0	t	na	2
t/t	0	na	na	2
t/t	0	t	na	2
0/0	0	0	0	3
0/0	0	0	l	0

Fruits (cont.)	Serving	Calories	Prot (g)	Carb (g)
Lime juice, raw	Yield from 1 lime	10	0	3
Orange juice, California, from concentrate	1 cup	110	2	25
Orange juice, canned	1 cup	105	1	25
Orange juice, from concentrate	1 cup	110	2	25
Orange juice, fresh	1 cup	112	2	27
Orange-grapefruit, canned	1 cup	106	1	25
Passion-fruit juice, purple, fresh	1 cup	126	1	33.5
Passion-fruit juice, yellow, fresh	1 cup	148	2	36
Pineapple juice, canned	1 cup	140	1	34
Pineapple juice, from concentrate	1 cup	130	1	32
Prune juice, canned	½ cup	91	1	22
Tangerine juice, fresh	1 cup	106	1	25

Fat/Sat Fat (g)	Chol (mg)	Fiber (g)	Sugars (g)	Sodium (mg)
0/0	0	0	1	0
t/t	0	na	na	2
t/t	0	t	na	5
t/t	0	t	na	2
t/t	0	t	na	2
t/t	0	t	na	7
t/t	0	t	na	15
t/t	0	t	na	15
t/t	0	t	na	3
t/t	0	t	na	3
t/t	0	1	na	5
t/t	0	t	na	2

HIGH-RESPONSE COST, HIGH-YIELD FOODS: GRAINS, GRAIN CAKES, PASTA, AND NOODLES

Food	Serving	Calories	Prot (g)	Carb (g)
Grains				
Amaranth, dry	¼ cup	182	7	32
Barley, pearled, cooked	½ cup	97	2	22
Bulgur, cooked	½ cup	76	3	17
Couscous, cooked	½ cup	88	3	18
Millet, cooked	½ cup	104	3	20.5
Quinoa, cooked	½ cup	106	6	17
Rice, brown, long-grain, cooked	½ cup	108	2.5	22
Rice, brown, medium-grain, cooked	½ cup	109	2	23
Wild rice, cooked	½ cup	83	3	17.5
Grain Cakes				
Brown rice, buckwheat, w/ salt	2 cakes	68	2	14
Brown rice, buckwheat, w/o salt	2 cakes	68	2	14
Brown rice, corn	2 cakes	69	1.5	15

Fat/Sat Fat (g)	Chol (mg)	Fiber (g)	Sugars (g)	Sodium (mg)
3/1	0	7	na	10
t/t	0	3	na	2
t/t	0	4	na	5
t/t	0	1	na	4
1/t	0	1	na	2
1.5/0	0	1.5	na	6
1/t	0	2	na	5
1/t	0	2	na	1
t/t	0	1.5	na	2

1/t	0	t	na	21
1/t	0	1	na	1
t/t	0	t	na	52

Grains (cont.)	Serving	Calories	Prot (g)	Carb (g)
Brown rice, multigrain, w/ salt	2 cakes	70	1.5	14
Brown rice, multigrain, w/o salt	2 cakes	70	1.5	14
Brown rice, plain, w/ salt	2 cakes	70	1	15
Brown rice, plain, w/o salt	2 cakes	70	1	15
Brown rice, rye	2 cakes	69	1	14
Brown rice, sesame seed, w/o salt	2 cakes	71	1	15
Corn cakes	2 cakes	70	1	15
Corn cakes, very low sodium	2 cakes	70	1	15
Popcorn cakes	2 cakes	77	2	16

Pasta and Noodles

	Serving	Calories	Prot (g)	Carb (g)
Chinese noodles, chow mein, cooked	½ cup	119	2	13
Corn pasta, cooked	½ cup	88	2	19.5
Egg noodles, enriched, cooked	½ cup	106	4	20

Fat/Sat Fat (g)	Chol (mg)	Fiber (g)	Sugars (g)	Sodium (mg)
l/t	0	t	na	45
l/t	0	na	na	I
t/t	0	I	na	59
t/t	0	I	na	5
l/t	0	I	na	20
l/t	0	na	na	I
t/t	0	t	na	88
t/t	0	na	na	5
l/t	0	I	na	58

7/I	0	I	na	99
t/t	0	3	na	0
l/t	26	I	na	6

Grains (cont.)	Serving	Calories	Prot (g)	Carb (g)
Egg noodles, spinach, enriched, cooked	½ cup	106	4	19
Japanese noodles, soba, cooked	½ cup	56	3	12
Japanese noodles, somen, cooked	½ cup	115	3.5	24
Macaroni, elbow, whole wheat, cooked	½ cup	87	4	18.5
Spinach pasta, refrigerated, cooked	½ cup	148	6	28.5
Spinach spaghetti, cooked	½ cup	91	3	18
Whole wheat spaghetti	½ cup	87	4	18.5

Fat/Sat Fat (g)	Chol (mg)	Fiber (g)	Sugars (g)	Sodium (mg)
l/t	26	2	na	10
t/t	0	na	na	34
t/t	0	na	na	142
t/t	0	2	na	2
l/t	38	na	na	7
t/t	0	na	na	10
t/t	0	3	na	2

HIGH-RESPONSE COST, HIGH-YIELD FOODS: LAMB, VEAL, AND GAME PRODUCTS

Food	Serving	Calories	Prot (g)	Carb (g)
Lamb, Lean Cuts				
Leg, shank half, lean only, trimmed to ¼" fat, choice, roasted	4 oz.	204	32	0
Leg, shank half, lean and fat, trimmed to ¼" fat, choice, roasted	4 oz.	246	30	0
Leg, sirloin half, lean only, trimmed to ¼" fat, choice, roasted	4 oz.	231	32	0
Leg, whole (shank and sirloin), lean only, trimmed to ¼" fat, choice, roasted	4 oz.	216	32	0
Loin, lean only, trimmed to ¼" fat, choice, broiled	4 oz.	245	34	0
Loin, lean only, trimmed to ¼" fat, choice, roasted	4 oz.	229	30	0

Fat/Sat Fat (g)	Chol (mg)	Fiber (g)	Sugars (g)	Sodium (mg)
7.5/3	99	0	0	75
13/5	102	0	0	74
10/4	104	0	0	80
9/3	101	0	0	77
11/4	108	0	0	95
11/4	99	0	0	75

Lamb & Veal (cont.)	Serving	Calories	Prot (g)	Carb (g)
Shoulder/arm, lean only, trimmed to ¼" fat, choice, broiled	4 oz.	227	31	0
Shoulder/arm, lean only, trimmed to ¼" fat, choice, roasted	4 oz.	218	29	0
Shoulder, whole (arm and shoulder), lean only, trimmed to ¼" fat, choice, broiled	4 oz.	238	31	0
Shoulder, whole (arm and shoulder), lean only, trimmed to ¼" fat, choice, roasted	4 oz.	231	28	0
Sirloin chop, lean only, broiled	4 oz.	213	31	0

Veal, Lean Cuts

	Serving	Calories	Prot (g)	Carb (g)
Breast, whole, lean only, boneless, braised	4 oz.	247	34	0
Cubed for stewing, lean only, braised	4 oz.	213	40	0
Ground, broiled	4 oz.	195	28	0

Fat/Sat Fat (g)	Chol (mg)	Fiber (g)	Sugars (g)	Sodium (mg)
10/4	104	0	0	93
10/4	97	0	0	76
12/4	105	0	0	94
12/5	99	0	0	77
9/3.5	96	0	0	75

Fat/Sat Fat (g)	Chol (mg)	Fiber (g)	Sugars (g)	Sodium (mg)
11/4	131	0	0	77
5/1	164	0	0	105
9/3	117	0	0	94

Lamb & Veal (cont.)	Serving	Calories	Prot (g)	Carb (g)
Leg, top round, lean only, braised	4 oz.	230	42	0
Leg, top round, lean only, pan-fried	4 oz.	207	37.5	0
Leg, top round, lean only, roasted	4 oz.	170	32	0
Loin, braised	4 oz.	156	23	0
Rib, braised	4 oz.	247	39	0
Rib, roasted	4 oz.	201	29	0
Shank, lean only, braised	4 oz.	201	36.5	0
Shoulder, arm, braised	4 oz.	228	40	0
Shoulder, arm, lean only roasted	4 oz.	186	30	0
Shoulder, blade, lean only, braised	4 oz.	224	37	0
Shoulder, blade, lean only, roasted	4 oz.	194	29	0
Shoulder, whole (arm and shoulder), lean only braised	4 oz.	226	38	0

Fat/Sat Fat (g)	Chol (mg)	Fiber (g)	Sugars (g)	Sodium (mg)
6/2	153	0	0	76
5/1.5	121	0	0	87
4/1	117	0	0	77
6/2	86	0	0	58
9/3	163	0	0	112
8/2	130	0	0	110
5/1	143	0	0	107
6/2	176	0	0	102
7/3	124	0	0	103
7/2	179	0	0	114
8/3	135	0	0	116
7/2	147	0	0	110

Lamb & Veal (cont.)	Serving	Calories	Prot (g)	Carb (g)
Shoulder, whole (arm and shoulder), lean only, roasted	4 oz.	193	29	0
Sirloin, lean only, braised	4 oz.	231	38.5	0
Sirloin, lean only, roasted	4 oz.	190	30	0

Variety Meats, Lean

	Serving	Calories	Prot (g)	Carb (g)
Veal liver, braised	4 oz.	187	24.5	3
Veal spleen, braised	4 oz.	146	27	0

Game Meats, Lean

	Serving	Calories	Prot (g)	Carb (g)
Bison, chuck roast, lean only, braised	4 oz.	218	38	0
Bison, ribeye, lean only	4 oz.	131	25	0
Bison, lean only, roasted	4 oz.	162	32	0
Bison, top round, lean only, broiled	4 oz.	197	34	0
Bison, top sirloin, lean only, broiled	4 oz.	193	32	0

Fat/Sat Fat (g)	Chol (mg)	Fiber (g)	Sugars (g)	Sodium (mg)
7.5/3	129	0	0	110
7/2	128	0	0	92
7/3	118	0	0	96

8/3	636	0	0	60
3/1	507	0	0	66

6/3	125	0	0	64
3/1	70	0	0	54
3/1	93	0	0	65
6/2	96	0	0	46
6/3	97	0	0	60

Lamb & Veal (cont.)	Serving	Calories	Prot (g)	Carb (g)
Rabbit, domesticated, various cuts, roasted	4 oz.	223	33	0
Rabbit, domesticated, various cuts, stewed	4 oz.	233	34	0
Rabbit, wild, various cuts, stewed	4 oz.	196	37	0
Venison, ground, pan-broiled	4 oz.	211	30	0
Venison, loin, lean only, broiled	4 oz.	170	34	0
Venison, roasted	4 oz.	179	34	0
Venison, shoulder roast, lean only, braised	4 oz.	216	41	0
Venison, tenderloin, lean only, broiled	4 oz.	168	34	0
Venison, top round, lean only, broiled	4 oz.	172	35.5	0

Fat/Sat Fat (g)	Chol (mg)	Fiber (g)	Sugars (g)	Sodium (mg)
9/3	93	0	0	53
9.5/3	97	0	0	42
4/1	139	0	0	51
9/4.5	111	0	0	88
3/1	89	0	0	64
4/1	127	0	0	61
4/2	128	0	0	59
3/1	99	0	0	64
2/1	96	0	0	51

HIGH-RESPONSE COST, HIGH-YIELD FOODS: LUNCH MEATS AND SAUSAGE

Food	Serving	Calories	Prot (g)	Carb (g)
Lunchmeats, Lean				
Bologna, fat free	1 serving	22	3.5	2
Bologna, pork and turkey, lite	2 slices	118	7	2
Bologna, turkey	2 slices	113	8	t
Chicken, smoked	2 oz.	94	10	t
Chicken, white, oven-roasted (Louis Rich)	1 serving	36	5	1
Chicken, white, oven-roasted deluxe (Louis Rich)	1 serving	28	5	1
Chicken breast Classic Baked (Louis Rich)	2 slices	43	9	2
Chicken breast, honey glazed (Oscar Mayer)	2 slices	28	5	1
Chicken breast, oven-roasted, fat-free	2 slices	33	7	1

Fat/Sat Fat (g)	Chol (mg)	Fiber (g)	Sugars (g)	Sodium (mg)
t/t	7	0	I	274
9/3	44	0	0	401
9/3	56	0	na	500
6/1.5	30	0	na	544
2/t	17	0	t	335
t/t	14	0	t	333
t/t	23	0	t	502
t/t	14	0	I	374
t/t	15	0	t	457

Lunch Meats (cont.)	Serving	Calories	Prot (g)	Carb (g)
Chicken breast, smoked, mesquite flavor	2 slices	34	7	1
Ham, extra lean	2 slices	73	11	t
Ham, 96% fat-free (Oscar Mayer)	2 slices	44	7	1
Hot dog, fat free	1 serving	37	6	2
Hot dog, light pork, turkey, beef	1 serving	111	7	2
Pastrami, beef, 98% fat free	6 slices	54	11	1
Salami, turkey	2 slices	82	8.5	t
Turkey breast, oven-roasted, fat-free (Louis Rich)	2 slices	101	21	2
Turkey breast, smoked (Oscar Meyer)	2 slices	21	4	1
Turkey breast and white turkey, smoked (Louis Rich)	2 slices	56	10	1
Turkey ham	2 slices	64	10	t
Turkey ham, cured turkey thigh meat	2 slices	73	11	t

Fat/Sat Fat (g)	Chol (mg)	Fiber (g)	Sugars (g)	Sodium (mg)
t/t	15	0	t	437
3/1	26	0	na	800
1/t	20	0	t	521
t/t	15	0	1	487
8.5/3	35	0	1	591
1/0	27	0	0	576
5/1	42	0	t	562
t/t	45	0	t	1318
t/t	8	0	t	285
1/t	24	0	t	514
2/t	38	0	t	632
3/1	32	0	na	568

Lunch Meats (cont.)	Serving	Calories	Prot (g)	Carb (g)
Sausage and Bacon, Lean				
Bacon, meatless	2 strips	31	1	1
Bacon, turkey	1 serving	35	2	t
Bratwurst, pork, beef and turkey, lite, smoked	2 oz.	129	9.5	3
Breakfast links, turkey sausage	2 links	129	9	1
Hot smoked turkey sausage	2 oz.	88	8	3
Meatless sausage	1 link	64	5	2
Meatless sausage	1 patty	97	7	4
Smoked sausage, turkey	1 serving	90	8	2
Smokies Sausage Little (pork, turkey) (Oscar Mayer)	2 links	54	2	t

Fat/Sat Fat (g)	Chol (mg)	Fiber (g)	Sugars (g)	Sodium (mg)
3/t	0	t	na	147
3/1	13	0	t	170
9/3	37	0	1	648
10/2	34	0	0	328
5/2	30	t	2	520
4.5/1	0	1	na	222
7/1	0	1	na	337
5.5/1.5	37	0	1.5	530
5/2	12	0	t	184

HIGH-RESPONSE COST, HIGH-YIELD FOODS: MILK, MILK PRODUCTS, AND YOGURT

Food	Serving	Calories	Prot (g)	Carb (g)
Milk and Milk Products				
Buttermilk, lowfat	I cup	98	8	12
Cocoa, sugar-free mix, mixed with water	I packet	54	2	11
Dry milk, nonfat, instant	⅓ cup	82	8	12
Evaporated milk, canned, nonfat	½ cup	100	10	15
Lowfat milk, 1%, protein fortified	I cup	118	10	14
Lowfat milk, 1%, regular	I cup	102	8	12
Nonfat milk (skim or fat-free)	I cup	86	8	12
Reduced fat milk, 2%	I cup	122	8	12
Yogurt				
Frozen yogurt, non-fat, w/ low-calorie sweetener	½ cup	100	4	18

Fat/Sat Fat (g)	Chol (mg)	Fiber (g)	Sugars (g)	Sodium (mg)
2/1	10	0	na	257
t/t	na	1	na	173
t/t	4	0	na	125
t/t	5	0	na	147
3/2	10	0	na	143
3/2	10	0	na	124
t/t	5	0	na	127
5/3	20	0	na	122

Fat/Sat Fat (g)	Chol (mg)	Fiber (g)	Sugars (g)	Sodium (mg)
1/t	3	2	na	75

Milk Products (cont.)	Serving	Calories	Prot (g)	Carb (g)
Light yogurt (Yoplait)	6 oz.	100	5	19
Nonfat, no-sugar yogurt, vanilla, lemon, maple, or coffee flavor	1 cup	105	10	18
Nonfat yogurt, strawberry, w/ aspartame and fructose (Kraft Breyers Light)	1 cup	125	8	22
Plain or sugar-free fruit-flavored yogurt, lowfat	1 cup	143	12	16
Plain yogurt, skim milk	1 cup	127	13	17

Fat/Sat Fat (g)	Chol (mg)	Fiber (g)	Sugars (g)	Sodium (mg)
0/0	t	0	14	85
t/t	5	0	na	144
t/t	11	0	17	102
4/2	14	0	na	159
t/t	5	0	na	175

HIGH-RESPONSE COST,
HIGH-YIELD FOODS: NUTS AND SEEDS

Food	Serving	Calories	Prot (g)	Carb (g)
Nuts and Seeds				
Almonds, dry roasted, w/ salt	1 tbsp	51	2	2
Almonds, dry roasted, w/o salt	1 tbsp	51	2	2
Brazil nuts, dried	1 tbsp	57	1	1
Cashews, dry roasted, w/ salt	1 tbsp	49	1	3
Cashews, dry roasted, w/o salt	1 tbsp	49	1	3
Hazelnuts or filberts	1 tbsp	53	1	1
Hickory nuts, dried	1 tbsp	49	1	1
Macadamia nuts, dry roasted, w/ salt	1 tbsp	60	1	1
Macadamia nuts, dry roasted, w/o salt	1 tbsp	60	1	1
Mixed nuts, dry roasted, w/ salt	1 tbsp	51	1	2
Mixed nuts, dry roasted, w/o salt	1 tbsp	51	1	2

Fat/Sat Fat (g)	Chol (mg)	Fiber (g)	Sugars (g)	Sodium (mg)
5/t	0	1	t	29
5/t	0	1	t	0
6/1	0	.5	na	0
4/1	0	t	na	55
4/1	0	t	na	1
5/t	0	1	t	0
5/.5	0	.5	na	0
6/1	0	1	t	22
6/1	0	1	t	0
4/1	0	1	na	57
4/1	0	1	na	1

Nuts & Seeds (cont.)	Serving	Calories	Prot (g)	Carb (g)
Peanuts, all types, boiled, w/ salt*	½ cup	286	12	19
Peanuts, all types, dry roasted, w/ salt*	10 peanuts	59	2	2
Peanuts, all types, dry roasted, w/o salt*	10 peanuts	59	2	2
Pecans	1 tbsp	47	1	1
Pistachio nuts, dry roasted, w/ salt	1 tbsp	45	2	2
Pistachio nuts, dry roasted, w/o salt	1 tbsp	45	2	2
Sunflower seeds, dried	1 tbsp	57	2	2
Sunflower seeds, dry roasted, w/ salt	1 tbsp	52	2	2
Sunflower seeds, dry roasted, w/o salt	1 tbsp	52	2	2
Sunflower seeds, toasted, w/ salt	1 tbsp	58	2	2
Walnuts, English	1 tbsp	41	1	1

*Peanuts are technically legumes but we tend to think of them as nuts.

Fat/Sat Fat (g)	Chol (mg)	Fiber (g)	Sugars (g)	Sodium (mg)
20/3	0	8	na	676
5/1	0	1	na	81
5/1	0	1	na	1
5/t	0	1	t	0
4/t	0	1	1	32
4/t	0	1	1	1
5/.5	0	1	na	0
5/.5	0	1	na	70
5/.5	0	1	na	0
5/.5	0	1	na	57
4/t	0	t	t	0

HIGH-RESPONSE COST,
HIGH-YIELD FOODS: PORK PRODUCTS

Food	Serving	Calories	Prot (g)	Carb (g)
Pork, Lean Cuts				
Center loin chop, w/ bone, lean only, braised	4 oz. edible portion	229	34	0
Center loin chop, w/ bone, lean only, broiled	4 oz. edible portion	229	34	0
Sirloin chop, w/ bone, lean only, braised	4 oz. edible portion	223	31	0
Sirloin chop, boneless, lean only, broiled	4 oz.	219	35	0
Sirloin roast, boneless, lean only, roasted	4 oz.	224	33	0
Tenderloin, lean only, broiled	4 oz.	212	34	0
Tenderloin, lean only, roasted	4 oz.	186	32	0
Tenderloin, lean and fat, broiled	4 oz.	228	34	0

Fat/Sat Fat (g)	Chol (mg)	Fiber (g)	Sugars (g)	Sodium (mg)
9/3	96	0	0	70
9/3	93	0	0	68
10/4	92	0	0	60
8/3	104	0	0	63
9/3	97	0	0	63
7/2.5	107	0	0	74
5.5/2	90	0	0	63
9/3	107	0	0	73

Pork Products (cont.)	Serving	Calories	Prot (g)	Carb (g)
Top loin chop, boneless, lean only, braised	4 oz.	229	33	0
Top loin chop, boneless, lean only, broiled	4 oz.	230	35	0

Variety Meats,* Lean

Pork heart, braised	1 heart	191	30	.5
Pork kidneys, braised	4 oz.	171	29	0
Pork liver, braised	4 oz.	187	29	4
Pork spleen, braised	4 oz.	169	32	0

* Although relatively low in fat, organ meats are high in dietary cholesterol.

Fat/Sat Fat (g)	Chol (mg)	Fiber (g)	Sugars (g)	Sodium (mg)
10/4	83	0	0	48
9/3	91	0	0	74

6.5/2	285	0	0	45
5/2	544	0	0	91
5/1.5	402	0	0	56
4/1	571	0	0	121

HIGH-RESPONSE COST,
HIGH-YIELD FOODS: POULTRY PRODUCTS

Food	Serving	Calories	Prot (g)	Carb (g)
Chicken				
Breast, meat only, roasted broiler or fryer	4 oz.	186	35	0
Cornish game hen, meat only, roasted	½ hen	147	26	0
Dark meat, roasted, broiler or fryer	4 oz.	232	31	0
Dark meat, roasted, roaster	4 oz.	201	26	0
Drumstick, meat only, roasted, broiler or fryer	4 oz.	194	32	0
Drumstick, meat only, roasted, broiler or fryer	1 drumstick	76	12	0
Leg, meat only, roasted, broiler or fryer	1 leg	181	26	0
Light meat, roasted, broiler or fryer	4 oz.	195	35	0
Light meat, roasted, roaster	4 oz.	173	31	0

Fat/Sat Fat (g)	Chol (mg)	Fiber (g)	Sugars (g)	Sodium (mg)
4/1	96	0	0	84
4/1	117	0	0	69
11/3	105	0	0	105
10/3	85	0	0	107
6/2	105	0	0	107
2/1	41	0	0	42
8/2	89	0	0	86
5/1	96	0	0	87
5/1	85	0	0	58

Poultry (cont.)	Serving	Calories	Prot (g)	Carb (g)
Light meat, stewed, stewer	4 oz.	241	37	0
Wing, meat only, roasted, broiler or fryer	1 wing	43	6	0

Duck and Goose

	Serving	Calories	Prot (g)	Carb (g)
Duck, wild, breast, w/o skin, cooked	4 oz.	140	22	0
Goose, w/o skin, roasted	4 oz.	268	33	0

Variety and Specialty Poultry

	Serving	Calories	Prot (g)	Carb (g)
Liver, chicken, cooked	4 oz.	176	28	1
Ostrich, cooked	4 oz.	160	30	0
Pheasant, w/o skin, cooked	4 oz.	152	27	0

Turkey

	Serving	Calories	Prot (g)	Carb (g)
Back meat, w/o skin, roasted	4 oz	192	32	0
Boneless, roast, light and dark meat	4 oz.	175	24	3
Breast meat, w/o skin, roasted	4 oz.	153	34	0

Fat/Sat Fat (g)	Chol (mg)	Fiber (g)	Sugars (g)	Sodium (mg)
9/2	79	0	0	66
2/t	18	0	0	19

Fat/Sat Fat (g)	Chol (mg)	Fiber (g)	Sugars (g)	Sodium (mg)
5/2	88	0	0	64
14/4	108	0	0	88

Fat/Sat Fat (g)	Chol (mg)	Fiber (g)	Sugars (g)	Sodium (mg)
6/0	716	0	1	56
3/0	108	0	0	88
4/0	76	0	0	40

Fat/Sat Fat (g)	Chol (mg)	Fiber (g)	Sugars (g)	Sodium (mg)
6/2	107	0	0	82
7/2	60	0	na	768
1/t	94	0	0	59

Poultry (cont.)	Serving	Calories	Prot (g)	Carb (g)
Canned, meat only, with broth	4 oz.	184	27	0
Dark meat, roasted	4 oz.	183	32	0
Ground turkey	1 patty, 4 oz.	193	22	0
Leg meat, w/o skin, roasted	4 oz.	180	33	0
Light meat, all classes, roasted	4 oz.	177	34	0
Meat, all classes, roasted	4 oz.	192	33	0
Neck meat, w/o skin, cooked	4 oz.	203	30	0
Turkey ham	4 oz.	134	18	4
Wing, w/o skin and bone	1 wing	98	19	0
Young hen, dark meat, w/o skin, roasted	4 oz.	217	32	0
Young hen, light meat, w/o skin, roasted	4 oz.	182	34	0
Young hen, meat only, roasted	4 oz.	198	33	0

Fat/Sat Fat (g)	Chol (mg)	Fiber (g)	Sugars (g)	Sodium (mg)
8/2	75	0	0	528
5/2	127	0	0	89
11/3	84	0	0	88
4/1	134	0	0	92
4/1	78	0	0	72
6/2	86	0	0	79
8/3	138	0	0	63
5/1	73	0	1	1031
2/1	61	0	0	47
9/3	90	0	0	85
4/1	77	0	0	68
6/2	82	0	0	76

Poultry (cont.)	Serving	Calories	Prot (g)	Carb (g)
Young tom, dark meat, w/o skin, roasted	4 oz.	209	32	0
Young tom, light meat, w/o skin, roasted	4 oz.	174	34	0
Young tom, meat w/o skin, roasted	4 oz.	190	33	0

Fat/Sat Fat (g)	Chol (mg)	Fiber (g)	Sugars (g)	Sodium (mg)
8/3	99	0	0	93
3/1	78	0	0	77
5/2	87	0	0	84,

HIGH-RESPONSE COST,
HIGH-YIELD FOODS: SOUPS

Food	Serving	Calories	Prot (g)	Carb (g)
Soups				
Beef broth or bouillon, canned, ready-to-serve	1 cup	17	3	t
Beef broth or bouillon, powder, prepared w/ water	1 cup	20	1	2
Beef broth, cube, prepared w/ water	1 cup	7	1	1
Beef mushroom, canned, prepared w/ water	1 cup	73	6	6
Beef noodle, canned, prepared w/ water	1 cup	83	5	9
Beef noodle, dehydrated, prepared w/ water	1 pkt	30	2	4
Black bean, canned, prepared w/ water	1 cup	116	6	20
Cauliflower, dehydrated, prepared w/ water	1 cup	69	3	11

Fat/Sat Fat (g)	Chol (mg)	Fiber (g)	Sugars (g)	Sodium (mg)
l/t	0	0	na	782
l/t	0	0	na	1362
t/t	0	0	na	1157
3/1	7	t	na	942
3/1	5	t	na	952
l/t	2	1	na	776
2/t	0	5	na	1198
2/t	0	na	na	842

Soups (cont.)	Serving	Calories	Prot (g)	Carb (g)
Chicken broth, canned, prepared w/ water	I cup	39	5	I
Chicken broth, cube, prepared w/ water	I cup	12	I	2
Chicken broth or boullion, dehydrated, prepared w/ water	I pkt	16	I	I
Chicken gumbo, canned, prepared w/ water	I cup	56	3	8
Chicken noodle, canned, prepared w/ water	I cup	75	4	9
Chicken noodle, chunky, ready-to-serve	I serving	114	8	14
Chicken noodle, dehydrated, prepared w/ water	I cup	43	2	7
Chicken noodle with celery and carrots, ready-to-serve	I serving	95	6	9

Fat/Sat Fat (g)	Chol (mg)	Fiber (g)	Sugars (g)	Sodium (mg)
1/t	0	0	na	776
t/t	0	na	na	792
1/t	0	0	na	1113
1/t	5	2	na	954
2/1	7	1	na	1106
3/1	24	na	na	875
1/t	8	t	na	433
3/1	21	na	na	985

Soups (cont.)	Serving	Calories	Prot (g)	Carb (g)
Chicken vegetable, canned, prepared w/ water	1 cup	75	4	9
Chicken vegetable, chunky, reduced fat, reduced sodium, ready-to-serve	1 serving	96	6	15
Chicken vegetable, dehydrated, prepared w/ water	1 cup	50	3	8
Chicken with rice, canned, prepared w/ water	1 cup	60	4	7
Clam chowder, Manhattan style, canned, prepared w/ water	1 cup	78	2	12
Clam chowder, Manhattan style, chunky, ready-to-serve	1 cup	134	7	19
Clam chowder, New England style, canned, prepared w/ water	1 cup	95	5	12
Consomme, canned, prepared w/ water	1 cup	29	5	2

Fat/Sat Fat (g)	Chol (mg)	Fiber (g)	Sugars (g)	Sodium (mg)
3/1	10	1	na	945
1/t	10	na	na	461
1/t	3	na	na	808
2/t	7	1	na	815
2/t	2	1.5	na	578
3/2	14	3	na	1001
3/t	5	1.5	na	915
0/0	0	0	na	636

Soups (cont.)	Serving	Calories	Prot (g)	Carb (g)
Crab soup, ready-to-serve	I cup	76	5	10
Cream of asparagus, dehydrated, prepared w/ water	I cup	58	2	9
Cream of celery, dehydrated, prepared w/ water	I cup	64	3	10
Cream of potato, canned, prepared w/ water	I cup	73	2	II
Gazpacho, ready-to-serve	I cup	46	7	4
Leek soup, dehydrated, prepared w/ water	I cup	71	2	II
Lentil soup, ready-to-serve	I cup	126	8	20
Minestrone, chunky, ready-to-serve	I cup	127	5	21
Minestrone, canned, prepared w/ water	I cup	82	4	II
Minestrone, dehydrated, prepared w/ water	I cup	79	4	12

Fat/Sat Fat (g)	Chol (mg)	Fiber (g)	Sugars (g)	Sodium (mg)
2/t	10	1	na	1235
2/t	0	na	na	801
2/t	0	na	na	838
2/1	5	.5	na	1000
t/t	0	.5	na	739
2/1	3	3	na	965
1.5/t	0	6	na	443
3/1	5	6	na	864
2.5/t	2	1	na	911
2/1	3	na	na	1026

Soups (cont.)	Serving	Calories	Prot (g)	Carb (g)
Mushroom, dehydrated, prepared w/ water	1 pkt	74	2	9
Mushroom barley, canned, prepared w/ water	1 cup	73	2	12
Mushroom with beef stock, canned, prepared w/ water	1 cup	85	3	9
Onion, canned, prepared w/ water	1 cup	58	4	8
Onion, dehydrated, prepared w/ water	1 cup	27	1	5
Oyster stew, canned, prepared w/ water	1 cup	58	2	4
Pea soup, canned, prepared w/ water	1 cup	165	9	27
Pea soup, dehydrated, prepared w/ water	1 cup	101	6	17
Split pea, ready-to-serve	1 cup	180	10	30
Tomato, canned, prepared w/ water	1 cup	85	2	17

Fat/Sat Fat (g)	Chol (mg)	Fiber (g)	Sugars (g)	Sodium (mg)
4/1	0	1	na	782
2/t	0	1	na	891
4/1.5	7	1	na	969
2/t	0	1	na	1053
t/t	0	1	na	849
4/2.5	14	na	na	981
3/1	0	3	na	918
1/t	2	2	na	927
2/1	5	5	na	420
2/t	0	.5	na	695

Soups (cont.)	Serving	Calories	Prot (g)	Carb (g)
Tomato, dehydrated, prepared w/ water	I pkt	78	2	15
Tomato bisque, canned, prepared w/ water	I cup	124	2	24
Tomato rice, canned, prepared w/ water	I cup	119	2	22
Tomato vegetable, dehydrated, prepared w/ water	I pkt	42	1	8
Turkey, chunky, ready-to-serve	I cup	135	10	14
Turkey noodle, canned, prepared w/ water	I cup	68	4	9
Turkey vegetable, canned, prepared w/ water	I cup	72	3	9
Vegetable, chunky ready-to-serve	I cup	122	3.5	19
Vegetable beef, canned, prepared w/ water	I cup	78	6	10
Vegetable beef, dehydrated, prepared w/ water	I cup	53	3	8

Fat/Sat Fat (g)	Chol (mg)	Fiber (g)	Sugars (g)	Sodium (mg)
2/1	0	t	na	708
2.5/.5	5	.5	na	1047
3/.5	2	1.5	na	815
1/t	0	t	na	856
4/1	9	na	na	923
2/t	5	1	na	815
3/1	2	.5	na	906
4/.5	0	1	na	1010
2/1	5	.5	na	791
1/.5	0	.5	na	1002

Soups (cont.)	Serving	Calories	Prot (g)	Carb (g)
Vegetable beef, microwaveable, ready-to-serve	I serving	128	18	10
Vegetable with beef broth, canned, prepared w/ water	I cup	82	3	13
Vegetarian vegetable, canned, prepared w/ water	I cup	72	2	12

Fat/Sat Fat (g)	Chol (mg)	Fiber (g)	Sugars (g)	Sodium (mg)
2/1	9	4	na	1098
2/t	2	.5	na	810
2/t	0	.5	na	822

HIGH-RESPONSE COST, HIGH-YIELD FOODS:
SOY AND VEGETARIAN FOODS

Food	Serving	Calories	Prot (g)	Carb (g)
Soy Foods				
Black bean burger	1 patty (2.7 oz.)	115	12	15
Hotdog, meatless	1 link	118	12	2
Soybeans, boiled, w/salt	½ cup	149	14	9
Soybeans, boiled, w/o salt	½ cup	149	14	9
Soybeans, dry roasted	2 tbsp	101	9	7
Soy burger	1 patty	125	13	9
Soy cheese, swiss	2 slices (0.7 oz.)	120	11	1
Soy cheese, mozzarella	2 slices (1 oz.)	120	15	2
Soy cheese, cheddar	2 slices (0.7 oz.)	120	11	1
Soy cheese, American	2 slices (0.7 oz.)	120	11	1
Soy milk, plain	1 cup	81	7	4

Fat/Sat Fat (g)	Chol (mg)	Fiber (g)	Sugars (g)	Sodium (mg)
1/t	1	5	1.5	499
7/1	0	2	t	224
8/2	0	5	na	204
8/2	0	5	na	1
5/1	0	2	na	0
4/1	0	3	1	385
8/na	na	na	na	na
6/na	na	na	na	na
8/na	na	na	na	na
8/na	na	na	na	na
5/t	0	3	na	29

Soy Foods (cont.)	Serving	Calories	Prot (g)	Carb (g)
Soy pasta	1 serving (2 oz. or ⅙ box)	200	14	34
Tempeh	½ cup	160	15	8
Tofu, silken, extra firm	1 slice	46	6	2
Tofu, silken, firm	1 slice	52	6	2
Tofu, silken, lite extra firm	1 slice	32	6	1
Tofu, silken, soft	1 slice	46	4	2
Tofu, silken, lite firm	1 slice	31	5	1
Vegetable burger	1 patty	138	18	7

Note: A "slice" of tofu is generally equal to ¼ of a block or ½ cup.

Fat/Sat Fat (g)	Chol (mg)	Fiber (g)	Sugars (g)	Sodium (mg)
2/1	0	1	2	85
9/2	0	na	na	7
2/t	0	t	1	53
2/t	0	n	1	30
t/t	0	0	t	82
2/t	0	n	1	4
1/t	0	0	t	71
4/1	0	6	na	411

HIGH-RESPONSE COST,
HIGH-YIELD FOODS: SUGAR-FREE FOODS

Food	Serving	Calories	Prot (g)	Carb (g)
Sugar-Free Foods				
Candy, hard, sugar-free	I candy	20	0	5
Gelatin dessert, sugar-free	½ cup	8	I	I
Gelatin, unflavored	I envelope	23	6	0
Jelly/preserves, low or reduced sugar	I tbsp	24	0	6
Sugar substitute	I pkt	4	0	I
Syrup, sugar-free	2 tbsp	9	0	2

Fat/Sat Fat (g)	Chol (mg)	Fiber (g)	Sugars (g)	Sodium (mg)
0/0	0	0	0	0
0/0	0	0	0	56
0/0	0	0	0	14
0/0	0	0	4.5	0
0/0	0	0	1	0
0/0	0	0	2	27

HIGH-RESPONSE COST, HIGH-YIELD FOODS: VEGETABLES, NON-STARCHY AND STARCHY

Food	Serving	Calories	Prot (g)	Carb (g)
Vegetables/Non-Starchy*				
Alfalfa sprouts, raw	1 cup	10	1	1
Artichoke, hearts, canned in water	4 oz.	42	3	8
Artichoke hearts, boiled, drained, w/ salt	½ cup	42	3	9
Artichoke, whole, globe or French boiled, drained w/salt	1 medium	60	4	13
Arugula, raw, chopped	1 cup	6	t	1
Asparagus, canned, drained	½ cup	23	3	3
Asparagus, from fresh, cuts and tips, cooked, w/ salt	½ cup	22	2	4
Asparagus, from fresh, cuts and tips, cooked, w/o salt	½ cup	22	2	4

* These vegetables can be eaten in liberal amounts on the food plans in this book.

Fat/Sat Fat (g)	Chol (mg)	Fiber (g)	Sugars (g)	Sodium (mg)
t/t	0	I	na	2
0/0	0	I	1.5	332
t/t	0	5	na	278
t/t	0	7	na	397
t/t	0	t	na	6
I/t	0	2	na	347
t/t	0	2	na	216
t/t	0	I	na	10

Vegetables (cont.)	Serving	Calories	Prot (g)	Carb (g)
Asparagus, from fresh, spears, boiled and drained, w/ salt	6 spears	22	2	4
Asparagus, from fresh, spears, boiled and drained, w/o salt	6 spears	22	2	4
Asparagus, from frozen, cuts and tips, boiled, drained, w/salt	½ cup	25	3	4
Asparagus, from frozen, spears, boiled, drained, w/salt	6 spears	25	3	4
Bamboo shoots, canned, drained slices, w/salt	½ cup	7	1	1
Bamboo shoots, canned, drained slices, w/o salt	½ cup	12	1	2
Bamboo shoots, raw, pieces	1 cup	41	4	8
Beans, snap, green, canned, w/ salt	½ cup	14	1	3
Beans, snap, green, canned, w/o salt	½ cup	14	1	3

Fat/Sat Fat (g)	Chol (mg)	Fiber (g)	Sugars (g)	Sodium (mg)
t/t	0	2	na	216
t/t	0	1	na	10
t/t	0	1	na	216
t/t	0	1	na	216
t/t	0	1	na	144
t/t	0	1	na	5
t/t	0	3	na	6
t/t	0	1	na	177
t/t	0	1	na	1

Vegetables (cont.)	Serving	Calories	Prot (g)	Carb (g)
Beans, snap, green, from fresh, boiled, w/ salt	½ cup	22	1	5
Beans, snap, green, from fresh, boiled, w/o salt	½ cup	22	1	5
Beans, snap, green, from frozen, boiled, w/ salt	½ cup	19	1	4
Beans, snap, green, from frozen, boiled, w/o salt	½ cup	19	1	4
Beans, snap, green, raw	1 cup	34	2	8
Beans, snap, yellow, canned, w/ salt	½ cup	14	1	3
Beans, snap, yellow, canned, w/o salt	½ cup	14	1	3
Beans, snap, yellow, from fresh, boiled, w/ salt	½ cup	22	1	5
Beans, snap, yellow, from fresh, boiled, w/o salt	½ cup	22	1	5

Fat/Sat Fat (g)	Chol (mg)	Fiber (g)	Sugars (g)	Sodium (mg)
t/t	0	2	na	149
t/t	0	2	na	2
t/t	0	2	na	165
t/t	0	2	na	6
t/t	0	4	na	7
t/t	0	1	na	169
t/t	0	1	na	1
t/t	0	2	na	149
t/t	0	2	na	2

Vegetables (cont.)	Serving	Calories	Prot (g)	Carb (g)
Beans, snap, yellow, from frozen, boiled, w/ salt	½ cup	19	1	4
Beans, snap, yellow, from frozen, boiled, w/o salt	½ cup	19	1	4
Beans, snap, yellow, raw	1 cup	34	2	8
Beets, raw	1 cup	58	2	13
Beets, raw (2" dia)	2 beets	71	3	16
Beets, canned, diced, drained	½ cup	24	1	6
Beets, canned, shredded, drained	½ cup	30	1	7
Beets, canned, sliced, drained	½ cup	26	1	6
Beets, canned, whole, drained	½ cup	25	1	6
Beets, canned, drained	2 beets	15	t	3
Beets, from fresh, sliced, boiled, drained	½ cup	37	1	8

Fat/Sat Fat (g)	Chol (mg)	Fiber (g)	Sugars (g)	Sodium (mg)
t/t	0	2	na	165
t/t	0	2	na	6
t/t	0	4	na	7
t/t	0	4	na	106
t/t	0	5	na	128
t/t	0	1	na	152
t/t	0	2	na	189
t/t	0	1	na	165
t/t	0	1	na	158
t/t	0	1	na	93
t/t	0	2	na	65

Vegetables (cont.)	Serving	Calories	Prot (g)	Carb (g)
Beets, canned, pickled, slices	½ cup	74	1	18
Beets, whole, from fresh, cooked	2 beets	44	2	10
Beet greens, boiled, drained, w/salt	½ cup	19	2	4
Beet greens, boiled, drained, w/o salt	½ cup	19	2	4
Beet greens, raw, chopped	1 cup	7	1	2
Broccoli, Chinese, cooked	½ cup	10	t	2
Broccoli, boiled, drained, w/o salt	1 large stalk (11"–12" long)	78	8	14
Broccoli, boiled, drained, w/o salt	1 medium stalk (7½"–8" long)	50	5	9
Broccoli, boiled, drained, w/o salt	1 small stalk (5" long)	39	4	7

Fat/Sat Fat (g)	Chol (mg)	Fiber (g)	Sugars (g)	Sodium (mg)
t/t	0	3	na	300
t/t	0	2	na	77
t/t	0	2	na	343
t/t	0	2	na	174
t/t	0	1	na	76
t/t	0	1	na	3
1/t	0	8	na	73
1/t	0	5	na	47
t/t	0	4	na	36

Vegetables (cont.)	Serving	Calories	Prot (g)	Carb (g)
Broccoli, chopped, boiled, drained, w/o salt	½ cup	22	2	4
Broccoli flowerets, raw	1 cup	20	2	4
Broccoli, frozen, chopped, boiled, drained, w/o salt	½ cup	26	3	5
Broccoli, frozen, spears, boiled, drained, w/o salt	½ cup	26	3	5
Broccoli, raw, chopped	1 cup	25	3	5
Broccoli, raw, spears	2 spears	17	2	3
Broccoli, raw, stalk	1 stalk	42	5	8
Brussels sprouts, boiled, drained, w/o salt	6 sprouts	49	3	11
Brussels sprouts, boiled, drained, w/o salt	½ cup	30	2	7
Brussels sprouts, frozen, boiled, drained, w/o salt	½ cup	33	3	6

Fat/Sat Fat (g)	Chol (mg)	Fiber (g)	Sugars (g)	Sodium (mg)
t/t	0	2	na	20
t/t	0	na	na	19
t/t	0	3	na	22
t/t	0	3	na	22
t/t	0	3	na	24
t/t	0	2	na	17
t/t	0	4.5	na	41
t/t	0	3	na	26
t/t	0	2	na	16
t/t	0	3	na	18

Vegetables (cont.)	Serving	Calories	Prot (g)	Carb (g)
Brussels sprouts, raw	1 cup	38	3	8
Brussels sprouts, raw	6 sprouts	49	4	10
Cabbage, Chinese (pak-choi), shredded, boiled, drained, w/o salt	½ cup	10	1	2
Cabbage, Chinese (pak-choi), shredded, raw	1 cup	9	1	2
Cabbage, Chinese (pe-tsai), shredded boiled, drained, w/o salt	½ cup	8	1	1
Cabbage, Chinese (pe-tsai), shredded, raw	1 cup	12	1	2
Cabbage, raw, chopped	1 cup	22	1	5
Cabbage, raw, shredded	1 cup	18	1	4
Cabbage, shredded, boiled, drained, w/o salt	½ cup	17	1	3

Fat/Sat Fat (g)	Chol (mg)	Fiber (g)	Sugars (g)	Sodium (mg)
t/t	0	3	na	22
t/t	0	4	na	29
t/t	0	1	na	29
t/t	0	1	na	46
t/t	0	1	na	5
t/t	0	2	na	7
t/t	0	2	na	16
t/t	0	2	na	13
t/t	0	2	na	6

Vegetables (cont.)	Serving	Calories	Prot (g)	Carb (g)
Cabbage, napa, cooked	½ cup	7	1	1
Cabbage, red, shredded, boiled, drained, w/o salt	½ cup	16	1	3
Cabbage, red, raw, chopped	1 cup	24	1	5
Cabbage, red, raw, shredded	1 cup	19	1	4
Cabbage, savoy, raw, shredded	1 cup	19	1	4
Cabbage, savoy, shredded, boiled, drained, w/o salt	½ cup	17	1	4
Carrots, baby, large, raw	6	34	1	7
Carrots, baby, medium, raw	6	23	t	5
Carrots, canned, mashed, w/o salt	½ cup	29	1	6
Carrots, canned, sliced, w/o salt	½ cup	18	t	4
Carrots, raw, chopped	1 cup	55	1	13

Fat/Sat Fat (g)	Chol (mg)	Fiber (g)	Sugars (g)	Sodium (mg)
t/t	0	na	na	6
t/t	0	1.5	na	6
t/t	0	2	na	10
t/t	0	1	na	8
t/t	0	2	na	20
t/t	0	2	na	17
t/t	0	2	na	31
t/t	0	1	na	21
t/t	0	2	na	48
t/t	0	1	na	31
t/t	0	4	na	45

Vegetables (cont.)	Serving	Calories	Prot (g)	Carb (g)
Carrots, raw, grated	1 cup	47	1	11
Carrots, raw, sliced	1 cup	52	1	12
Carrots, sliced, boiled, drained, w/o salt	½ cup	35	1	8
Carrots, frozen, sliced, boiled, w/o salt	½ cup	26	1	6
Cauliflower, raw	1 cup	25	2	5
Cauliflower, raw, flowerets	6	20	2	4
Cauliflower, boiled, drained, w/o salt	½ cup	14	1	3
Cauliflower, flowerets, boiled, drained, w/o salt	6 pieces	25	2	4
Cauliflower, frozen, boiled, drained, w/o salt	½ cup	17	1	3
Cauliflower, green, cooked, w/o salt	⅕ head	29	3	6
Cauliflower, green, raw	1 cup	20	2	4

Fat/Sat Fat (g)	Chol (mg)	Fiber (g)	Sugars (g)	Sodium (mg)
t/t	0	3	na	39
t/t	0	4	na	43
t/t	0	3	na	51
t/t	0	3	na	43
t/t	0	2.5	na	30
t/t	0	2	na	23
t/t	0	2	na	9
t/t	0	3	na	16
t/t	0	2	na	16
t/t	0	3	na	21
t/t	0	2	na	15

Vegetables (cont.)	Serving	Calories	Prot (g)	Carb (g)
Cauliflower, green, flowerets	6	47	4	9
Celery, diced, boiled, drained, w/o salt	½ cup	14	I	3
Celery, diced, raw	I cup	19	I	4
Celery, strips, raw	I cup	20	I	5
Chard, swiss, chopped, boiled, drained, w/o salt	½ cup	18	2	4
Chard, swiss, raw	I cup	7	I	I
Chayote, chopped, boiled, drained, w/o salt	½ cup	19	t	4
Chayote, chopped, raw	I cup	25	I	6
Collards, chopped, boiled, drained, w/o salt	½ cup	25	2	5
Collards, chopped, frozen, boiled, drained, w/o salt	½ cup	31	3	6
Collards, chopped, raw	I cup	II	I	2

Fat/Sat Fat (g)	Chol (mg)	Fiber (g)	Sugars (g)	Sodium (mg)
t/t	0	5	na	35
t/t	0	1	na	68
t/t	0	2	na	104
t/t	0	2	na	108
t/t	0	2	na	157
t/t	0	1	na	77
t/t	0	2	na	1
t/t	0	2	na	3
t/t	0	3	na	9
t/t	0	2	na	43
t/t	0	1	na	7

Vegetables (cont.)	Serving	Calories	Prot (g)	Carb (g)
Cucumber, peeled, raw, chopped	1 cup	16	1	3
Cucumber, peeled, raw, sliced	1 cup	14	1	3
Cucumber, peeled, raw, large (8¼" long)	1	34	2	7
Cucumber, peeled, raw, medium	1	24	1	5
Cucumber, peeled, raw, small (6⅜" long)	1	19	t	4
Cucumber, with peel, raw, slices	1 cup	14	1	3
Cucumber, with peel, raw, large (8¼" long)	1	39	2	8
Dandelion greens, chopped, boiled, drained, w/o salt	½ cup	17	1	3
Dandelion greens, raw, chopped	1 cup	25	1	5
Eggplant, cubes, boiled, drained, w/o salt	½ cup	14	t	3

Fat/Sat Fat (g)	Chol (mg)	Fiber (g)	Sugars (g)	Sodium (mg)
t/t	0	1	na	3
t/t	0	1	na	2
t/t	0	2	na	6
t/t	0	1	na	4
t/t	0	1	na	3
t/t	0	1	na	2
t/t	0	2	na	6
t/t	0	1.5	na	23
t/t	0	2	na	42
t/t	0	1	na	1

Vegetables (cont.)	Serving	Calories	Prot (g)	Carb (g)
Eggplant, raw, cubes	1 cup	21	1	5
Endive, raw, chopped	1 cup	9	t	2
Grape leaves, raw	1 cup	13	1	2
Jicama, raw, sliced	1 cup	46	1	11
Kale, chopped, boiled, drained, w/o salt	½ cup	18	1	4
Kale, frozen, chopped, boiled, drained, w/o salt	½ cup	20	2	3
Kale, raw, chopped	1 cup	34	2	7
Kale, scotch, chopped, boiled, drained, w/o salt	½ cup	18	1	4
Kale, scotch, raw, chopped	1 cup	28	2	6
Kohlrabi, sliced, boiled drained, w/o salt	½ cup	24	1	6
Kohlrabi, raw	1 cup	36	2	8

Fat/Sat Fat (g)	Chol (mg)	Fiber (g)	Sugars (g)	Sodium (mg)
t/t	0	2	na	2
t/t	0	2	na	11
t/t	0	1.5	na	1
t/t	0	6	na	5
t/t	0	1	na	15
t/t	0	1	na	10
t/t	0	1	na	29
t/t	0	1	na	29
t/t	0	1	na	47
t/t	0	1	na	17
t/t	0	5	na	27

Vegetables (cont.)	Serving	Calories	Prot (g)	Carb (g)
Leeks (bulb and lower-leaf portion), boiled, drained, w/o salt	1 leek	38	1	9
Leeks, chopped (bulb and lower-leaf portion), boiled, drained, w/o salt	½ cup	16	t	4
Leeks, chopped, raw (bulb and lower-leaf portion)	1 cup	54	1	13
Leeks, raw (bulb and lower-leaf portion)	1 leek	54	1	13
Lettuce, shredded, raw, butterhead, boston, and bibb types	1 cup	7	1	1
Lettuce, shredded, raw, cos or romaine	1 cup	8	1	1
Lettuce, shredded, raw, iceberg	1 cup	7	1	1
Lettuce, shredded, raw, looseleaf	1 cup	10	1	2

Fat/Sat Fat (g)	Chol (mg)	Fiber (g)	Sugars (g)	Sodium (mg)
t/t	0	1	na	12
t/t	0	.5	na	5
t/t	0	2	na	18
t/t	0	2	na	18
t/t	0	1	na	3
t/t	0	1	na	4
t/t	0	1	na	5
t/t	0	1	na	5

Vegetables (cont.)	Serving	Calories	Prot (g)	Carb (g)
Lettuce, shredded, raw, radicchio	1 cup	9	1	2
Mushrooms, raw, Crimini or Italian	6 pieces	18	2	3
Mushrooms, canned, drained	½ cup	19	1	4
Mushrooms, boiled, drained, w/o salt	½ cup	21	2	4
Mushrooms, boiled, drained, w/o salt	6 pieces	19	2	4
Mushrooms, raw, enoki	6 pieces (large)	10	1	2
Mushrooms, raw, enoki	6 pieces (medium)	6	t	1
Mushrooms, raw, slices or pieces	1 cup	18	2	3
Mushrooms, raw, whole	1 cup	24	3	4
Mushrooms, raw	6 pieces (large)	35	4	6
Mushrooms, raw	6 pieces (medium)	27	3	4
Mushrooms, raw portabella	4 slices	20	3	4

Fat/Sat Fat (g)	Chol (mg)	Fiber (g)	Sugars (g)	Sodium (mg)
t/t	0	t	na	9
t/t	0	.5	l	5
t/t	0	2	na	332
t/t	0	2	na	2
t/t	0	2	na	l
t/t	0	l	na	l
t/t	0	.5	na	l
t/t	0	l	na	3
t/t	0	l	na	4
t/t	0	2	na	6
t/t	0	l	na	4
0/0	0	3	l	l0

Vegetables (cont.)	Serving	Calories	Prot (g)	Carb (g)
Mushrooms, cooked, pieces, shiitake, w/o salt	½ cup	40	1	10
Mushrooms, cooked, whole, shiitake, w/o salt	6 pieces	59	2	15
Mushrooms, dried, shiitake	6 mushrooms	67	2	17
Mushrooms, canned, straw, drained	½ cup	29	3	4
Okra, frozen, boiled, drained, w/o salt	½ cup	26	2	5
Okra, raw	1 cup	33	2	8
Okra, raw	6 pods	24	1	5
Okra, slices, boiled, drained, w/o salt	½ cup	26	1	6
Okra, whole, boiled, drained, w/o salt	6 pods	20	1	5
Onions, boiled, drained, w/o salt	½ cup	46	1	11
Onions, boiled, drained, w/o salt	1 large	56	2	13
Onions, boiled, drained, w/o salt	1 medium	41	1	10

Fat/Sat Fat (g)	Chol (mg)	Fiber (g)	Sugars (g)	Sodium (mg)
t/t	0	1.5	na	3
t/t	0	2	na	4
t/t	0	3	na	3
t/t	0	2	na	349
t/t	0	3	na	3
t/t	0	3	na	8
t/t	0	2	na	6
t/t	0	2	na	4
t/t	0	2	na	3
t/t	0	1.5	na	3
t/t	0	2	na	4
t/t	0	1	na	3

Vegetables (cont.)	Serving	Calories	Prot (g)	Carb (g)
Onions, boiled, drained, w/o salt	1 small	26	1	6
Onions, canned, chopped	½ cup	21	1	5
Onions, dehydrated flakes	¼ cup	49	1	12
Onions, frozen, chopped, boiled, drained, w/o salt	½ cup	29	1	7
Onions, raw, chopped	1 cup	61	2	14
Onions, raw, sliced	1 cup	44	1	10
Onions, raw, sliced (¼" thick)	1 slice	14	t	3
Onions, raw, sliced (⅛" thick)	1 slice	5	t	1
Onions, raw, whole	1 large	57	2	13
Onions, raw, whole	1 medium	42	1	9
Onions, raw, whole	1 small	27	1	6
Onions, raw, chopped, spring or scallions (tops and bulbs)	1 cup	32	2	7

Fat/Sat Fat (g)	Chol (mg)	Fiber (g)	Sugars (g)	Sodium (mg)
t/t	0	1	na	2
t/t	0	1	na	416
t/t	0	1	na	3
t/t	0	2	na	13
t/t	0	3	na	5
t/t	0	2	na	3
t/t	0	1	na	1
t/t	0	t	na	0
t/t	0	3	na	5
t/t	0	2	na	3
t/t	0	1	na	2
t/t	0	3	na	16

Vegetables (cont.)	Serving	Calories	Prot (g)	Carb (g)
Onions, raw, whole spring or scallions (tops and bulbs)	1 large	8	t	2
Onions, raw, whole spring or scallions (tops and bulbs)	1 medium	5	t	1
Onions, raw, whole spring or scallions (tops and bulbs)	1 small	2	t	t
Palm, hearts, canned	½ cup	20	2	3
Palm, hearts, canned,	3 pieces	28	2.5	5
Parsley, freeze-dried	¼ cup	4	t	1
Parsley, raw	1 cup	22	2	4
Parsley, raw	6 sprigs	2	t	t
Parsnips, raw	1 cup	100	2	24
Parsnips, sliced, boiled, drained, w/o salt	½ cup	63	1	15
Peas and carrots, canned, w/o salt	½ cup	48	3	11
Peas and carrots, canned, w/ salt	½ cup	48	3	11

Fat/Sat Fat (g)	Chol (mg)	Fiber (g)	Sugars (g)	Sodium (mg)
t/t	0	1	na	4
t/t	0	t	na	2
t/t	0	t	na	1
t/t	0	2	na	311
t/t	0	2	na	422
t/t	0	.5	na	5
t/t	0	2	na	34
t/t	0	t	na	3
t/t	0	6.5	na	13
t/t	0	3	na	8
t/t	0	4	na	5
t/t	0	3	na	332

Vegetables (cont.)	Serving	Calories	Prot (g)	Carb (g)
Peas and carrots, frozen, boiled, drained, w/o salt	½ cup	38	2	8
Peas, edible-podded, fresh, boiled, drained, w/o salt	½ cup	34	3	6
Peas, edible-podded, frozen, boiled, drained, w/o salt	½ cup	42	3	7
Peas, green, canned, w/o salt	½ cup	59	4	11
Peas, green, fresh, boiled, drained, w/o salt	½ cup	67	4	13
Peas, green, frozen, boiled, drained, w/o salt	½ cup	62	4	11
Peas, pigeon, fresh, boiled, w/o salt	½ cup	102	6	20
Peas and onions, canned	½ cup	31	2	5
Peas and onions, frozen, boiled, drained, w/o salt	½ cup	41	2	8
Peppers, chili, green, canned	½ cup	15	t	3

Fat/Sat Fat (g)	Chol (mg)	Fiber (g)	Sugars (g)	Sodium (mg)
t/t	0	2.5	na	54
t/t	0	2	na	3
t/t	0	2.5	na	4
t/t	0	3.5	na	2
t/t	0	4	na	2
t/t	0	4	na	70
t/t	0	6	na	4
t/t	0	1	na	265
t/t	0	2	na	33
t/t	0	1	na	276

Vegetables (cont.)	Serving	Calories	Prot (g)	Carb (g)
Peppers, hot chili, sun-dried	6 peppers	10	t	2
Peppers, hot chili, green, chopped, canned, pods	½ cup	14	1	3
Peppers, hot chili, green, whole, canned	1 pepper	15	1	4
Peppers, hot chili, green, chopped, raw	1 cup	60	3	14
Peppers, hot chili, green, whole, raw	1 pepper	18	1	4
Peppers, chili, red, chopped, canned	½ cup	14	t	3
Peppers, hot chili, red, whole, canned	1 pepper	15	1	4
Peppers, hot chili, red, chopped, raw	1 cup	60	3	14
Peppers, hot chili, red, whole, raw	1 pepper	18	1	4
Peppers, Hungarian, raw	1 pepper	8	t	2
Peppers, jalapeno, chopped, canned	½ cup	18	1	3

Fat/Sat Fat (g)	Chol (mg)	Fiber (g)	Sugars (g)	Sodium (mg)
t/t	0	1	na	3
t/t	0	1	na	798
t/t	0	1	na	856
t/t	0	2	na	11
t/t	0	1	na	3
t/t	0	1	na	798
t/t	0	1	na	856
t/t	0	2	na	11
t/t	0	1	na	3
t/t	0	na	na	0
t/t	0	2	na	1136

Vegetables (cont.)	Serving	Calories	Prot (g)	Carb (g)
Peppers, jalapeno, sliced, canned	½ cup	14	t	2
Peppers, jalapeno, whole, canned	1 pepper	6	t	1
Peppers, jalapeno, whole, raw	1 pepper	4	t	1
Peppers, sweet, green, halves, canned	½ cup	13	1	3
Peppers, sweet, green, strips, boiled, drained, w/o salt	½ cup	19	1	5
Peppers, sweet, green, chopped, boiled, drained, w/o salt	½ cup	19	1	5
Peppers, sweet, green, chopped, raw	1 cup	40	1	10
Peppers, sweet, green, slices, raw	1 cup	25	1	6
Peppers, sweet, green, large, raw	1 pepper	44	1	11
Peppers, sweet, green, medium, raw	1 pepper	32	1	8

Fat/Sat Fat (g)	Chol (mg)	Fiber (g)	Sugars (g)	Sodium (mg)
t/t	0	1	na	869
t/t	0	1	na	368
t/t	0	t	na	0
t/t	0	1	na	958
t/t	0	1	na	1
t/t	0	1	na	1
t/t	0	3	na	3
t/t	0	2	na	2
t/t	0	3	na	3
t/t	0	2	na	2

Vegetables (cont.)	Serving	Calories	Prot (g)	Carb (g)
Peppers, sweet, green, small, raw	I pepper	20	I	5
Peppers, sweet, green, rings, raw	6 rings	16	t	4
Peppers, sweet, green, rings, raw	6 strips	4	t	I
Peppers, sweet, red, strips, boiled, drained, w/o salt	½ cup	19	I	5
Peppers, sweet, red, chopped, boiled, drained, w/o salt	½ cup	19	I	5
Peppers, sweet, red, chopped, raw	I cup	40	I	10
Peppers, sweet, red, slices, raw	I cup	25	I	6
Peppers, sweet, red, large, raw	I pepper	44	I	11
Peppers, sweet, red, medium, raw	I pepper	32	I	8
Peppers, sweet, red, small, raw	I pepper	20	I	5
Peppers, sweet, yellow, large, raw	I pepper	50	2	12

Fat/Sat Fat (g)	Chol (mg)	Fiber (g)	Sugars (g)	Sodium (mg)
t/t	0	l	na	l
t/t	0	l	na	l
t/t	0	t	na	0
t/t	0	l	na	l
t/t	0	l	na	l
t/t	0	3	na	3
t/t	0	2	na	2
t/t	0	3	na	3
t/t	0	2	na	2
t/t	0	1.5	na	l
t/t	0	2	na	4

Vegetables (cont.)	Serving	Calories	Prot (g)	Carb (g)
Peppers, sweet, yellow, strips, raw	6 strips	8	t	2
Radishes, oriental, sliced, boiled, drained, w/o salt	½ cup	12	t	3
Radishes, oriental, whole, raw	1 radish	61	2	14
Radishes, slices, raw	1 cup	23	1	4
Radish, large, raw	1 radish	2	t	t
Radish, medium, raw	1 radish	1	t	t
Radishes, white icicle, slices, raw	1 cup	14	1	3
Radishes, white icicle, whole, raw	1 radish	2	t	t
Rhubarb, raw, diced	1 cup	26	1	6
Rutabagas, cubes, boiled, drained, w/o salt	½ cup	33	1	7
Rutabagas, mashed, boiled, drained, w/o salt	½ cup	47	2	11
Sauerkraut, canned	½ cup	13	1	3
Seaweed, kelp, raw	1 cup	34	1	8

Fat/Sat Fat (g)	Chol (mg)	Fiber (g)	Sugars (g)	Sodium (mg)
t/t	0	t	na	1
t/t	0	1	na	10
t/t	0	5	na	71
t/t	0	2	na	28
t/t	0	t	na	2
t/t	0	t	na	1
t/t	0	1	na	16
t/t	0	t	na	3
t/t	0	2	na	5
t/t	0	1.5	na	17
t/t	0	2	na	24
t/t	0	2	na	469
t/t	0	1	na	186

Vegetables (cont.)	Serving	Calories	Prot (g)	Carb (g)
Shallots, chopped, raw	1 tbsp	7	t	2
Spinach, canned, w/o salt	½ cup	22	2	3
Spinach, boiled, drained, w/o salt	½ cup	21	3	3
Spinach, frozen, chopped or leaf, boiled, drained, w/o salt	½ cup	27	3	5
Spinach, raw	1 cup	7	1	1
Sprouts, alfalfa, raw	1 cup	10	1	1
Sprouts, mung, boiled drained	½ cup	13	1	2.5
Sprouts, mung, raw	1 cup	31	3	6
Squash, spaghetti, boiled or baked, drained, w/o salt	½ cup	21	t	5
Summer squash, all varieties, sliced, boiled, drained, w/o salt	½ cup	18	1	4
Summer squash, all varieties, sliced, raw	1 cup	23	1	5

Fat/Sat Fat (g)	Chol (mg)	Fiber (g)	Sugars (g)	Sodium (mg)
t/t	0	na	na	l
t/t	0	3	na	88
t/t	0	2	na	63
t/t	0	3	na	82
t/t	0	l	na	24
t/0	0	l	na	2
t/0	0	na	na	na
t/0	0	na	na	na
t/t	0	l	na	14
t/t	0	l	na	l
t/t	0	2	na	2

Vegetables (cont.)	Serving	Calories	Prot (g)	Carb (g)
Summer squash, crookneck and straightneck, diced, canned	½ cup	14	1	3
Summer squash, crookneck and straightneck, mashed, canned, w/o salt	½ cup	16	1	4
Summer squash, crookneck and straightneck, slices, canned, w/o salt	½ cup	14	1	3
Summer squash, crookneck and straightneck, slices, frozen, w/o salt	½ cup	24	1	5
Summer squash, crookneck and straightneck, slices, raw	1 cup	25	1	5
Taro shoots, slices, cooked, w/o salt	½ cup	10	t	2
Taro shoots, slices, raw	1 cup	9	1	2
Tomatillos, medium, raw	1 tomatillo	11	t	2

Fat/Sat Fat (g)	Chol (mg)	Fiber (g)	Sugars (g)	Sodium (mg)
t/t	0	1.5	na	5
t/t	0	2	na	6
t/t	0	1.5	na	5
t/t	0	1	na	6
t/t	0	2.5	na	3
t/t	0	na	na	1
t/t	0	na	na	1
t/t	0	1	na	0

Vegetables (cont.)	Serving	Calories	Prot (g)	Carb (g)
Tomatillos, chopped, raw	I cup	42	I	8
Tomatoes, crushed, canned	½ cup	39	2	9
Tomatoes, green, chopped, raw	I cup	43	2	9
Tomatoes, green, slice or wedge, raw	I piece	5	t	I
Tomatoes, green, whole, raw	I large tomato	44	2	9
Tomatoes, green, whole, raw	I medium tomato	30	I	6
Tomatoes, green, whole, small, raw	I small tomato	22	I	5
Tomatoes, orange, chopped, raw	I cup	25	2	5
Tomatoes, orange, raw	I tomato	18	I	4
Tomatoes, red, canned, stewed	½ cup	36	I	9
Tomatoes, red, canned, wedges in tomato juice	½ cup	34	I	8

Fat/Sat Fat (g)	Chol (mg)	Fiber (g)	Sugars (g)	Sodium (mg)
t/t	0	2.5	na	1
t/t	0	2	na	161
t/t	0	2	na	23
t/t	0	t	na	3
t/t	0	2	na	24
t/t	0	1	na	16
t/t	0	1	na	12
t/t	0	1	na	66
t/t	0	1	na	47
t/t	0	1	na	282
t/t	0	na	na	283

Vegetables (cont.)	Serving	Calories	Prot (g)	Carb (g)
Tomatoes, red, whole, canned, w/o salt	½ cup	23	1	5
Tomatoes, red, whole, canned, w/ salt	½ cup	23	1	5
Tomatoes, red, canned, with green chiles	½ cup	18	1	4
Tomatoes, red, boiled, w/o salt	½ cup	32	1	7
Tomatoes, red, boiled, w/ salt	½ cup	32	1	7
Tomatoes, red, slice (¼" thick)	1 slice	4	t	1
Tomatoes, red (¼ of a medium tomato), raw	1 wedge	7	t	1
Tomatoes, red whole, boiled, w/o salt	2 medium tomatoes	66	3	14
Tomatoes, red, whole, raw	1 large tomato	38	2	8
Tomatoes, red, whole, raw	1 medium tomato	26	1	6

Fat/Sat Fat (g)	Chol (mg)	Fiber (g)	Sugars (g)	Sodium (mg)
t/t	0	1	na	12
t/t	0	1	na	178
t/t	0	na	na	483
t/t	0	1	na	13
t/t	0	1	na	296
t/t	0	t	na	2
t/t	0	t	na	3
1/t	0	2.5	na	27
t/t	0	2	na	16
t/t	0	1	na	11

Vegetables (cont.)	Serving	Calories	Prot (g)	Carb (g)
Tomatoes, red, whole, raw	1 small tomato	19	1	4
Tomatoes, red, stewed	½ cup	40	1	7
Tomatoes, cherry, raw	1 cup	31	1	7
Tomatoes, cherry, raw	1 tomato	4	t	1
Tomatoes, red, chopped, raw	1 cup	38	2	8
Tomatoes, roma (Italian), raw	1 tomato	13	t	3
Tomatoes, sun-dried	½ cup	70	4	15
Tomatoes, sun-dried	1 piece	5	t	1
Tomatoes, yellow, chopped, raw	1 cup	21	1	4
Tomatoes, yellow, whole, raw	1 tomato	32	2	6
Tomato paste, w/o salt	¼ cup	53	2	12
Tomato paste, w/ salt	¼ cup	53	2	12

Fat/Sat Fat (g)	Chol (mg)	Fiber (g)	Sugars (g)	Sodium (mg)
t/t	0	l	na	8
l/t	0	l	na	230
t/t	0	2	na	13
t/t	0	t	na	2
t/t	0	2	na	16
t/t	0	l	na	6
t/t	0	3	na	566
t/t	0	t	na	42
t/t	0	l	na	32
t/t	0	1.5	na	49
t/t	0	2.5	na	57
t/t	0	2.5	na	517

Vegetables (cont.)	Serving	Calories	Prot (g)	Carb (g)
Tomato puree, w/o salt	½ cup	50	2	12
Tomato puree, w/ salt	½ cup	50	2	12
Tomato sauce, canned	½ cup	37	2	9
Tomato sauce, canned, Spanish style	½ cup	40	2	9
Tomato sauce, canned, w/ mushrooms	½ cup	43	2	10
Tomato sauce, canned, w/ onions	½ cup	51	2	12
Tomato sauce, canned, w/ onions, green peppers, and celery	½ cup	51	1	11
Tomato sauce, canned, w/ tomato tidbits	½ cup	39	2	9
Turnips, cubes, boiled, drained, w/o salt	½ cup	16	t	4

Fat/Sat Fat (g)	Chol (mg)	Fiber (g)	Sugars (g)	Sodium (mg)
t/t	0	2.5	na	43
t/t	0	2.5	na	499
t/t	0	2	na	741
t/t	0	2	na	576
t/t	0	2	na	554
t/t	0	2	na	675
t/t	0	2	na	683
t/t	0	2	na	18
t/t	0	2	na	39

Vegetables (cont.)	Serving	Calories	Prot (g)	Carb (g)
Turnips, mashed, boiled, drained, w/o salt	½ cup	24	1	6
Turnips, frozen, boiled, drained, w/o salt	½ cup	18	1	3
Turnip greens and turnips, frozen, boiled, drained, w/o salt	½ cup	15	2	2
Vegetables, mixed, canned	½ cup	38	2	8
Vegetables, mixed, frozen, boiled, drained, w/ salt	½ cup	54	3	12
Vegetables, mixed, frozen, boiled, drained, w/o salt	½ cup	54	3	12
Water chestnuts, Chinese, slices, canned	½ cup	35	1	9
Watercress, chopped, raw	1 cup	4	1	t
Watercress, raw	10 sprigs	3	t	t

Fat/Sat Fat (g)	Chol (mg)	Fiber (g)	Sugars (g)	Sodium (mg)
t/t	0	2	na	58
t/t	0	2	na	28
t/t	0	1.5	na	13
t/t	0	2	na	121
t/t	0	4	na	247
t/t	0	4	na	32
t/t	0	2	na	6
t/t	0	t	na	14
t/t	0	t	na	10

Vegetables (cont.)	Serving	Calories	Prot (g)	Carb (g)
Zucchini, frozen, boiled, drained, w/o salt	½ cup	19	1	4
Zucchini, sliced, boiled, drained, w/o salt	½ cup	14	t	4
Zucchini, mashed, boiled, drained, w/o salt	½ cup	19	1	5
Zucchini, chopped, raw	1 cup	17	1	4

Vegetable Juices

	Serving	Calories	Prot (g)	Carb (g)
Carrot juice, canned	1 cup	94	2	22
Clam and tomato juice	1 can (5.5 oz.)	80	1	18
Mixed vegetable and fruit juice drink	1 serving	110	t	28
Tomato juice, w/o salt	1 cup	41	2	10
Tomato juice, w/ salt	1 cup	41	2	10
Vegetable juice cocktail, canned	1 cup	46	1.5	11

Fat/Sat Fat (g)	Chol (mg)	Fiber (g)	Sugars (g)	Sodium (mg)
t/t	0	1	na	2
t/t	0	1	na	3
t/t	0	2	na	4
t/t	0	1.5	na	4

Fat/Sat Fat (g)	Chol (mg)	Fiber (g)	Sugars (g)	Sodium (mg)
t/t	0	2	na	68
t/t	0	t	na	601
t/t	0	t	na	20
t/t	0	2	na	24
t/t	0	1	na	877
t/t	0	2	na	653

Vegetables (cont.)	Serving	Calories	Prot (g)	Carb (g)
Vegetables/Starchy				
Acorn squash, cubes, baked, w/o salt	½ cup	57	1	15
Acorn squash, mashed, baked, w/o salt	½ cup	42	1	11
Beans/Legumes				
Adzuki, boiled, w/ salt	½ cup	147	9	28
Adzuki, boiled, w/o salt	½ cup	147	9	28
Black beans, boiled w/ salt	½ cup	114	8	20
Black beans, boiled w/o salt	½ cup	114	8	20
Black beans, canned Ranch Style (ConAgra)	½ cup	100	6	19
Broadbeans (fava), boiled, w/ salt	½ cup	94	6	17
Broadbeans (fava), boiled, w/o salt	½ cup	94	6	17
Broadbeans (fava), canned	½ cup	91	7	16

Fat/Sat Fat (g)	Chol (mg)	Fiber (g)	Sugars (g)	Sodium (mg)
t/t	0	4.5	na	4
t/t	0	3	na	4

Fat/Sat Fat (g)	Chol (mg)	Fiber (g)	Sugars (g)	Sodium (mg)
t/t	0	8	na	281
t/t	0	8	na	9
t/t	0	7.5	na	204
t/t	0	7.5	na	1
t/0	0	5	1	420
t/t	0	5	na	205
t/t	0	5	na	4
t/t	0	5	na	580

Vegetables (cont.)	Serving	Calories	Prot (g)	Carb (g)
Chickpeas (garbanzos), boiled, w/ salt	½ cup	134	7	22
Chickpeas (garbanzos), boiled, w/o salt	½ cup	134	7	22
Chickpeas (garbanzos), canned	½ cup	143	6	27
Cranberry beans, boiled, w/ salt	½ cup	120	8	22
Cranberry beans, boiled, w/o salt	½ cup	120	8	22
Cranberry beans, canned	½ cup	108	7	20
Great Northern beans, boiled, w/ salt	½ cup	104	7	19
Great Northern beans, boiled, w/o salt	½ cup	104	7	19
Great Northern beans, canned	½ cup	149	10	28
Kidney beans, boiled, w/ salt	½ cup	112	8	20

Fat/Sat Fat (g)	Chol (mg)	Fiber (g)	Sugars (g)	Sodium (mg)
2/t	0	6	na	199
2/t	0	6	na	6
1/t	0	5	na	359
t/t	0	9	na	210
t/t	0	9	na	1
t/t	0	8	na	432
t/t	0	6	na	211
t/t	0	6	na	2
t/t	0	6	na	5
t/t	0	6	na	211

Vegetables (cont.)	Serving	Calories	Prot (g)	Carb (g)
Kidney beans, boiled, w/o salt	½ cup	112	8	20
Kidney beans, canned	½ cup	104	7	19
Lentils, boiled, w/o salt	½ cup	115	9	20
Lentils, sprouted, raw	1 cup	82	7	17
Lima beans, baby, boiled, w/ salt	½ cup	115	7	21
Lima beans, baby, boiled, w/o salt	½ cup	115	7	21
Lima beans, large, boiled, w/ salt	½ cup	108	7	20
Lima beans, large, boiled, w/o salt	½ cup	108	7	20
Lima beans, large, canned	½ cup	95	6	18
Mung beans, boiled, w/ salt	½ cup	106	7	19
Mung beans, boiled, w/o salt	½ cup	106	7	19
Navy beans, boiled, w/ salt	½ cup	129	8	24

Fat/Sat Fat (g)	Chol (mg)	Fiber (g)	Sugars (g)	Sodium (mg)
t/t	0	6	na	2
t/t	0	4.5	na	444
t/t	0	8	na	2
t/t	0	na	na	8
t/t	0	7	na	217
t/t	0	7	na	3
t/t	0	7	na	224
t/t	0	7	na	2
t/t	0	6	na	405
t/t	0	8	na	240
t/t	0	8	na	2
t/t	0	6	na	216

Vegetables (cont.)	Serving	Calories	Prot (g)	Carb (g)
Navy beans, boiled, w/o salt	½ cup	129	8	24
Navy beans, canned	½ cup	148	10	27
Pink beans, boiled, w/ salt	½ cup	126	8	24
Pink beans, boiled, w/o salt	½ cup	126	8	24
Pinto beans, boiled, w/ salt	½ cup	117	7	22
Pinto beans, boiled, w/o salt	½ cup	117	7	22
Pinto beans, canned	½ cup	103	6	18
Split peas, boiled, w/o salt	½ cup	116	8	21
White beans (small), boiled, w/o salt	½ cup	127	8	23
White beans, boiled, w/ salt	½ cup	124	9	23
White beans, boiled, w/o salt	½ cup	124	9	23
White beans, canned	½ cup	153	10	29

Fat/Sat Fat (g)	Chol (mg)	Fiber (g)	Sugars (g)	Sodium (mg)
t/t	0	6	na	1
t/t	0	7	na	587
t/t	0	4.5	na	201
t/t	0	4.5	na	2
t/t	0	7	na	203
t/t	0	7	na	2
1/t	0	5.5	na	353
t/t	0	8	na	2
t/t	0	9	na	2
t/t	0	6	na	217
t/t	0	6	na	5
t/t	0	6	na	7

Vegetables (cont.)	Serving	Calories	Prot (g)	Carb (g)
Vegetables/Starchy				
Breadfruit, cooked	½ cup	113	1	30
Butternut squash, cubes, baked, w/o salt	½ cup	41	1	11
Butternut squash, frozen, boiled, mashed, w/o salt	½ cup	47	1	12
Corn, canned, w/ red and green peppers	½ cup	85	3	21
Corn, canned, white, w/o salt	½ cup	83	3	20
Corn, canned, white, sweet, whole kernel, canned	½ cup	66	2	15
Corn, canned, white, sweet, whole kernel, w/o salt	½ cup	82	3	20
Corn, fresh, white, sweet, boiled, drained w/o salt	½ cup	89	3	21
Corn, frozen, white, sweet, boiled, drained, w/o salt	½ cup	66	2	16

Fat/Sat Fat (g)	Chol (mg)	Fiber (g)	Sugars (g)	Sodium (mg)
t/t	0	5	na	2
t/t	0	na	na	4
t/t	0	na	na	2
t/t	0	na	na	394
t/t	0	2	na	3
l/t	0	2	na	265
l/t	0	1	na	15
l/t	0	2	na	14
t/t	0	2	na	4

Vegetables (cont.)	Serving	Calories	Prot (g)	Carb (g)
Corn, white, sweet, on the cob	1 ear	59	2	14
Corn, canned, yellow, sweet	½ cup	66	2	15
Corn, fresh, yellow, sweet, boiled, drained, w/o salt	½ cup	88	3	20
Corn on the cob, fresh, yellow, sweet, boiled, drained, w/o salt	1 ear	83	3	19
Corn cut off the cob, frozen, yellow, sweet, boiled, drained, w/o salt	½ cup	66	2	16
Corn, air-popped popcorn	2 cups	61	2	12
Hubbard squash, baked, cubes, w/o salt	½ cup	51	3	11
Hubbard squash, boiled, mashed, w/o salt	½ cup	35	2	8
Potato, baked with skin, w/ salt	1 medium	161	4	37

Fat/Sat Fat (g)	Chol (mg)	Fiber (g)	Sugars (g)	Sodium (mg)
t/t	0	1	na	3
l/t	0	2	na	175
l/t	0	2	na	14
l/t	0	2	na	13
t/t	0	2	na	4
t/t	0	2	na	1
t/t	0	na	na	8
t/t	0	3	na	6
t/t	0	4	2	422

Vegetables (cont.)	Serving	Calories	Prot (g)	Carb (g)
Potato, baked with skin, w/o salt	1 medium	161	4	37
Potato, boiled w/o skin, w/o salt	1 medium	144	3	33
Potatoes, canned, drained	½ cup	54	1	12
Potatoes, micro-waved with skin, w/ salt	1 medium	156	3	36
Potatoes, red, baked w/ flesh and skin	1 medium	154	4	34
Potatoes, Russet, baked w/ flesh and skin	1 medium	168	5	37
Potatoes, white, baked w/ flesh and skin	1 medium	163	4	36
Pumpkin, canned, w/o salt	½ cup	42	1	10
Pumpkin, boiled, mashed, w/o salt	½ cup	25	1	6
Succotash, boiled, drained, w/o salt	½ cup	110	5	23

Fat/Sat Fat (g)	Chol (mg)	Fiber (g)	Sugars (g)	Sodium (mg)
t/t	0	4	2	17
t/t	0	3	na	8
t/t	0	2	na	197
t/t	0	2.5	na	379
t/t	0	3	2.5	14
t/t	0	4	na	14
t/t	0	4	3	12
t/t	0	4	na	6
t/t	0	1	na	1
t/t	0	4	na	16

Vegetables (cont.)	Serving	Calories	Prot (g)	Carb (g)
Succotash, frozen, boiled, drained, w/o salt	½ cup	79	4	17
Sweet potato, baked in skin, w/o salt	½ cup	103	2	24
Sweet potato, baked in skin, w/o salt	1 medium	117	2	28
Sweet potato, canned, mashed	½ cup	129	3	30
Sweet potatoes, frozen, cubes, baked, w/o salt	½ cup	88	1	21
Winter squash, all varieties, baked, w/o salt	½ cup	40	1	9

Fat/Sat Fat (g)	Chol (mg)	Fiber (g)	Sugars (g)	Sodium (mg)
t/t	0	3.5	na	38
t/t	0	3	na	10
t/t	0	3	na	11
t/t	0	2	na	96
t/t	0	2	na	7
t/t	0	3	na	1

LOW-RESPONSE COST, LOW-YIELD FOODS: BEEF

Food	Serving	Calories	Prot (g)	Carb (g)
Beef				
Brisket, point half, lean and fat, trimmed to ¼" fat, all grades, braised	4 oz.	458	25	0
Chuck arm pot roast, lean and fat, trimmed to ½" fat, prime, braised	4 oz.	443	30	0
Chuck blade roast, lean and fat, trimmed to ½" fat, prime, braised	4 oz.	473	29	0
Corned beef, canned	4 oz.	284	31	0
Corned beef loaf, jellied	4 oz.	171	26	0
Ground, regular	4 oz.	320	28	0
Hot dog, beef	1 hot dog	141	5	2
Hot dog, meat	1 hot dog	151	5	2
Meatloaf	4 oz.	260	24	6

Fat/Sat Fat (g)	Chol (mg)	Fiber (g)	Sugars (g)	Sodium (mg)
39/15	104	0	na	74
35/14	112	0	na	66
39/16	117	0	na	71
17/7	98	0	na	1141
7/3	53	0	na	1067
22/9	107	0	na	87
13/5	23	0	1.5	490
13/4	40	0	na	567
16/6	68	1	4	556

Beef (cont.)	Serving	Calories	Prot (g)	Carb (g)
Rib, large end (ribs 6–9), lean and fat, trimmed to ⅛" fat, prime, broiled	4 oz.	458	23	0
Rib, large end (ribs 6–9), lean and fat, trimmed to ⅛" fat, prime, roasted	4 oz.	445	26	0
Rib, large end (ribs 6–9), lean and fat, trimmed to ¼" fat, prime, broiled	4 oz.	468	23	0
Rib, large end (ribs 6–9), lean and fat, trimmed to ¼" fat, prime, roasted	4 oz.	456	25.5	0
Rib, large end (ribs 6–9), lean and fat, trimmed to ½" fat, prime, broiled	4 oz.	482	22.5	0
Rib, large end (ribs 6–9), lean and fat, trimmed to ½" fat, prime, roasted	4 oz.	461	25	0

Fat/Sat Fat (g)	Chol (mg)	Fiber (g)	Sugars (g)	Sodium (mg)
40/16	97	0	na	70
37/15	96	0	na	73
41/17	97	0	na	69
38.5/16	96	0	na	71
43/18	99	0	na	68
39/17	96	0	na	71

Beef (cont.)	Serving	Calories	Prot (g)	Carb (g)
Rib, small end (ribs 10–12), lean and fat, trimmed to ⅛" fat, all grades, broiled	4 oz.	374	27	0
Rib, small end (ribs 10–12), lean and fat, trimmed to ⅛" fat, all grades, roasted	4 oz.	386	25.5	0
Rib, small end (ribs 10–12), lean and fat, trimmed to ⅛" fat, prime, broiled	4 oz.	401	27	0
Rib, small end (ribs 10–12), lean and fat, trimmed to ⅛" fat, prime, roasted	4 oz.	466	25	0
Rib, small end (ribs 10–12), lean and fat, trimmed to ¼" fat, prime, broiled	4 oz.	409	27	0
Rib, small end (ribs 10–12), lean and fat, trimmed to ¼" fat, prime, roasted	4 oz.	473	25	0

Fat/Sat Fat (g)	Chol (mg)	Fiber (g)	Sugars (g)	Sodium (mg)
28.5/11.5	95	0	na	70
31/12	94	0	na	71
32/13	94	0	na	71
40/16	95	0	na	74
32.5/13	95	0	na	70
41/17	95	0	na	74

Beef (cont.)	Serving	Calories	Prot (g)	Carb (g)
Rib, small end (ribs 10–12), lean and fat, trimmed to ½" fat, prime, broiled	4 oz.	413	27	0
Rib, small end (ribs 10–12), lean and fat, trimmed to ½" fat, prime, roasted	4 oz.	476	25	0
Rib, whole (ribs 6–12), lean and fat, trimmed to ¼" fat, all grades, broiled	4 oz.	388	25	0
Rib, whole (ribs 6–12), lean and fat, trimmed to ¼" fat, all grades, roasted	4 oz.	406	25.5	0
Rib, whole (ribs 6–12), lean and fat, trimmed to ½" fat, prime, broiled	4 oz.	462	24	0
Rib, whole (ribs 6–12), lean and fat, trimmed to ½" fat, prime, roasted	4 oz.	482	24	0

Fat/Sat Fat (g)	Chol (mg)	Fiber (g)	Sugars (g)	Sodium (mg)
33/14	95	0	na	70
41/17	96	0	na	73
31/13	93	0	na	71
33/13	95	0	na	71
40/17	97	0	na	68
42/18	97	0	na	71

Beef (cont.)	Serving	Calories	Prot (g)	Carb (g)
Sandwich steaks	4 oz.	346	18	0
Short ribs, lean and fat, choice, braised	4 oz.	534	24	0

Fat/Sat Fat (g)	Chol (mg)	Fiber (g)	Sugars (g)	Sodium (mg)
30/13	80	0	0	76
47.5/20	107	0	na	57

LOW-RESPONSE COST, LOW-YIELD FOODS: BEVERAGES

Food	Serving	Calories	Prot (g)	Carb (g)
Alcoholic				
Beer, light	I can or bottle (12 fl. oz.)	99	I	5
Beer, low-carb	I can or bottle (12 fl. oz.)	96	t	2.5
Beer, regular	I can or bottle (12 fl. oz.)	146	I	13
Cocktail mix, non-alcoholic, concentrated, frozen	I fl. oz.	103	0	26
Coffee liqueur, 53 proof	I jigger (1.5 fl. oz.)	175	t	24
Coffee liqueur, 63 proof	I jigger (1.5 fl. oz.)	160	t	17
Coffee liqueur w/cream, 34 proof	I jigger (1.5 fl. oz.)	154	I	10
Crème de menthe, 72 proof	I jigger (1.5 fl. oz.)	186	0	21
Daiquiri, canned	I can (6.8 fl. oz.)	259	0	32.5

Fat/Sat Fat (g)	Chol (mg)	Fiber (g)	Sugars (g)	Sodium (mg)
0/0	0	0	na	11
0/0	na	na	na	na
0/0	0	t	na	18
0/0	0	0	26	0
t/t	0	0	na	4
t/t	0	0	na	4
7/4.5	7	0	na	43
t/t	0	0	na	3
0/0	0	0	na	83

Beverages (cont.)	Serving	Calories	Prot (g)	Carb (g)
Gin, rum, vodka, whiskey, 80 proof	1 jigger (1.5 fl. oz.)	97	0	0
Gin, rum, vodka, whiskey, 86 proof	1 jigger (1.5 fl. oz.)	105	0	0
Gin, rum, vodka, whiskey, 90 proof	1 jigger (1.5 fl. oz.)	110	0	0
Gin, rum, vodka, whiskey, 94 proof	1 jigger (1.5 fl.oz.)	116	0	0
Gin, rum, vodka, whiskey, 100 proof	1 jigger (1.5 fl. oz.)	124	0	0
Hard cider	1 bottle (12 fl. oz.)	195	0	19
Martini	1 fl. oz.	68	0	1
Pina Colada, canned	1 can (6.8 fl. oz.)	526	1	61
Tequila Sunrise, canned	1 can (6.8 fl. oz.)	232	1	24
Whiskey Sour Mix, powder	1 packet	65	0	17
Whiskey Sour, canned	1 can (6.8 fl. oz.)	249	0	28
Wine, dessert, dry	1 glass (3.5 fl. oz.)	130	t	4

Fat/Sat Fat (g)	Chol (mg)	Fiber (g)	Sugars (g)	Sodium (mg)
0/0	0	0	na	0
0/0	0	0	na	0
0/0	0	0	na	0
0/0	0	0	na	0
0/0	0	0	na	0
0/0	0	na	na	na
0/0	0	0	0	1
17/14.5	0	t	na	158
t/t	0	0	na	120
0/0	0	0	17	47
0/0	0	t	na	92
0/0	0	0	na	9

Beverages (cont.)	Serving	Calories	Prot (g)	Carb (g)
Wine, dessert, sweet	1 glass (3.5 fl. oz.)	158	t	12
Wine, table, all varieties	1 glass (3.5 fl. oz.)	72	t	1
Wine, table, red	1 glass (3.5 fl. oz.)	74	t	2
Wine, table, rose	1 glass (3.5 fl. oz.)	73	t	1
Wine, table, white	1 glass (3.5 fl. oz.)	70	t	1

Coffee and Tea / Flavored

	Serving	Calories	Prot (g)	Carb (g)
Cappuccino flavored coffee, powdered w/sugar	2 tsp. rounded	62	t	11
French café flavored coffee, powdered	1 serving	62	t	7
French-flavor coffee, powder	2 tsp. rounded	57	1	6
French vanilla café flavored coffee, powder	1 serving	65	t	10
Mocha flavored coffee, powder	2 tsp. rounded	51	t	8

Fat/Sat Fat (g)	Chol (mg)	Fiber (g)	Sugars (g)	Sodium (mg)
0/0	0	0	na	9
0/0	0	0	na	8
0/0	0	0	na	5
0/0	0	0	na	5
0/0	0	0	na	5

Fat/Sat Fat (g)	Chol (mg)	Fiber (g)	Sugars (g)	Sodium (mg)
2/t	0	0	4	98
3.5/1	0	t	4	93
3/1	0	0	3	82
2/1	0	t	8	56
2/1	0	t	6	31

Beverages (cont.)	Serving	Calories	Prot (g)	Carb (g)
Suisse Mocha flavored coffee, powder	I serving	57	t	9
Lemon flavored tea, instant w/sugar	I cup (8 fl. oz.)	88	t	22
Lemon flavored iced tea, ready-to-drink	I cup (8 fl. oz.)	89	0	20

Soft Drinks

Chocolate-flavor soda	I can or bottle (12 fl. oz.)	155	0	39
Cola, w/ caffeine	I can or bottle (12 fl. oz.)	155	0	40
Cola, w/ higher caffeine	I can or bottle (12 fl. oz.)	155	0	40
Cola, w/o caffeine	I can or bottle (12 fl. oz.)	155	0	40
Cola, w/o caffeine, supersized, large	I drink (32 fl. oz.)	413	0	106
Cola, w/o caffeine, supersized, extra large	I drink (44 fl. oz.)	568	I	145

Fat/Sat Fat (g)	Chol (mg)	Fiber (g)	Sugars (g)	Sodium (mg)
2/t	0	t	7	33
0/0	0	0	na	8
1/t	na	0	18	0

0/0	0	0	39	325
0/0	0	0	40	15
0/0	0	0	40	15
0/0	0	0	40	15
0/0	0	0	106	39
0/0	0	0	145	54

Beverages (cont.)	Serving	Calories	Prot (g)	Carb (g)
Cream Soda	I can or bottle (12 fl. oz.)	189	0	49
Ginger Ale	I can or bottle (12 fl. oz.)	124	0	32
Grape Soda	I can or bottle (12 fl. oz.)	160	0	42
Lemon-lime Soda, w/o caffeine	I can or bottle (12 fl. oz.)	147	0	38
Lemon-lime Soda, w/ caffeine	I can or bottle (12 fl. oz.)	147	0	38
Orange Soda	I can or bottle (12 fl. oz.)	179	0	46
Pepper-type, w/ caffeine	I can or bottle (12 fl. oz.)	151	0	38
Root Beer	I can or bottle (12 fl. oz.)	152	0	39

Fat/Sat Fat (g)	Chol (mg)	Fiber (g)	Sugars (g)	Sodium (mg)
0/0	0	0	49	45
0/0	0	0	32	26
0/0	0	0	na	56
0/0	0	0	38	40
0/0	0	0	38	40
0/0	0	0	na	45
t/t	0	0	na	37
0/0	0	0	na	48

LOW-RESPONSE COST, LOW-YIELD FOODS: BREAD PRODUCTS, CRACKERS, AND MUFFINS

Food	Serving	Calories	Prot (g)	Carb (g)
Bread Products				
Biscuits, buttermilk, refrigerated dough	I serving	108	2	14.5
Biscuits, buttermilk, refrigerated dough	I serving, large	195	4	25
Biscuits, plain, refrigerated dough, higher fat, baked	I biscuit (2½" dia.)	93	2	13
Biscuits, plain or buttermilk, prepared from recipe	I biscuit (4" dia.)	358	7	45
Biscuits, plain or buttermilk, commercially prepared	I biscuit, large	280	5	37
Bread, white	I slice	67	2	13
Cornbread, prepared from dry mix	I piece	188	4	29
Cornbread, prepared from recipe, made w/ low-fat (2%) milk	I piece	173	4	28
Dinner rolls (includes brown-and-serve)	I roll (1 oz.)	84	2	14

Fat/Sat Fat (g)	Chol (mg)	Fiber (g)	Sugars (g)	Sodium (mg)
4.5/1	na	na	na	343
9/2	na	na	na	605
4/1	0	t	na	325
16/4	3	1.5	na	586
13/2	1	1	na	810
1/0	0	0	t	7
6/2	37	1.5	na	467
5/1	26	na	na	428
2/t	0	1	na	146

Bread Products (cont.)	Serving	Calories	Prot (g)	Carb (g)
French baguette	1 slice	77	3	16
French rolls	1 roll	105	3	19
French toast, frozen, ready-to-heat	1 piece	126	4	19
Hamburger rolls	1 serving	117	3.5	22
Hotdog bun	1 roll	123	4	22
Hotdog roll, foot long	1 roll	258	7	43
Italian bread	1 slice, large (4½" x 3¼" x ¾")	81	3	15
Italian bread, garlic, crusty	1 serving	186	4	21
Kaiser rolls	1 roll (3½" dia.)	167	6	30
Rye dinner roll	1 roll, large (3½" to 4" dia.)	123	4	23
Stuffing, bread	½ cup	178	3	22
Stuffing, chicken flavor	½ cup	107	3.5	20

Fat/Sat Fat (g)	Chol (mg)	Fiber (g)	Sugars (g)	Sodium (mg)
1/0	0	t	t	192
2/t	0	1	na	231
3.5/1	48	1	na	292
2/t	na	1	5	256
2/t	0	1	na	241
6/1.5	1	3	na	448
1/t	0	1	na	175
10/2	6	na	na	200
2/t	0	1	na	310
1.5/t	0	2	na	384
9/2	0	3	na	543
1/t	1	1	3	429

Bread Products (cont.)	Serving	Calories	Prot (g)	Carb (g)
Stuffing, cornbread	½ cup	179	3	22
Taco shells, corn, fried	1 medium (5" dia)	98	1.5	13
Tortillas, ready-to-bake or -fry, white flour	1 tortilla (7"–8" dia.)	150	4	25.5
Tortillas, ready-to-bake or -fry, white flour	1 tortilla (10" dia.)	228	6	39

Crackers

	Serving	Calories	Prot (g)	Carb (g)
Butter-type	1 serving	79	1	10
Cheese, regular	1 cup, bite size	312	6	36
Cheese, sandwich-type, w/ peanut butter filling	4 crackers	135	4	16
French onion snack	1 serving	128	2	23
Italian ranch snack	1 serving	128	2	23
Matzo, plain	1 matzo	111	3	23
Oyster	½ cup	98	2	16
Oyster, low-salt	½ cup	98	2	16
Salsa snack	1 serving	128	2	23

Fat/Sat Fat (g)	Chol (mg)	Fiber (g)	Sugars (g)	Sodium (mg)
9/2	0	3	na	455
5/1	na	2	na	77
3/1	0	1.5	na	220
5/1	0	2	na	335

4/1	0	t	1	124
16/6	8	1.5	na	617
6.5/1.5	1	1	na	278
3/t	1	1	2	275
3/1	1	1	2	311
t/t	0	1	na	1
3/1	0	1	na	293
3/1	0	1	na	143
3/t	1	t	2	321

Bread Products (cont.)	Serving	Calories	Prot (g)	Carb (g)
Rye, sandwich-type, w/ peanut butter filling	4 crackers	135	2.5	17
Saltines	1 serving	59	1.5	10
Snack-type, sandwich-type w/ cheese filling	4 crackers	134	3	17
Wheat, sandwich-type, w/ cheese filling	4 crackers	139	3	16
Wheat, sandwich-type, w/ peanut butter filling	4 crackers	139	4	15
Wheat, thin-type	1 serving	136	2	20

Muffins

	Serving	Calories	Prot (g)	Carb (g)
Blueberry, commercially prepared	1 large	385	8	67
Blueberry, commercially prepared	1 medium	313	6	54
Blueberry, commercially prepared	1 small	183	4	32
Blueberry, commercially prepared	1 mini	47	1	8

Fat/Sat Fat (g)	Chol (mg)	Fiber (g)	Sugars (g)	Sodium (mg)
6/2	3	1	na	292
1/t	0	t	na	178
6/2	1	t	na	392
7/1	2	1	na	256
7/1	0	1	na	226
6/1	0	1	3	168

Fat/Sat Fat (g)	Chol (mg)	Fiber (g)	Sugars (g)	Sodium (mg)
9/2	42	4	na	621
7/1.5	34	3	na	505
4/1	20	2	na	295
1/t	5	t	na	76

Bread Products (cont.)	Serving	Calories	Prot (g)	Carb (g)
Blueberry, prepared from recipe, made w/ low-fat milk (2%)	1 muffin	162	4	23
Blueberry, toaster-type	1 muffin	103	1.5	17.5
Corn, commercially prepared	1 large	424	8	71
Corn, commercially prepared	1 medium	345	7	57.5
Corn, commercially prepared	1 small	201	4	33.5
Corn, commercially prepared	1 mini	52	1	9
Corn, prepared from recipe, made w/ low-fat milk (2%)	1 muffin (2" dia. x 2")	180	4	25
Corn, toaster-type	1 muffin	114	2	19
English muffin, plain, includes sourdough	1 muffin	134	4	26
English muffin, plain, includes sourdough	1 muffin	133	4	26

Fat/Sat Fat (g)	Chol (mg)	Fiber (g)	Sugars (g)	Sodium (mg)
6/1	21	na	na	251
3/t	2	t	na	158
12/2	36	5	na	724
9.5/1.5	29	4	na	589
5.5/1	17	2	na	344
1/t	4	1	na	89
7/1	24	na	na	333
4/t	4	t	na	142
1/t	0	1.5	na	264
1/t	0	1.5	na	262

Bread Products (cont.)	Serving	Calories	Prot (g)	Carb (g)
English muffin, raisin-cinnamon and apple-cinnamon	1 muffin	139	4	28
English muffin, raisin-cinnamon and apple-cinnamon, toasted	1 muffin	137	4	27.5
Plain, prepared from recipe, made w/ low-fat milk (2%)	1 muffin	169	4	24

Fat/Sat Fat (g)	Chol (mg)	Fiber (g)	Sugars (g)	Sodium (mg)
2/t	0	2	na	255
1.5/t	0	1.5	na	253
7/1	22	1.5	na	266

LOW-RESPONSE COST,
LOW-YIELD FOODS: CAKES AND PIES

Food	Serving	Calories	Prot (g)	Carb (g)
Cakes				
Angelfood cake, commercially prepared	1 piece (1/12 of 12 oz. cake)	72	2	16
Boston cream pie, commercially prepared	1 piece (1/6 of pie)	232	2	39
Cherry fudge cake w/ chocolate frosting	1 piece (1/8 cake)	187	2	27
Chocolate cake, commercially prepared	1 piece (1/8 of 18 oz. cake)	235	3	35
Chocolate snack cake, crème filling	1 serving	368	3	45
Devil's food cookie cakes, fat free	1 serving	49	1	12
Fruitcake, commercially prepared	1 piece	139	1	26
Gingerbread cake, prepared from recipe	1 piece	263	3	36

Fat/Sat Fat (g)	Chol (mg)	Fiber (g)	Sugars (g)	Sodium (mg)
t/t	0	t	na	210
8/2	34	1	na	132
8/3.5	30	1	na	160
10.5/3	27	2	na	214
19/11	14	2	32	241
t/t	0	t	7	28
4/t	2	2	na	116
12/3	24	na	na	242

Cakes & Pies (cont.)	Serving	Calories	Prot (g)	Carb (g)
Pineapple upside-down cake, prepared from recipe	1 piece (⅑ of 8" square)	367	4	58
Pound cake, commercially prepared, butter	1 piece (1/12 of 12 oz. cake)	109	1.5	14
Pound cake, commercially prepared, other than all butter, unenriched	1 piece (1/12 of 12 oz. cake)	109	1.5	15
Shortcake, biscuit-type, prepared from recipe	2 oz.	196	3.5	27.5
Snack cakes, crème-filled, chocolate w/ frosting	1 cupcake	188	2	30
Snack cakes, crème-filled, sponge	1 cupcake	157	1	27
Snack cakes, cup-cakes, chocolate, w/ frosting, low-fat	1 cupcake	131	2	29
Sponge cake, commercially prepared	1 piece (1/12 of 16 oz. cake)	110	2	23
Sponge cake, prepared from recipe	1 piece (1/12 of 16 oz. cake)	187	5	36

Fat/Sat Fat (g)	Chol (mg)	Fiber (g)	Sugars (g)	Sodium (mg)
14/3	25	1	na	367
5.5/3	62	t	na	111
5/1	16	t	na	112
8/2	2	na	na	287
7/1	9	t	na	213
5/1	7	t	na	157
1.5/t	0	2	na	178
1/t	39	t	na	93
3/1	107	na	na	144

Cakes & Pies (cont.)	Serving	Calories	Prot (g)	Carb (g)
White cake, prepared from recipe, w/ coconut frosting	1 piece (1/12 of 9" dia cake)	399	5	71
White cake, prepared from recipe, w/o frosting	1 piece (1/12 of 9" dia cake)	264	4	42
Yellow cake, commercially prepared, w/ chocolate frosting	1 piece (1/8 of 18 oz. cake)	243	2	35.5
Yellow cake, commercially prepared, w/ vanilla frosting	1 piece (1/8 of 18 oz. cake)	239	2	38
Yellow cake, prepared from recipe, w/o frosting	1 piece (1/12 of 8" dia cake)	245	4	36

Pies

	Serving	Calories	Prot (g)	Carb (g)
Apple, frozen, ready to bake	1 serving	292	3	41
Apple, commercially prepared, enriched flour	1 piece (1/8 of 9" dia)	296	2	42.5
Apple, commercially prepared, enriched flour	1 piece (1/6 of 8" dia)	277	2	40

Fat/Sat Fat (g)	Chol (mg)	Fiber (g)	Sugars (g)	Sodium (mg)
11.5/4	I	I	na	318
9/2	I	I	na	242
11/3	35	I	na	216
9/1.5	35	t	na	220
10/3	37	t	na	233

13/6	9	I	26	361
14/5	0	2	na	333
13/4	0	2	na	311

Cakes & Pies (cont.)	Serving	Calories	Prot (g)	Carb (g)
Apple, prepared from recipe	1 piece (⅛ of 9" dia)	411	4	57.5
Banana cream, prepared from recipe	1 piece (⅛ of 9" dia)	387	6	47
Blueberry, commercially prepared	1 piece (⅙ of 8" dia)	271	2	41
Blueberry, prepared from recipe	1 piece (⅛ of 9" dia)	360	4	49
Cherry, commercially prepared	1 piece (⅛ of 9" dia)	325	2.5	50
Cherry, commercially prepared	1 piece (⅙ of 8" dia)	304	2	46.5
Cherry, prepared from recipe	1 piece (⅛ of 9" dia)	486	5	69
Chocolate crème, commercially prepared	1 piece (⅙ of 8" dia)	344	3	38
Chocolate mousse, prepared from mix, no-bake type	1 piece (⅛ of 9" dia)	247	3	28

Fat/Sat Fat (g)	Chol (mg)	Fiber (g)	Sugars (g)	Sodium (mg)
19/5	0	na	na	327
20/5	73	I	na	346
12/2	0	I	na	380
17/4	0	na	na	272
14/3	0	I	na	308
13/3	0	I	na	288
22/5	0	na	na	344
22/6	6	2	na	154
15/8	33	na	na	437

Cakes & Pies (cont.)	Serving	Calories	Prot (g)	Carb (g)
Coconut cream, prepared from mix, no-bake type	1 piece (⅛ of 9" dia)	259	3	27
Coconut cream, commercially prepared	1 piece (⅛ of 7" pie)	143	1	18
Coconut custard, commercially prepared	1 piece (⅙ of 8" dia)	270	6	31
Egg custard, commercially prepared	1 piece (⅙ of 8" dia)	221	6	22
Fried pies, cherry	1 pie (5" x 3¾")	404	4	55
Fried pies, fruit	1 pie (5" x 3¾")	404	4	55
Fried pies, lemon	1 pie (5" x 3¾")	404	4	55
Lemon meringue, commercially prepared	1 piece (⅙ of 8" dia)	303	2	53
Lemon meringue, prepared from recipe	1 piece (⅛ of 9" dia)	362	5	50

Fat/Sat Fat (g)	Chol (mg)	Fiber (g)	Sugars (g)	Sodium (mg)
16.5/8	22	t	na	309
8/3	0	1	na	122
14/6	36	2	na	348
12/2	35	2	na	252
21/3	0	3	na	479
21/3	0	3	na	479
21/3	0	3	na	479
10/2	51	1	na	165
16/4	67	na	na	307

Cakes & Pies (cont.)

Cakes & Pies (cont.)	Serving	Calories
Mince, prepared from recipe	1 piece (⅛ of 9" dia)	477
Peach	1 piece (⅙ of 8" dia)	261
Pecan, commercially prepared	1 piece (⅙ of 8" dia)	452
Pecan, prepared from recipe	1 piece (⅛ of 9" dia)	503
Pumpkin, commercially prepared	1 piece (⅙ of 8" dia)	229
Pumpkin, prepared from recipe	1 piece (⅛ of 9" dia)	316
Vanilla cream, prepared from recipe	1 piece (⅛ of 9" dia)	350

Fat/Sat Fat (g)	Chol (mg)	Fiber (g)	Sugars (g)	Sodium (mg)
18/4	0	4	na	419
12/2	0	1	na	316
21/4	36	4	na	479
27/5	106	na	na	320
10/2	22	3	na	307
14/5	65	na	na	349
18/5	78	1	na	328

LOW-RESPONSE COST, LOW-YIELD FOODS: CANDY

Food	Serving	Calories	Prot (g)	Carb (g)
Candy				
Almond and coconut candy bar	I package (1.76 oz.)	235	2	29
Almond and coconut candy bar	I bar, snack size	91	I	II
Butterscotch candy	3 pieces	63	0	14
Caramel candy bar	I bar (1.25 oz.)	162	2	22
Caramel candy bar	I bar (1.6 oz.)	208	3	29
Caramel candy	I piece	39	t	8
Caramel cookie bars	I package (2 oz.)	284	3	37
Caramel cookie bars	2 bars (2.06 oz.)	289	3	38
Caramels in milk chocolate	I package (1.91 oz.)	256	3	37
Caramels in milk chocolate	2 rolls (3 pieces per roll)	171	2	24.5
Caramels in milk chocolate	7 pieces	199	2	28.5

Fat/Sat Fat (g)	Chol (mg)	Fiber (g)	Sugars (g)	Sodium (mg)
13/9	2	2.5	24	70
5/3	1	1	9	27
t/t	1	0	na	63
7/4	9	t	20	43
9.5/6	12	t	26	55
1/1	1	t	7	25
14/5	3	1	27	110
14/5	3	1	28	112
11/8	6	t	34.5	102
7.5/5	4	t	23	68
9/6	5	t	27	79

Candy (cont.)	Serving	Calories	Prot (g)	Carb (g)
Carob candy bar	1 bar (3 oz.)	470	7	49
Chocolate covered coconut candy bar	1 bar, snack size	92	1	11
Chocolate covered coconut candy bar	1 package (1.9 oz.)	258	2	31
Chocolate fudge, prepared from recipe	1 piece	70	t	13
Chocolate nougat bar	1 bar (0.8 oz)	96	1	18
Chocolate nougat bar	1 bar (1.813 oz.)	212	2	39
Chocolate nougat bar	1 bar, fun size	71	t	13
Chocolate wafer bar	1 bar, miniature (0.35 oz.)	52	1	6
Chocolate wafer bar	1 bar (1.5 oz.)	217	3	27
Chocolate wafer bar	1 bar (1.625 oz.)	238	3	30
Chocolate wafer bar	1 bar (2.8 oz.)	403	5	50

Fat/Sat Fat (g)	Chol (mg)	Fiber (g)	Sugars (g)	Sodium (mg)
27/25	3	3	na	93
5/4	0	1	9	28
14/11	1	2	24	77
2/1	3	t	na	10
3/2	3	t	15	45
7/3	6	1	34	99
2/1	2	t	11	33
3/2	1	t	5	7
11/7	4	1	22	27
12/8	4	1	24	30
21/14	7	1.5	41	51

Candy (cont.)	Serving	Calories	Prot (g)	Carb (g)
Chocolate wafer bar	1 bar (3.375 oz.)	496	6	62
Dark chocolate bar	1 bar (1.45 oz.)	218	2	24
Dark chocolate bar	1 bar (2.6 oz.)	388	4	43
Dinner mints	1 piece	29	t	6
Dinner mints	5 pieces	147	1	31
Fruit chews	1 package, fun size	166	t	35
Fruit chews	1 package (2.07 oz.)	234	t	50
Fruit chews	1 serving	158	t	34
Gumdrops	10 gumdrops	139	0	36
Gumdrops	1 cup of gumdrops	703	0	180
Gummy bears	10 gummy bears	85	0	22
Jelly beans	10 small	40	0	10
Jelly beans	10 large (1 oz.)	103	0	26

Fat/Sat Fat (g)	Chol (mg)	Fiber (g)	Sugars (g)	Sodium (mg)
26/17	9	2	50	62
13/8	2	3	20	2
24/14	4	5	35	4
1/1	0	t	na	1
6/3	0	1	na	5
3/t	0	0	28	24
5/1	0	0	39	33
3/t	0	0	27	22
0/0	0	0	na	16
0/0	0	0	na	80
0/0	0	0	na	10
t/t	0	0	na	3
t/t	0	0	na	7

Candy (cont.)	Serving	Calories	Prot (g)	Carb (g)
Marshmallows, miniature	10 pieces	22	t	6
Marshmallows, miniature	1 cup	159	1	41
Marshmallows, regular	1 piece	23	t	6
Milk chocolate coated peanuts	10 pieces	208	5	20
Milk chocolate coated peanuts	1 cup	773	20	74
Milk chocolate coated raisins	10 pieces	39	t	7
Milk chocolate coated raisins	1 cup	702	7	123
Milk chocolate bar, miniature	1 bar	36	t	4
Milk chocolate bar	1 bar (1.55 oz.)	226	3	26
Milk chocolate bar w/ almonds	1 bar (1.45 oz.)	216	4	22
Milk chocolate bar w/ almonds	1 bar (1.55 oz.)	231	4	23
Milk chocolate bar w/ rice cereal	1 bar, miniature	50	1	6

Fat/Sat Fat (g)	Chol (mg)	Fiber (g)	Sugars (g)	Sodium (mg)
t/t	0	0	4	3
t/t	0	0	28	24
t/t	0	0	4	3
13/6	4	2	na	16
50/22	13	7	na	61
1.5/t	0	t	6	4
27/16	5	8	112	65
2/1	2	t	na	6
14/8	10	1.5	na	36
14/7	8	2.5	18	30
15/7	8	3	19	33
3/1.5	2	t	5.5	15

Candy (cont.)	Serving	Calories	Prot (g)	Carb (g)
Milk chocolate bar w/ rice cereal	1 bar (1.4 oz.)	198	2.5	25
Milk chocolate bar w/ rice cereal	1 bar (1.45 oz.)	223	3	28.5
Milk chocolate bar w/ rice cereal	1 bar (1.55 oz.)	218	3	28
Milk chocolate bar w/ rice cereal	1 bar (1.65 oz.)	233	3	30
Peanut bar	1 bar (1.4 oz.)	209	6	19
Peanut bar	1 bar (1.6 oz.)	235	7	21
Peanut butter candies pieces	¼ cup	234	6	28
Peanut butter candies pieces	10 pieces	40	1	5
Peanut butter candies pieces	1 package (1.63 oz.)	229	6	27.5
Peanut butter cookie bars	2 bars (1.89 oz.)	286	5	28
Peanut butter cups	1 piece miniature	36	1	4
Peanut butter cups	1 cup (0.6 oz.)	88	2	9

Fat/Sat Fat (g)	Chol (mg)	Fiber (g)	Sugars (g)	Sodium (mg)
11/6	8	1	22	58
12/7	9	1	25	65
12/7	8	1	24	64
12/7	9	1.5	26	68
13/2	0	2	17	62
15/2	0	3	19	70
12/8	0	1	25	91
2/1	0	t	4	16
11/7.5	0	1	24.5	89
17/6	3	2	19	147
2/1	0	t	3	22
5/2	1	1	8	53

Candy (cont.)	Serving	Calories	Prot (g)	Carb (g)
Peanut butter cups	2 cups (1.6 oz.)	232	5	25
Peanut chocolate candies	1 cup	877	16	103
Peanut chocolate candies	1 package, fun size	108	2	13
Peanut chocolate candies	1 package (1.67 oz.)	243	4	28
Peanut chocolate candies	1 package (1.74 oz.)	253	5	30
Peppermint patty	1 patty (1.5 oz.)	165	1	35
Plain chocolate candies	1 cup	1023	9	148
Plain chocolate candies	1 box (1.48 oz.)	207	2	30
Plain chocolate candies	1 package (1.69 oz.)	236	2	34
Peppermints mints	3 pieces	59	0	15
Semi-sweet chocolate	1 cup chips (6 oz. pkg)	805	7	106
Semi-sweet chocolate	1 cup of mini chips	829	7	109

Fat/Sat Fat (g)	Chol (mg)	Fiber (g)	Sugars (g)	Sodium (mg)
14/5	3	2	21	141
45/18	15	6	86	82
5/2	2	1	11	10
12/5	4	2	24	23
13/5	4	2	25	24
3/2	0	1	27	12
44/27	29	5	132	127
9/4.5	6	1	27	26
10/6	7	1	30.5	29
t/t	na	na	9	6
50/30	0	10	95.5	18
52/31	0	10	98	19

Candy (cont.)	Serving	Calories	Prot (g)	Carb (g)
Semi-sweet chocolate	1 oz. or 60 pieces	136	1	18
Toffee bar	1 bar (1.4 oz.)	209	1	24
Sugar coated almonds	6 pieces	96	2	15
Sweet chocolate bar	1 bar (1.45 oz.)	207	2	24
Strawberry twists candy	4 pieces from 5 oz. package	556	1	30
Strawberry twists candy	4 pieces from 8 oz. package	659	1	36

Fat/Sat Fat (g)	Chol (mg)	Fiber (g)	Sugars (g)	Sodium (mg)
8.5/5	0	2	16	3
12.5/7	21	t	23	124
4/t	0	1	na	4
14/8	0	2	na	7
1/0	0	0	15	109
1/0	0	0	18	129

LOW-RESPONSE COST, LOW-YIELD FOODS: CEREALS AND CEREAL BARS

Food	Serving	Calories	Prot (g)	Carb (g)
Cereals—Cold				
Apple cinnamon	¾ cup	118	2	25
Apple flavored cereal	1 cup	117	1	27
Chocolate-flavored crisp cereal	¾ cup	118	1	27
Chocolate-flavored puff cereal	1 cup	117	1	26
Cookie crisp-type cereal	1 cup	117	1	26
Corn-based puff cereal	1 cup	118	1	28
Frosted flakes	¾ cup	114	1	28
Frosted rice crisp cereal	¾ cup	114	1	27
Frosted wheat flake cereal	¾ cup	112	1.5	27
Fruit-flavored cereal	1 cup	118	1	26
Graham cracker cereal	¾ cup	112	1.5	25

Fat/Sat Fat (g)	Chol (mg)	Fiber (g)	Sugars (g)	Sodium (mg)
1.5/t	0	1	13	120
1/t	0	1	15	143
1/t	0	1	14	190
1/t	0	1	14	171
1/t	0	t	13	178
t/t	0	t	14	120
t/t	0	1	12	148
t/t	0	t	12	218
t/t	0	1	12	204
1/t	0	1	14	141
1/t	0	1	10.5	269

Cereals (cont.)	Serving	Calories	Prot (g)	Carb (g)
Granola, plain	1 cup	499	12	78.5
Granola w/ raisins	1 cup	468	11	76
Honey nut flavored cereal	1 cup	214	4	46
Honey roasted oat cereal	¾ cup	118	2	24.5
Oat, corn, puffed	1⅓ cup	115	2	26
Oat, corn-puffed mixture, pre-sweetened, w/ marshmallows	1 cup	115	2	25
Oat, corn, and wheat squares, maple-flavored	1 cup	129	2	24
Oatmeal crisp w/ almonds cereal	1 cup	218	5.5	42
Oatmeal crisp w/ apples cereal	1 cup	207	5	45
Peanut butter crunch cereal	1 cup	150	2.5	28
Puffed rice, presweetened	¾ cup	108	1	24

Fat/Sat Fat (g)	Chol (mg)	Fiber (g)	Sugars (g)	Sodium (mg)
18/4.5	0	7	na	293
16/4	0	6	na	226
3/t	0	3	na	249
2/t	0	1.5	6	193
1/0	0	1	11	215
1/t	0	0	13	206
3/0	0	1	11	130
5/1	0	4	15	237
2/t	0	4	19	253
3/1	0	1	12	267
1/0	0	0	12	158

Cereals (cont.)	Serving	Calories	Prot (g)	Carb (g)
Puffed wheat, presweetened, fruit-flavored	¾ cup	107	1	25
Waffle crisp cereal	1 cup	129	2	24

Cereals—Hot

	Serving	Calories	Prot (g)	Carb (g)
Corn grits, instant, cheddar cheese flavor, prepared w/ water	1 packet	99	2	20
Oatmeal, instant, w/ apples and cinnamon, prepared w/ water	1 packet	125	3	26
Oatmeal, instant, w/ cinnamon and spice, prepared w/ water	1 packet	177	5	35
Oatmeal, instant, w/ maple and brown sugar, prepared w/ water	1 packet	153	4	31
Oatmeal, instant, w/ raisins and spice, prepared w/ water	1 packet	161	4	32
Oatmeal, microwave, apple spice	1 packet	166	4	35

Fat/Sat Fat (g)	Chol (mg)	Fiber (g)	Sugars (g)	Sodium (mg)
0/0	0	0	15	41
3/t	0	t	9.5	130

1.5/t	0	1	na	510
1/t	0	2.5	na	121
2/t	0	3	na	280
2/t	0	3	na	234
2/t	0	2	na	226
2/t	0	3	15	306

Cereals (cont.)	Serving	Calories	Prot (g)	Carb (g)
Oatmeal, microwave, brown sugar and cinnamon	1 packet	155	4	31
Oatmeal, microwave, cinnamon and double raisin	1 packet	169	4	35

Cereal Bars

	Serving	Calories	Prot (g)	Carb (g)
Cereal bar, fruit	1 bar (1 oz.)	103	1	20
Cereal bar, mixed berry	1 bar (1 oz.)	104	1	20
Chocolate chip crisped rice bar	1 bar (1 oz.)	113	1	20
Granola bar, hard, almond	1 bar	119	2	15
Granola bar, hard, chocolate chip	1 bar	105	2	17
Granola bar, hard, peanut	1 bar (1 oz.)	136	3	18
Granola bar, hard, peanut butter	1 bar	116	2	15
Granola bar, hard, plain	1 bar (1 oz.)	132	3	18

Fat/Sat Fat (g)	Chol (mg)	Fiber (g)	Sugars (g)	Sodium (mg)
2/t	0	3	12	255
2/t	0	3	15.5	275

Fat/Sat Fat (g)	Chol (mg)	Fiber (g)	Sugars (g)	Sodium (mg)
2/t	0	1	na	83
2/t	0	t	9	83
4/1	0	1	na	78
6/3	0	1	na	61
4/3	0	1	na	83
6/1	0	1	na	79
6/1	0	1	na	68
5.5/1	0	1.5	na	82

Cereals (cont.)	Serving	Calories	Prot (g)	Carb (g)
Granola bar, soft, chocolate chip w/ milk chocolate coating	1 bar (1.25 oz.)	163	2	22
Granola bar, soft, chocolate chip w/ milk chocolate coating	1 bar (1 oz.)	130	2	18
Granola bar, soft, peanut butter w/ milk chocolate coating	1 bar (1.3 oz.)	188	4	20
Granola bar, soft, chocolate chip, uncoated	1 bar (1.5 oz.)	181	3	30
Granola bar, soft, chocolate chip, uncoated	1 bar (1 oz.)	118	2	19
Granola bar, soft, chocolate chip, graham and marshmallow, uncoated	1 bar (1 oz.)	120	2	20
Granola bar, soft, nut and raisin, uncoated	1 bar (1 oz.)	127	2	18

Fat/Sat Fat (g)	Chol (mg)	Fiber (g)	Sugars (g)	Sodium (mg)
9/5	2	1	na	70
7/4	1	1	na	56
11.5/6	4	1	na	71
7/4	0	2	na	117
5/3	0	1	na	76
4/2.5	0	1	na	88
6/3	0	2	na	71

Cereals (cont.)	Serving	Calories	Prot (g)	Carb (g)
Granola bar, soft, peanut butter, uncoated	1 bar (1 oz.)	119	3	18
Granola bar, soft, peanut butter and chocolate chip, uncoated	1 bar (1 oz.)	121	3	17
Granola bar, soft, plain, uncoated	1 bar (1 oz.)	124	2	19
Granola bar, soft, raisin, uncoated	1 bar (1.5 oz.)	193	3	28.5
Granola bar, soft, raisin, uncoated	1 bar (1 oz.)	125	2	18.5

Fat/Sat Fat (g)	Chol (mg)	Fiber (g)	Sugars (g)	Sodium (mg)
4/1	0	1	na	115
6/1.5	0	1	na	92
5/2	0	1	na	78
8/4	0	2	na	121
5/3	0	1	na	79

LOW-RESPONSE COST, LOW-YIELD FOODS: CHEESES

Food	Serving	Calories	Prot (g)	Carb (g)
Cheeses—Full Fat				
Cheese, blue	1 oz.	100	6	1
Cheese, brick	1 oz.	105	6.5	1
Brie	1 oz.	95	6	t
Camembert	1 oz.	85	6	t
Caraway	1 oz.	107	7	1
Cheddar	1 oz.	114	7	t
Colby	1 oz.	112	7	1
Cream cheese	1 tbsp	51	1	0
Creamed cottage, large or small curd, full fat	½ cup, small curd, not packed	116	14	3
Creamed cottage, full fat w/ fruit	½ cup, not packed	140	11	15
Edam	1 oz.	101	7	t
Feta	1 oz.	75	4	1
Fontina	1 oz.	110	7	t
Goat, hard type	1 oz.	128	9	1

Fat/Sat Fat (g)	Chol (mg)	Fiber (g)	Sugars (g)	Sodium (mg)
8/5	21	0	na	395
8/5	27	0	na	159
8/5	28	0	na	178
7/4	20	0	na	239
8/5	26	0	na	196
9/6	30	0	na	176
9/6	27	0	na	171
5/3	16	0	0	43
5/3	17	0	na	456
4/2	12	0	na	458
8/5	25	0	na	274
6/4	25	0	na	316
9/5	33	0	na	227
10/7	30	0	na	98

Cheeses (cont.)	Serving	Calories	Prot (g)	Carb (g)
Goat, semisoft type	1 oz.	103	6	1
Goat, soft type	1 oz.	76	5	t
Gouda	1 oz.	101	7	1
Gruyere	1 oz.	117	8.5	t
Limburger	1 oz.	93	6	t
Low-sodium, cheddar or Colby	1 oz.	113	7	t
Monterey	1 oz.	106	7	t
Mozzarella, whole milk	1 oz.	80	5.5	1
Mozzarella, whole milk, low moisture	1 oz.	90	6	1
Muenster	1 oz.	104	7	t
Neufchatel	1 oz.	74	3	1
Parmesan, grated	2 tbsp	46	4	t
Parmesan, hard	1 oz.	111	10	1
Port de Salut	1 oz.	100	7	t
Provolone	1 oz.	100	7	1
Ricotta, whole milk	½ cup	214	14	4

Fat/Sat Fat (g)	Chol (mg)	Fiber (g)	Sugars (g)	Sodium (mg)
8/6	22	0	na	146
6/4	13	0	na	104
8/5	32	0	na	232
9/5	31	0	na	95
8/5	26	0	na	227
9/6	28	0	na	6
8.5/5	25	0	na	152
6/4	22	0	na	106
7/4	25	0	na	118
8.5/5	27	0	na	178
7/4	22	0	na	113
3/2	8	0	na	186
7/5	19	0	na	454
8/5	35	0	na	151
8/5	20	0	na	248
16/10	63	0	na	103

Cheeses (cont.)	Serving	Calories	Prot (g)	Carb (g)
Romano	1 oz.	110	9	1
Roquefort	1 oz.	105	6	t
Swiss	1 oz.	107	8	1

Cheese—Processed

	Serving	Calories	Prot (g)	Carb (g)
American, processed pasteurized, w/o di sodium phosphate	1 oz.	106	6	0
American, processed pasteurized, w/ di sodium phosphate	1 oz.	106	6	0
American spread, w/o di sodium phosphate	1 oz.	82	5	2.5
American spread, w/ di sodium phosphate	1 oz.	82	5	2.5
Cheddar, pasteurized process, low-sodium	1 slice	79	5	0
Cheese Spread	1 oz.	85	5	3
Cheese Sauce	2 tbsp	91	4	3
Imitation cheese, American or cheddar, low cholesterol	1 cubic inch	70	4	0

Fat/Sat Fat (g)	Chol (mg)	Fiber (g)	Sugars (g)	Sodium (mg)
8/5	29	0	na	340
9/5	26	0	na	513
8/5	26	0	na	74

9/6	27	0	0	184
9/6	27	0	0	421
6/4	16	0	na	381
6/4	16	0	na	461
7/4	20	0	0	1
6/4	22	0	2	420
7/4	25	t	2	541
6/1	3	0	0	121

Cheeses (cont.)	Serving	Calories	Prot (g)	Carb (g)
Pimiento processed cheese	1 oz.	106	6	t
Swiss processed cheese	1 oz.	95	7	t

Fat/Sat Fat (g)	Chol (mg)	Fiber (g)	Sugars (g)	Sodium (mg)
9/5.5	27	0	0	405
7/4.5	24	0	na	193

LOW-RESPONSE COST, LOW-YIELD FOODS: COOKIES

Food	Serving	Calories	Prot (g)	Carb (g)
Cookies				
Animal crackers	1 serving	22	t	4
Apricot filled cookies	1 serving	100	1	16
Butter cookies, commercially pre- pared, unenriched	1 cookie	23	t	3
Brownies, prepared from recipe	1 brownie (2" square)	112	1	12
Brownies, commercially prepared	1 package, twin wrapped	247	3	39
Brownies, commercially prepared	1 brownie, large (2¾" square x ⅞")	227	3	36
Chocolate chip cookie, refrigerated dough	1 serving	127	1	18
Chocolate chip cookie, refrigerated dough, baked	1 cookie, medium (2¼" dia)	59	1	8

Fat/Sat Fat (g)	Chol (mg)	Fiber (g)	Sugars (g)	Sodium (mg)
1/t	0	t	na	19
3/1	7	t	8	80
1/.5	6	0	na	18
7/2	18	na	na	82
10/3	10	1	na	190
9/2	10	1	na	175
6/2	na	1	10	88
3/1	3	t	na	28

Cookies (cont.)	Serving	Calories	Prot (g)	Carb (g)
Chocolate chip cookie, prepared from recipe, made w/ margarine	1 cookie, medium (2¼" dia)	78	1	9
Chocolate chip cookie, prepared from recipe, made w/ margarine	1 bar (2" square)	156	2	19
Chocolate chip cookie, prepared from recipe, made w/ butter	1 cookie, medium (2¼" dia)	78	1	9
Chocolate chip cookie, commercially prepared, soft type	1 cookie	69	1	9
Chocolate sandwich cookie with extra crème filling	1 cookie	65	t	9
Chocolate sandwich cookie with crème filling, regular, chocolate-coated	1 cookie	82	1	11
Chocolate sandwich cookie with crème filling	1 cookie	47	t	7
Chocolate wafers	1 wafer	26	t	4

Fat/Sat Fat (g)	Chol (mg)	Fiber (g)	Sugars (g)	Sodium (mg)
5/1	5	t	na	58
9/3	10	1	na	116
5/2	11	na	na	55
4/1	0	t	na	49
3/t	0	t	na	64
4/1	0	1	na	55
2/t	0	t	na	60
1/t	0	t	na	35

Cookies (cont.)	Serving	Calories	Prot (g)	Carb (g)
Coconut macaroons, prepared from recipe	I cookie, medium (2" dia)	97	I	17
Fig bars	I cookie	56	I	11
Fortune cookie	I cookie	30	t	7
Fudge, cake-type	I cookie	73	I	16
Gingersnaps	I cookie	29	t	5
Gingersnaps	I large (3½"–4" dia)	133	2	25
Graham crackers, plain or honey (includes cinnamon)	I cracker (2½" square)	30	t	5
Graham crackers, plain or honey (includes cinnamon)	I large rectangular piece or 2 squares or 4 small rectangular pieces	59	I	11
Graham crackers, chocolate-coated	I cracker (2½" square)	68	I	9
Lemon drop cookies	I serving	93	I	15
Lemon snaps	I serving	152	2	20

Fat/Sat Fat (g)	Chol (mg)	Fiber (g)	Sugars (g)	Sodium (mg)
3/3	0	t	na	59
1/t	0	1	na	56
t/t	0	t	4	22
1/t	0	1	na	40
1/t	0	t	na	46
3/1	0	1	na	209
1/t	0	t	1	42
1/t	0	t	3	85
3/2	0	t	na	41
3/1	9	t	7	95
7/2	7	t	9	117

Cookies (cont.)	Serving	Calories	Prot (g)	Carb (g)
Marshmallow pies	1 pie (3" dia x ¾")	164	2	26
Mint crème cookies	1 serving	108	1	19
Molasses cookies	1 medium	65	1	11
Molasses cookies	1 large (3½"– 4" dia)	138	2	24
Molasses iced cookies	1 serving	114	1	20
Oatmeal cookies	1 serving	111	2	17
Oatmeal cookies, apple filled	1 serving	99	1	16
Oatmeal cookies, refrigerated dough, baked	1 cookie	57	1	8
Oatmeal cookies, prepared from recipe, w/o raisins	1 cookie (2⅝" dia)	67	1	10
Oatmeal cookies, prepared from recipe, w/ raisins	1 cookie (2⅝" dia)	65	1	10
Oatmeal cookies, commercially prepared, soft-type	1 cookie	61	1	10

Fat/Sat Fat (g)	Chol (mg)	Fiber (g)	Sugars (g)	Sodium (mg)
7/2	0	I	na	66
4/I	0	I	13	72
2/t	0	t	na	69
4/I	0	t	na	147
4/I	0	t	10	130
4/I	4	I	9	114
3/I	2	I	8	103
2/I	3	t	na	39
3/I	5	na	na	90
2/t	5	na	na	81
2/I	I	t	na	52

Cookies (cont.)	Serving	Calories	Prot (g)	Carb (g)
Oatmeal cookies, commercially pre-pared, regular	1 cookie, large	81	1	12
Oatmeal cookies, commercially pre-pared, regular	1 cookie, big (3½"–4" dia)	113	2	17
Oatmeal raisin cookie	1 serving	107	1	17
Oatmeal iced cookie	1 serving	123	1	18
Peanut butter cookie	1 serving	101	2	12
Peanut butter cookie, refrigerated dough, baked	1 cookie	60	1	7
Peanut butter cookie, commercially prepared, regular	1 cookie	72	1	9
Peanut butter cookie, commercially prepared, soft-type	1 cookie	69	1	9
Peanut butter sandwich cookie	1 cookie	67	1	9
Raisin cookie, soft-type	1 cookie	60	1	10

Fat/Sat Fat (g)	Chol (mg)	Fiber (g)	Sugars (g)	Sodium (mg)
3/1	0	1	na	69
5/1	0	1	na	96
4/1	3	1	9	98
5/1	3	1	10	92
5/1	8	1	7	85
3/1	4	t	na	52
4/1	0	t	na	62
4/1	0	t	na	50
3/1	0	t	na	52
2/1	0	t	na	51

Cookies (cont.)	Serving	Calories	Prot (g)	Carb (g)
Pecan ice box cookie	1 serving	120	1	15
Raspberry filled cookies	1 serving	101	1	16
Shortbread cookie, commercially pre-pared, plain	1 cookie (1⅝" square)	40	t	5
Shortbread cookie, commercially pre-pared, pecan	1 cookie (2" dia)	76	1	8
Strawberry filled cookie	1 serving	100	1	16
Sugar cookie, refrigerated dough, baked	1 cookie, pre-sliced cookie dough	111	1	15
Sugar cookie, prepared from recipe, made w/ margarine	1 cookie (3" dia)	66	1	8
Sugar cookie, refrigerated dough, baked	1 cookie, rolled cookie dough	73	1	10
Sugar cookie, commercially pre-pared, regular	1 cookie	72	1	10

Fat/Sat Fat (g)	Chol (mg)	Fiber (g)	Sugars (g)	Sodium (mg)
6/1	6	t	7	75
3/1	7	t	8	84
2/t	2	t	na	36
5/1	5	t	na	39
3/1	7	t	8	84
5/1	7	t	na	108
3/1	4	t	na	69
3/1	5	t	na	70
3/1	8	t	na	54

Cookies (cont.)	Serving	Calories	Prot (g)	Carb (g)
Sugar wafer cookie w/ crème filling	1 wafer, small (2½" x ¾" x ¼")	18	t	2
Sugar wafer cookie w/ crème filling	1 wafer, large (3½" x 1" x ½")	46	t	6
Vanilla sandwich cookie, w/ crème filling	1 cookie, round (1¾" dia)	48	t	7
Vanilla sandwich cookie, w/ crème filling	1 cookie, oval (3⅛" x 1¼" x ⅜")	72	1	11
Vanilla wafer	1 wafer	28	t	4

Fat/Sat Fat (g)	Chol (mg)	Fiber (g)	Sugars (g)	Sodium (mg)
1/t	0	0	na	5
2/t	0	t	na	13
2/t	0	t	na	35
3/t	0	t	na	52
1/t	0	t	na	18

LOW-RESPONSE COST, LOW-YIELD FOODS: DINNERS, CANNED AND FROZEN

Food	Serving	Calories	Prot (g)	Carb (g)
Dinners Canned				
Beef ravioli in tomato and meat sauce	I serving	229	8	37
Beef ravioli in tomato and meat sauce, mini ravioli	I serving	239	9	41
Beef stew	I serving	218	11	16
Chicken and dumplings, canned	I serving	218	15	23
Chow mein, no noodles or rice	2 cups	160	16	12
Corned beef hash	I cup	387	21	22
Macaroni w/ beef in tomato sauce	I serving	184	8	31
Macaroni and cheese	I serving	199	7.5	29
Roast beef hash	I cup	385	21	23
Spaghetti and meatballs in tomato sauce	I serving	250	9	34

Fat/Sat Fat (g)	Chol (mg)	Fiber (g)	Sugars (g)	Sodium (mg)
5/2	15	4	5	1174
5/2	18	3	5	1197
12/5	37	3.5	2	947
7/2	36	3	na	946
7/3	40	6	4	2380
24/10	76	3	1	1003
3/1	17	3	5	799
6/3	8	3	2	1058
24/10	73	3.5	t	793
9/4	22	2	7	941

Dinners (cont.)	Serving	Calories	Prot (g)	Carb (g)
Sweet and sour vegetables, fruit and sauce w/ chicken	I serving	165	6	32

Frozen

	Serving	Calories	Prot (g)	Carb (g)
Beef macaroni	I serving	211	14	33
Beef pot pie	I serving	449	13	44
Beef strips w/ Oriental-style vegetables	I serving	433	26	71
Beef stroganoff and noodles w/ carrots and peas	I serving	600	30	59
Chicken Alfredo with fettucini and vegetables	I serving	373	19	33
Chicken cordon bleu, filled w/ cheese and ham	I serving	344	25.5	15
Chicken enchilada and Mexican-style rice w/ Monterey jack cheese sauce	I serving	376	12.5	48
Chicken fajita	I serving	129	8	17

Fat/Sat Fat (g)	Chol (mg)	Fiber (g)	Sugars (g)	Sodium (mg)
2/na	23	na	na	564

Fat/Sat Fat (g)	Chol (mg)	Fiber (g)	Sugars (g)	Sodium (mg)
2/1	14	5	9	444
24/9	38	2	na	737
5/na	na	na	na	1584
27/11	70	4	8	1141
18/7	57	4	na	588
20.5/6	81	na	na	754
15/3	25	4.5	na	1002
3/1	13	na	na	350

Dinners (cont.)	Serving	Calories	Prot (g)	Carb (g)
Chicken mesquite w/ barbeque, corn medley, potatoes au gratin	1 serving	321	18	45
Chicken pot pie	1 serving	484	13	43
Creamed chipped beef	1 serving	175	10	7
Dinner-type meal (TV), generic, frozen	1 meal (16 oz.)	512	27	54
Fried chicken w/ mashed potatoes and corn in sauce	1 serving	470	21	35
Entrée or meal (8–11 oz.), less than 340 calories	1 carton (9.5 oz)	298	18	40
Escalloped chicken and noodles	1 serving	419	17	31
Fried chicken meal w/ mashed potatoes, corn in seasoned sauce	1 serving	470	21	35
Italian sausage lasagna	1 serving	456	21	40
Lasagna w/ meat and sauce	1 serving	277	19	26

Fat/Sat Fat (g)	Chol (mg)	Fiber (g)	Sugars (g)	Sodium (mg)
7/3	26	4	na	793
29/12	41	2	8	857
12/5	44	na	na	621
21/7	59	6	9	1402
27/9	89	2	3	1500
6/2	39	3	2	535
25/6.5	76	na	na	1211
27/9	89	2	3	1500
24/8	48	3	na	903
11/5	41	3	na	735

Dinners (cont.)	Serving	Calories	Prot (g)	Carb (g)
Meat loaf dinner w/ tomato sauce, mashed potatoes and carrots in seasoned sauce	I serving	612	29	33.5
Mesquite beef with barbecue sauce, mashed potatoes, and sweetened corn	I serving	320	21	38
Mexican style dinner w/ tamales, beef enchiladas and chili sauce, beans and rice	I serving	508	14	68
Roasted chicken w/ garlic sauce, pasta and vegetable medley	I serving	214	17	21.5
Salisbury steak in gravy, w/ macaroni and cheese	I serving	386	22.5	26
Salisbury steak in gravy, w/ mashed potatoes and corn in seasoned sauce	I serving	782	27	47

Fat/Sat Fat (g)	Chol (mg)	Fiber (g)	Sugars (g)	Sodium (mg)
40/15	113	6	12	1943
9/3	3	5	16	491
20/7	26	8	na	1812
7/1	28	4	na	467
21/8	63	na	na	1015
54/21	131	7	7	2195

Dinners (cont.)	Serving	Calories	Prot (g)	Carb (g)
Sliced beef meal, w/ gravy, mashed potatoes and peas in seasoned sauce	1 serving	270	26	19
Stuffed peppers w/ beef, in tomato sauce	1 serving	189	8	21
Tuna noodle casserole	1 cup	259	13	34
Turkey and gravy w/ dressing and broccoli	1 serving	504	31	52
Turkey and gravy w/ dressing meal, w/ mashed potatoes and corn in seasoned sauce	1 serving	280	14	34
Turkey pot pie	1 serving	699	26	70
Veal parmigiana meal w/ tomato sauce, mashed potatoes and peas in seasoned sauce	1 serving	362	13	35

Fat/Sat Fat (g)	Chol (mg)	Fiber (g)	Sugars (g)	Sodium (mg)
10/4	71	4	12	742
8/3	22	5	na	579
8/2	42	2	1	1043
19/9	79	0	11	2037
10/2.5	52	3	6.5	1061
35/11	64	4	na	1390
19/6	26	7	15	964

LOW-RESPONSE COST,
LOW-YIELD FOODS: DONUTS AND PASTRIES

Food	Serving	Calories	Prot (g)	Carb (g)
Donuts				
Cake-type, wheat, sugared or glazed	1 donut, medium (3" dia)	162	3	19
Cake-type, wheat, sugared or glazed	1 donut (2" dia)	101	2	12
Cake-type, plain, sugared or glazed	1 donut, medium (3" dia)	192	2	23
Cake-type, plain, chocolate-coated or frosted	1 donut, large (3½ " dia)	270	3	27
Donuts, cake-type, plain, chocolate-coated or frosted	1 donut, medium (3" dia)	204	2	21
Cake-type, plain, chocolate-coated or frosted	1 donut (2" dia)	133	1	13
Cake-type, plain, unsugared, old fashioned	1 donut stick	219	3	26
Cake-type, plain, unsugared, old fashioned	1 donut, large (4" dia)	299	3.5	35

Fat/Sat Fat (g)	Chol (mg)	Fiber (g)	Sugars (g)	Sodium (mg)
9/1	9	1	na	160
5/1	6	1	na	99
10/3	14	1	na	181
18/5	35	1	na	245
13/3	26	1	na	184
9/2	17	1	na	120
12/2	19	1	na	284
16/2.5	26	1	na	388

Donuts (cont.)	Serving	Calories	Prot (g)	Carb (g)
Cake-type, plain, unsugared, old fashioned	1 donut, mini (1½" dia) or donut hole	59	1	7
Cake-type, plain, unsugared, old fashioned	1 donut, medium (3¼" dia)	198	2	23
Cake-type, plain, unsugared, old fashioned	1 donut, long type (twist) (4½" long)	219	3	26
Cake-type, chocolate, sugared or glazed	1 donut, medium (3" dia)	175	2	24
Cake-type, chocolate, sugared or glazed	1 donut, (3¾" dia)	250	3	34
Yeast-leavened, w/ crème filling	1 donut oval (3½" x 2½")	307	5	25.5
Donut, yeast-leavened, w/ jelly filling	1 donut oval (3½" x 2½")	289	5	33
Donut stick, cake-type, plain	1 donut stick	219	3	26
Donut stick, yeast-leavened, glazed, enriched	1 donut stick	226	3.5	25

Fat/Sat Fat (g)	Chol (mg)	Fiber (g)	Sugars (g)	Sodium (mg)
3/t	5	t	na	76
11/2	17	1	na	257
12/2	19	1	na	284
8/2	24	1	na	143
12/3	34	1	na	204
21/5	20	1	na	263
16/4	22	1	na	249
12/2	19	1	na	284
13/3	3	1	na	192

Donuts (cont.)	Serving	Calories	Prot (g)	Carb (g)
Donut twist, yeast-leavened, glazed, enriched	1 donut twist (4½" lg)	219	3	26
Donut hole, yeast-leavened, glazed, enriched	1 donut hole	52	1	6
French crullers, glazed	1 cruller (3" dia)	169	1	24

Pastries

	Serving	Calories	Prot (g)	Carb (g)
Apple turnovers, frozen, ready to bake	1 serving	284	4	31
Cream puffs, prepared from recipe	1 cream puff	335	9	30
Coffeecake, cheese	1 piece (⅙ of 16 oz. cake)	258	5	34
Coffeecake, cinnamon w/ crumb topping, commercially prepared	1 piece (⅑ of 20 oz. cake)	263	4	29
Coffeecake, crème-filled w/ chocolate frosting	1 piece (⅙ of 19 oz. cake)	298	4.5	48

Fat/Sat Fat (g)	Chol (mg)	Fiber (g)	Sugars (g)	Sodium (mg)
12/2	19	1	na	284
3/1	1	t	na	44
7.5/2	5	t	na	141

16/4	na	2	11	176
20/5	174	t	na	443
11.5/4	65	1	na	258
15/4	20	1	na	221
10/2.5	62	2	na	291

Donuts (cont.)	Serving	Calories	Prot (g)	Carb (g)
Coffeecake, fruit	1 piece (⅛ cake)	156	3	26
Croissant, apple	1 croissant, medium	145	4	21
Croissant, butter	1 croissant, large	272	5.5	31
Croissant, butter	1 croissant, medium	231	5	26
Croissant, butter	1 croissant, small	171	3	19
Croissant, butter	1 croissant, mini	114	2	13
Croissant, cheese	1 croissant, large	277	6	31.5
Croissant, cheese	1 croissant, medium	236	5	27
Croissant, cheese	1 croissant, small	174	4	20
Danish pastry, cheese	1 pastry	266	6	26
Danish pastry, cinnamon	1 pastry, large (7" dia.)	572	10	63

Fat/Sat Fat (g)	Chol (mg)	Fiber (g)	Sugars (g)	Sodium (mg)
5/1	4	1	na	193
5/3	18	1	na	156
14/8	45	2	na	498
12/7	38	1.5	na	424
9/5	28	1	na	312
6/3	19	1	na	208
14/7	38	2	na	372
12/6	32	1.5	na	316
9/4	24	1	na	233
15.5/5	11	1	na	320
32/8	30	2	na	527

Donuts (cont.)	Serving	Calories	Prot (g)	Carb (g)
Danish pastry, cinnamon	1 pastry, (4¼" dia)	262	4.5	29
Danish pastry, cinnamon	1 pastry, small or frozen (3" dia)	141	2	16
Danish pastry, cinnamon	1 piece (⅛ of 15 oz. ring)	214	4	24
Danish pastry, fruit	1 pastry, large (7" dia)	527	8	68
Danish pastry, fruit	1 pastry (4¼" dia)	263	4	34
Danish pastry, fruit	1 pastry, small or frozen (3" dia)	130	2	17
Danish pastry, fruit	1 piece (⅛ of 15 oz. ring)	197	3	25
Danish pastry, nut	1 pastry (4¼" dia)	280	5	30
Danish pastry, nut	1 piece (⅛ of 15 oz. ring)	228	4	24

Fat/Sat Fat (g)	Chol (mg)	Fiber (g)	Sugars (g)	Sodium (mg)
14.5/4	14	1	na	241
8/2	7	t	na	44
12/3	11	1	na	197
26/7	162	3	na	503
13/3	81	1	na	251
6/2	40	1	na	124
10/3	60	1	na	188
16/4	30	1	na	236
13/3	24	1	na	192

Donuts (cont.)	Serving	Calories	Prot (g)	Carb (g)
Eclairs, custard-filled w/ chocolate glaze, prepared from recipe	1 small éclair, (3½" x 2")	293	7	27
Eclairs, custard-filled w/ chocolate glaze, prepared from recipe	1 medium éclair, (5" x 2" x 1¾")	262	6	24
Sweet rolls, cinnamon, refrigerated dough w/ frosting, baked	1 roll	109	2	17
Sweet rolls, cinnamon, refrigerated dough w/ frosting	1 roll	100	2	15
Sweet rolls, cinnamon, commercially prepared w/ raisins	1 roll (2¾" square)	223	4	31
Sweet rolls, cinnamon, commercially prepared w/ raisins	1 roll, large	309	5	42
Sweet rolls, cheese	1 roll	238	5	29
Toaster pastry, apple cinnamon	1 pastry	205	2	37
Toaster pastry, apple cinnamon Danish swirl	1 pastry	256	3	37

Fat/Sat Fat (g)	Chol (mg)	Fiber (g)	Sugars (g)	Sodium (mg)
18/5	142	1	na	377
16/4	127	1	na	337
4/1	0	na	na	250
4/1	0	na	na	230
10/2	40	1	na	230
14/3	55	2	na	318
5/4	50	1	na	236
5/1	0	1	18	174
11/3	0	1	11	190

Donuts (cont.)	Serving	Calories	Prot (g)	Carb (g)
Toaster pastry, blueberry	1 pastry	212	2	36
Toaster pastry, blueberry, frosted	1 pastry	203	2	37
Toaster pastry, frosted chocolate fudge, low-fat	1 pastry	190	3	40
Toaster pastry, brown-sugar-cinnamon	1 pastry	206	3	34
Toaster pastry, brown-sugar-cinnamon, frosted	1 pastry	211	2.5	34
Toaster pastry, cheese Danish	1 pastry	252	3	37
Toaster pastry, cherry	1 pastry	204	2	37
Toaster pastry, cherry, frosted	1 pastry	204	2	37
Toaster pastry, chocolate fudge, frosted	1 pastry	201	2	37
Toaster pastry, chocolate vanilla crème, frosted	1 pastry	203	3	37

Fat/Sat Fat (g)	Chol (mg)	Fiber (g)	Sugars (g)	Sodium (mg)
7/1	0	1	16	207
5/1	0	1	16	207
3/1	0	1	19	249
7/2	0	1	na	212
7/1	0	1	15	185
11/3	1	t	12	180
5/1	0	1	16	220
5/1	0	t	18	220
5/1	0	1	20	203
5/1	0	1	20	229

Donuts (cont.)	Serving	Calories	Prot (g)	Carb (g)
Toaster pastry, fruit	1 pastry	204	2	37
Toaster pastry, grape, frosted	1 pastry	203	2	37.5
Toaster pastry, milk chocolate	1 pastry	205	3	36
Toaster pastry, raspberry, frosted	1 pastry	205	2	37
Toaster pastry, strawberry Danish	1 pastry	254	3	37
Toaster pastry, strawberry, frosted	1 pastry	203	2	37
Toaster pastry, strudel	1 pastry	214	4	24
Toaster pastry, wild berry, frosted	1 pastry	210	2	39

Fat/Sat Fat (g)	Chol (mg)	Fiber (g)	Sugars (g)	Sodium (mg)
5/1	0	1	na	218
5/1	0	t	18	198
6/1.5	0	1	18	227
5.5/1	0	t	18	211
11/3	0	1	16	170
5/1	0	t	20	169
12/3	11	1	na	197
5/1	0	t	21	168

LOW-RESPONSE COST,
LOW-YIELD FOODS: EGGS

Food	Serving	Calories	Prot (g)	Carb (g)
Eggs				
Fried	I large	92	6	t
Omelet	I large	93	6	I
Scrambled	I large	101	7	I

Fat/Sat Fat (g)	Chol (mg)	Fiber (g)	Sugars (g)	Sodium (mg)
7/2	211	0	0	162
7/2	214	0	0	165
7/2	215	0	0	171

LOW-RESPONSE COST, LOW-YIELD FOODS: FAST FOODS

Food	Serving	Calories	Prot (g)	Carb (g)
Breakfast Foods				
Biscuit, apple, cinnamon, and raisin	1 biscuit	250	2	42
Biscuit, chicken	1 biscuit	590	24	62
Biscuit, country ham	1 biscuit	440	14	44
Biscuit with egg	1 biscuit	373	12	32
Biscuit with egg and bacon	1 biscuit	458	17	29
Biscuit with egg and ham	1 biscuit	230	11	16
Biscuit with egg, cheese, and bacon	1 biscuit	331	11	23
Biscuit with gravy	1 biscuit	530	10	56
Biscuit with ham	1 biscuit	386	13	44
Biscuit with jelly	1 biscuit	440	6	57
Biscuit, omelet variety	1 biscuit	540	20	45
Biscuit with sausage	1 biscuit	485	12	40
Biscuit, steak	1 biscuit	580	15	56

Fat/Sat Fat (g)	Chol (mg)	Fiber (g)	Sugars (g)	Sodium (mg)
8/2	0	na	na	350
27/7	45	na	na	1820
22/7	30	na	na	1710
22/5	245	1	na	891
31/8	353	1	na	999
14/3	156	t	na	720
22/8	181	na	na	875
30/9	15	na	na	1550
18/11	25	1	na	1433
21/6	0	na	na	1000
32/12	225	na	na	1350
32/14	35	1	na	1071
32/10	30	na	na	1580

Fast Foods (cont.)	Serving	Calories	Prot (g)	Carb (g)
Cinnamon roll	1 roll	535	9	96
Croissant with egg and cheese	1 croissant	368	13	24
Croissant with egg, cheese and bacon	1 croissant	413	16	24
Croissant with egg, cheese, and ham	1 croissant	474	19	24
Croissant with egg, cheese, and sausage	1 croissant	523	20	25
Danish pastry, cinnamon	1 pastry	349	5	47
Danish pastry, cheese	1 pastry	353	6	29
Danish pastry, fruit	1 pastry	335	5	45
Egg and cheese sandwich	1 sandwich	340	16	26
Egg, scrambled	2 eggs	199	13	2
English muffin, with butter	1 muffin	189	5	30
English muffin with cheese and sausage	1 muffin	393	15	29

Fat/Sat Fat (g)	Chol (mg)	Fiber (g)	Sugars (g)	Sodium (mg)
21/7	17	na	na	770
25/14	216	na	na	551
28/15	215	na	na	889
33.5/17.5	213	na	na	1081
38/18	216	na	na	1115
17/3.5	27	na	na	326
25/5	20	na	na	319
16/3	19	na	na	333
19/7	291	na	na	804
15/6	400	0	na	211
6/2	13	na	na	386
24/10	59	1.5	na	1036

Fast Foods (cont.)	Serving	Calories	Prot (g)	Carb (g)
English muffin with egg, cheese and Canadian bacon	1 muffin	289	17	27
English muffin with egg, cheese and sausage	1 muffin	487	22	31
French toast sticks	5 pieces	513	8	58
Ham, egg, and cheese sandwich	1 sandwich	347	19	31
Pancakes with butter and syrup	2 cakes	520	8	91
Quesadilla, breakfast	1 quesadilla	400	17	38
Sourdough sandwich with bacon	1 sandwich	380	14	29
Sourdough sandwich with ham	1 sandwich	220	12	30
Sourdough sandwich with sausage	1 sandwich	330	10	29

Burgers

	Serving	Calories	Prot (g)	Carb (g)
Bacon cheeseburger, ⅓ lb.	1 sandwich	800	39	41
Bacon cheeseburger, ⅔ lb.	1 sandwich	1148	63	42

Fat/Sat Fat (g)	Chol (mg)	Fiber (g)	Sugars (g)	Sodium (mg)
12.5/5	234	1.5	3	729
31/12	274	na	na	1135
29/5	75	3	na	499
16/7	246	na	na	1005
14/6	58	na	na	1104
20/9	190	3	3	1050
7/1.5	10	2	na	890
7/1.5	30	1	na	1270
19/6	30	1	na	810

55/18	120	na	na	1413
82/31	198	na	na	2042

Fast Foods (cont.)	Serving	Calories	Prot (g)	Carb (g)
Cheeseburger, large double patty, w/ condiments	1 sandwich	704	38	40
Cheeseburger, large, single patty, w/ condiments	1 sandwich	563	28	38
Cheeseburger, large, single patty, w/ ham and condiments	1 sandwich	744	40	38
Cheeseburger, regular, double patty, plain	1 sandwich	461	22	44
Cheeseburger, regular, double patty, w/ condiments	1 sandwich	650	30	53
Cheeseburger, regular, single patty, w/ condiments	1 sandwich	295	16	27
Cheeseburger, triple patty, plain	1 sandwich	796	56	27
Cheeseburger w/ mushrooms and Swiss cheese, ⅓ lb.	1 sandwich	637	37	43

Fat/Sat Fat (g)	Chol (mg)	Fiber (g)	Sugars (g)	Sodium (mg)
44/18	142	na	na	1148
33/15	88	na	na	1108
48/21	122	na	na	1712
22/9.5	80	na	na	891
35/13	93	na	na	921
14/6	37	na	na	616
51/22	161	na	na	1213
38/15	92	na	na	1459

Fast Foods (cont.)	Serving	Calories	Prot (g)	Carb (g)
Chili cheeseburger, ⅓ lb.	I sandwich	855	42	48
Hamburger, large, double patty, w/ condiments	I sandwich	540	34	40
Hamburger, large, single patty, w/ condiments	I sandwich	427	23	37
Hamburger, large, triple patty, w/ condiments	I sandwich	692	50	28.5
Hamburger, regular, double patty, plain	I sandwich	544	30	43
Hamburger, regular, double patty, w/ condiments	I sandwich	576	32	39
Hamburger, regular, single patty, plain	I sandwich	275	12	30.5
Hamburger, regular, single patty, w/ condiments	I sandwich	272	12	34

Chicken

	Serving	Calories	Prot (g)	Carb (g)
Chicken club sandwich	I sandwich	470	30	47

Fat/Sat Fat (g)	Chol (mg)	Fiber (g)	Sugars (g)	Sodium (mg)
57/23	121	na	na	1704
26.5/10.5	122	na	na	791
21/8	71	2	8	731
41/16	142	na	na	712
28/10	99	na	na	554
32/12	103	na	na	742
12/4	35	na	na	387
10/3.5	30	2	7	534

19/4	65	2	6	920

Fast Foods (cont.)	Serving	Calories	Prot (g)	Carb (g)
Chicken fillet sandwich, plain	1 sandwich	515	24	39
Chicken fillet sandwich, w/ cheese	1 sandwich	632	29	41.5
Chicken sandwich w/ bacon and Swiss cheese	1 sandwich	610	31	49
Chicken pieces, breaded and fried, plain	6 pieces	319	18	15
Chicken pieces, breaded and fried, w/ barbecue sauce	6 pieces	330	17	25
Chicken pieces, breaded and fried, w/ honey	6 pieces	329	17	27
Chicken pieces, breaded and fried, w/ mustard sauce	6 pieces	322	17	21
Chicken pieces, breaded and fried, w/ sweet and sour sauce	6 pieces	346	17	29
Chicken strips	4 strips	290	29	14
Chicken wings, hot	6 drum-mettes	443	37.5	t

Fat/Sat Fat (g)	Chol (mg)	Fiber (g)	Sugars (g)	Sodium (mg)
29/8.5	60	na	na	957
39/12	78	na	na	1238
33/8	110	2	na	1550
21/5	61	0	0	513
18/5.5	61	na	na	829
18/5.5	61	na	na	537
19/6	61	na	na	790
18/5.5	61	na	na	677
13/2.5	65	1	3	730
32/8	117	t	0	114

Fast Foods (cont.)	Serving	Calories	Prot (g)	Carb (g)
Dark meat, breaded and fried	2 pieces	431	30	16
Light meat, breaded and fried	2 pieces	247	18	10
Roast chicken, Caesar-style, sandwich	1 sandwich	820	43	75

Desserts

	Serving	Calories	Prot (g)	Carb (g)
Apple turnover, iced	1 turnover	420	4	65
Banana split	1 serving	510	8	96
Cherry turnover, iced	1 turnover	410	4	63
Dessert thick frost-type shakes, junior size	1 shake (6 oz.)	170	4	28
Dessert thick frost-type shakes, small size	1 shake (12 oz.)	330	8	56
Dessert thick frost-type shakes, medium size	1 shake (16 oz.)	440	11	73
Ice cream cone, chocolate, small	1 cone	240	6	37

Fat/Sat Fat (g)	Chol (mg)	Fiber (g)	Sugars (g)	Sodium (mg)
27/7	166	na	na	755
15/4	74	na	na	487
38/9	140	5	na	2160

Fat/Sat Fat (g)	Chol (mg)	Fiber (g)	Sugars (g)	Sodium (mg)
16/4.5	0	2	na	230
12/8	30	3	82	180
16/4.5	0	1	na	250
4/2.5	20	0	21	100
8/5	35	0	43	200
11/7	50	0	56	260
8/5	20	0	25	115

Fast Foods (cont.)	Serving	Calories	Prot (g)	Carb (g)
Ice cream cone, chocolate, medium	1 cone	340	8	53
Ice cream cone, dipped, small	1 cone	340	6	42
Ice cream cone, dipped, medium	1 cone	490	8	59
Ice cream cone, vanilla, small	1 cone	230	6	38
Ice cream cone, vanilla, medium	1 cone	330	8	53
Ice cream cone, vanilla, large	1 cone	410	10	65
Ice milk, vanilla, soft serve, w/ cone	1 cone	164	4	24
Malt, chocolate, small	1 malt (418 g.)	650	15	111
Malt, chocolate, medium	1 malt (567 g.)	880	19	153
Peach cobbler	1 cobbler	310	2	60
Shake, chocolate, regular	1 shake (10 fl. oz.)	264	7	43
Shake, chocolate, large	1 shake (22 fl. oz.)	582	15.5	94

Fat/Sat Fat (g)	Chol (mg)	Fiber (g)	Sugars (g)	Sodium (mg)
11/7	30	0	34	160
17/9	20	1	31	130
24/13	30	1	43	190
7/4.5	20	0	27	115
9/6	30	0	38	160
12/8	40	0	49	200
6/3.5	28	t	na	92
16/10	55	0	95	370
22/14	70	0	131	500
7/1	0	na	na	360
8/5	27	2	na	202
17/11	60	4	na	444

Fast Foods (cont.)	Serving	Calories	Prot (g)	Carb (g)
Shake, chocolate, extra large	1 shake (32 fl. oz.)	1150	30	187
Shake, strawberry, regular	1 shake (10 fl. oz.)	320	10	53
Shake, strawberry, large	1 shake (22 fl. oz.)	704	21	118
Shake, strawberry, extra large	1 shake (32 fl. oz.)	1120	28	178
Shake, vanilla, regular	1 shake (10 fl. oz.)	231	7	37
Shake, vanilla, large	1 shake (22 fl. oz.)	508	16	82
Shake, vanilla, extra large	1 shake (32 fl. oz.)	1140	28	178
Sundae, caramel	1 sundae	304	7	49
Sundae, hot fudge	1 sundae	284	6	48
Sundae, strawberry	1 sundae	268	6	45

Mexican Foods

Burrito w/ beans	1 burrito	224	7	36
Burrito w/ beans and cheese	1 burrito	189	8	27

Fat/Sat Fat (g)	Chol (mg)	Fiber (g)	Sugars (g)	Sodium (mg)
33/22	135	3	163	550
8/5	31	1	na	235
17/11	68	2.5	na	517
32/22	135	2	158	380
6/4	23	1	na	171
14/8.5	50	2	na	376
32/22	135	t	152	810
9/4.5	25	0	na	195
9/5	21	0	na	182
8/4	21	0	na	92

7/3	2	na	na	493
6/3	14	na	na	583

Fast Foods (cont.)	Serving	Calories	Prot (g)	Carb (g)
Burrito w/ beans and chili peppers	1 burrito	206	8	29
Burrito w/ beans and meat	1 burrito	254	11	33
Burrito w/ beans, cheese, and beef	1 burrito	165	7	20
Burrito w/ beans, cheese, and chili peppers	1 burrito	331	17	42.5
Burrito w/ beef	1 burrito	262	13	29
Burrito w/ beef and chili peppers	1 burrito	213	11	25
Burrito w/ beef, cheese, and chili peppers	1 burrito	316	20	32
Burrito, w/ fruit (apple or cherry)	1 burrito, small	231	2.5	35
Burrito, w/ fruit (apple or cherry)	1 burrito, large	484	5	73
Burrito, grilled, stuffed w/ beef	1 burrito	730	28	79
Burrito, grilled, stuffed w/ chicken	1 burrito	680	35	76

Fat/Sat Fat (g)	Chol (mg)	Fiber (g)	Sugars (g)	Sodium (mg)
7/4	16	na	na	522
9/4	24	na	na	668
7/3.5	62	na	na	495
11.5/5.5	79	na	na	1030
10/5	32	na	na	746
8/4	27	na	na	558
12/5	85	na	na	1046
10/5	4	na	na	212
20/10	8	na	na	443
33/11	55	10	7	2080
26/7	70	7	6	1950

Fast Foods (cont.)	Serving	Calories	Prot (g)	Carb (g)
Burrito, grilled, stuffed w/ steak	1 burrito	680	31	76
Chili con carne	1 cup	256	25	22
Chimichanga w/ beef	1 chimi-changa	425	20	43
Chimichanga w/ beef and cheese	1 chimi-changa	443	20	39
Chimichanga w/ beef and red chili peppers	1 chimi-changa	424	18	46
Chimichanga w/ beef, cheese, and red chili peppers	1 chimi-changa	364	15	38
Enchilada w/ cheese	1 enchilada	319	10	28.5
Enchilada w/ cheese and beef	1 enchilada	323	12	30
Enchilada w/ cheese, beef, and beans	1 enchilada	344	18	34
Frijoles w/ cheese	1 cup	225	11	29
Nachos w/ cheese	6–8 nachos	346	9	36
Nachos w/ cheese and jalapeno peppers	6–8 nachos	608	17	60

Fat/Sat Fat (g)	Chol (mg)	Fiber (g)	Sugars (g)	Sodium (mg)
28/8	55	8	6	1940
8/3	134	na	na	1007
20/8.5	9	na	na	910
23/11	51	na	na	957
19/8	10	na	na	1169
17.5/8	50	na	na	895
19/10.5	44	na	na	784
18/9	40	na	na	1319
16/8	50	na	na	1251
8/4	37	na	na	882
19/8	18	na	na	816
34/14	84	na	na	1736

Fast Foods (cont.)	Serving	Calories	Prot (g)	Carb (g)
Nachos w/ cheese, beans, ground beef, and peppers	6–8 nachos	569	20	56
Nachos w/ cinnamon and sugar	6–8 nachos	592	7	63
Taco	1 taco, small	369	21	27
Taco	1 taco, large	568	32	41
Taco salad	2 cups	372	18	31
Taco salad w/ chili con carne	2 cups	386	23	35
Tostada w/ beans and cheese	1 tostada	223	10	27
Tostada w/ beans, beef, and cheese	1 tostada	333	16	30
Tostada w/ beef, and cheese	1 tostada	315	19	23

Pizzas

	Serving	Calories	Prot (g)	Carb (g)
Individual, pan pizza	1 pizza	722	33	70
Regular, Italian sausage	1 slice	340	16	28
Regular, pepperoni	1 slice	280	13	28

Fat/Sat Fat (g)	Chol (mg)	Fiber (g)	Sugars (g)	Sodium (mg)
31/12	20	na	na	1800
36/18	39	na	na	439
20.5/11	56	na	na	802
32/17	87	na	na	1233
20/9	58	na	na	1016
17.5/8	7	na	na	1180
10/5	30	na	na	543
17/11	74	na	na	871
16/10	41	na	na	897

34/12	66	6	3	1760
18/8	30	2	2	910
13/6	20	2	2	790

Fast Foods (cont.)	Serving	Calories	Prot (g)	Carb (g)
Stuffed crust, Italian sausage	1 slice	400	19	40
Stuffed crust, pepperoni	1 slice	360	17	39
Thin crust, cheese	1 slice	400	19	41
Thin crust, Italian sausage	1 slice	290	12	22
Thin crust, pepperoni	1 slice	190	9	21

Sandwiches, other

	Serving	Calories	Prot (g)	Carb (g)
Corndog	1 sandwich	460	17	56
Hot dog, plain	1 sandwich	242	10	18
Hot dog w/ chili	1 sandwich	296	14	31
Roast beef sandwich, plain	1 sandwich	346	21.5	33
Roast beef sandwich w/ cheddar	1 sandwich	480	23	43
Roast beef sandwich, giant-size	1 sandwich (8 oz.)	480	32	41
Roast beef sandwich w/ Swiss cheese	1 sandwich	810	37	73

Fat/Sat Fat (g)	Chol (mg)	Fiber (g)	Sugars (g)	Sodium (mg)
20/8	35	3	2	1180
16/7	30	3	2	1120
19/9	37	2	5	992
17/7	30	2	1	800
9/4	15	2	1	610

Fat/Sat Fat (g)	Chol (mg)	Fiber (g)	Sugars (g)	Sodium (mg)
19/5	79	na	na	973
15/5	44	na	na	670
13/5	51	na	na	480
14/4	51	na	na	792
24/8	90	2	na	1240
23/10	110	3	na	1440
42/13	130	5	na	1780

Fast Foods (cont.)	Serving	Calories	Prot (g)	Carb (g)
Roast ham sand-wich w/ Swiss cheese	1 sandwich	730	36	74
Roast turkey w/ bacon and ranch dressing	1 sandwich	880	48	74
Roast turkey w/ Swiss cheese	1 sandwich	760	43	75
Ham and cheese sandwich	1 sandwich	352	21	33
Submarine sandwich w/ cold cuts	1 sub	456	22	51
Submarine sandwich w/ cold cuts, double meat	1 sub	580	31	49
Submarine sandwich w/ meat balls, double meat	1 sub	780	35	61
Submarine sandwich w/ roast beef	1 sub	410	29	44
Submarine sandwich w/ tuna salad	1 sub	584	30	55

Seafood

Battered fish	1 piece	230	11	16

Fat/Sat Fat (g)	Chol (mg)	Fiber (g)	Sugars (g)	Sodium (mg)
34/8	125	5	na	2180
44/10	155	5	na	2320
33/6	130	5	na	1920
15/6	58	na	na	771
19/7	36	na	na	1651
32/11	105	4	7	2540
41/18	85	5	10	1760
13/7	73	na	na	845
28/5	49	na	na	1293

13/4	30	0	0	700

Fast Foods (cont.)	Serving	Calories	Prot (g)	Carb (g)
Clams, breaded and fried	1 cup	601	17	52
Fish sandwich w/ tartar sauce	1 sandwich	431	17	41
Fish sandwich w/ tartar sauce and cheese	1 sandwich	523	21	48
Oysters, battered or breaded, fried	6 oysters	368	13	40
Scallops, breaded and fried	6 scallops	386	16	38
Shrimp, breaded and fried	6 shrimp	454	19	40

Sides

French fries, fried in vegetable oil	1 small serving	291	4	34
French fries, fried in vegetable oil	1 medium serving	458	6	53
French fries, fried in vegetable oil	1 large serving	578	7	67
French fries, cheddar-style	1 serving (6 oz.)	460	6	54
French fried, chili cheese	1 serving	667	17	51

Fat/Sat Fat (g)	Chol (mg)	Fiber (g)	Sugars (g)	Sodium (mg)
35/9	117	na	na	1112
23/5	55	na	na	615
29/8	68	na	na	939
18/5	108	na	na	677
19/5	108	na	na	919
25/5	200	na	na	1446

Fat/Sat Fat (g)	Chol (mg)	Fiber (g)	Sugars (g)	Sodium (mg)
16/3	0	3	0	168
25/5	0	5	0	265
31/6.5	0	6	0	335
24/6	5	4	na	1290
44/14	60	na	na	840

Fast Foods (cont.)	Serving	Calories	Prot (g)	Carb (g)
Hash browns	½ cup	151	2	16
Hush puppies	5 pieces	257	5	35
Mozzarella sticks	4 sticks	470	18	34
Onion rings, breaded and fried	8–9 onion rings	276	4	31
Potato, baked and topped w/ cheese sauce	1 potato	474	15	47
Potato, baked and topped w/ cheese sauce and bacon	1 potato	451	18	44
Potato, baked and topped w/ cheese sauce and broccoli	1 potato	403	14	47
Potato, baked and topped w/ cheese sauce and chili	1 potato	482	23	56
Potato, baked and topped w/ sour cream and chives	1 potato	393	7	50

Fat/Sat Fat (g)	Chol (mg)	Fiber (g)	Sugars (g)	Sodium (mg)
9/4	9	na	na	290
12/3	135	na	na	965
29/14	60	2	na	1330
15.5/7	14	na	na	430
29/11	18	na	na	382
26/10	30	na	na	972
21/8.5	20	na	na	485
22/13	32	na	na	699
22/10	24	na	na	181

LOW-RESPONSE COST, LOW-YIELD FOODS: FATS

Fats Food	Serving	Calories	Prot (g)	Carb (g)
Fats				
Bacon grease	1 tbsp	114	0	0
Beef tallow	1 tbsp	115	0	0
Butter, light, stick w/ salt	1 tbsp	69	t	0
Butter, light, stick w/o salt	1 tbsp	69	t	0
Butter, whipped, w/ salt	1 pat (1" sq x ⅓" high)	27	t	0
Butter, w/o salt	1 pat (1" sq x ⅓" high)	36	t	0
Butter, w/ salt	1 pat (1" sq x ⅓" high)	36	t	0
Coconut oil	1 tbsp	116	0	0
Lard	1 tbsp	115	0	0
Margarine, 80% fat stick, includes regular and hydrogenated corn and soybean oils	1 tbsp	99	t	0

Fat/Sat Fat (g)	Chol (mg)	Fiber (g)	Sugars (g)	Sodium (mg)
12/6	12	0	0	18
13/6	14	0	0	0
7.5/6	15	0	0	63
7.5/6	15	0	0	6
3/2	8	0	0	31
4/3	11	0	0	1
4/3	11	0	0	41
14/12	0	0	0	0
13/5	12	0	0	0
12/3	0	0	0	90

Fats (cont.)	Serving	Calories	Prot (g)	Carb (g)
Margarine, 70% vegetable oil spread, soybean and soybean (hydrogenated)	1 tbsp	87	t	0
Margarine, regular, hard, coconut (hydrogenated and regular) and safflower and palm (hydrogenated)	1 tbsp	102	t	0
Margarine, regular, hard, corn (hydrogenated and regular)	1 tbsp	102	t	0
Margarine, regular, hard, corn (hydrogenated)	1 tbsp	102	t	0
Margarine, regular, hard, corn and soybean (hydrogenated) and cottonseed (hydrogenated), w/salt	1 tbsp	102	t	0

Fat/Sat Fat (g)	Chol (mg)	Fiber (g)	Sugars (g)	Sodium (mg)
9/3	0	0	0	99
12/9	0	0	0	132
12/3	0	0	0	132
12/3	0	0	0	132
12/3	0	0	0	132

Fats (cont.)	Serving	Calories	Prot (g)	Carb (g)
Margarine, regular, hard, corn and soybean (hydrogenated) and cottonseed (hydrogenated), w/o salt	1 tbsp	102	t	0
Margarine, regular, hard, lard (hydrogenated)	1 tbsp	102	t	0
Margarine, regular, hard, safflower and soybean (hydrogenated and regular) and cottonseed (hydrogenated)	1 tbsp	102	t	0
Margarine, regular, hard, safflower and soybean (hydrogenated)	1 tbsp	102	t	0
Margarine, regular, hard, safflower and soybean (hydrogenated) and cottonseed (hydrogenated)	1 tbsp	102	t	0

Fat/Sat Fat (g)	Chol (mg)	Fiber (g)	Sugars (g)	Sodium (mg)
12/3	0	0	0	0
12/3	6	0	0	132
12/3	0	0	0	132
12/3	0	0	0	132
12/3	0	0	0	132

Fats (cont.)	Serving	Calories	Prot (g)	Carb (g)
Margarine, regular, hard, soybean (hydrogenated and regular)	1 tbsp	102	t	0
Margarine, regular, hard, soybean (hydrogenated)	1 tbsp	102	t	0
Margarine, regular, liquid, soybean (hydrogenated and regular) and cottonseed	1 tbsp	102	t	0
Margarine, regular, unspecified oils, w/ salt	1 tbsp	102	t	0
Margarine, regular, unspecified oils, w/o salt	1 tbsp	102	t	0
Margarine, soft, corn (hydrogenated and regular)	1 tbsp	102	t	0
Margarine, soft, safflower (hydrogenated and regular)	1 tbsp	102	t	0

Fat/Sat Fat (g)	Chol (mg)	Fiber (g)	Sugars (g)	Sodium (mg)
12/3	0	0	0	132
12/3	0	0	0	132
12/3	0	0	0	111
12/3	0	0	0	132
12/3	0	0	0	0
12/3	0	0	0	155
12/3	0	0	0	153

Fats (cont.)	Serving	Calories	Prot (g)	Carb (g)
Margarine, soft, soybean (hydrogenated and regular), w/o salt	1 tbsp	102	t	0
Margarine, soft, soybean (hydrogenated and regular), w/ salt	1 tbsp	102	t	0
Margarine, soft, soybean (hydrogenated) and safflower	1 tbsp	102	t	0
Margarine-butter blend, 60% corn oil margarine and 40% butter	1 tbsp	102	t	t
Margarine-like spread approx. 40% fat, corn (hydrogenated and regular)	1 tbsp	51	t	t
Margarine-like spread approx. 40% fat, soybean (hydrogenated)	1 tbsp	51	t	t
Margarine-like spread approx. 40% fat, unspecified oils	1 tbsp	51	t	t

Fat/Sat Fat (g)	Chol (mg)	Fiber (g)	Sugars (g)	Sodium (mg)
12/3	0	0	0	3
12/3	0	0	0	153
12/3	0	0	0	153
12/3	12	0	0	126
6/t	0	0	0	126
6/t	0	0	0	126
6/t	0	0	0	126

Fats (cont.)	Serving	Calories	Prot (g)	Carb (g)
Margarine-like spread approx. 60% fat, stick, soybean (hydrogenated and regular)	1 tbsp	78	t	0
Margarine-like spread approx. 60% fat, tub, unspecified oils	1 tbsp	78	t	0
Shortening, multipurpose, soybean (hydrogenated) and palm (hydrogenated)	1 tbsp	113	0	0
Shortening, house-hold, soybean (hydrogenated) and palm	1 tbsp	113	0	0
Shortening, house-hold, soybean (hydrogenated) and cottonseed (hydrogenated)	1 tbsp	113	0	0

Fat/Sat Fat (g)	Chol (mg)	Fiber (g)	Sugars (g)	Sodium (mg)
9/3	0	0	0	144
9/3	0	0	0	144
13/4	0	0	0	0
13/3	0	0	0	0
13/3	0	0	0	0

LOW-RESPONSE COST,
LOW-YIELD FOODS: FISH AND SHELLFISH

Food	Serving	Calories	Prot (g)	Carb (g)
Fish				
Anchovy, canned in oil, drained	I can (2 oz.)	95	13	0
Catfish, breaded and fried	4 oz.	260	20.5	9
Croaker, breaded and fried	4 oz.	250	21	8.5
Fish fillet, fried, generic	I fillet	211	13	15.5
Fish sticks, frozen, preheated	4 sticks	305	17.5	27
Sardine, canned in oil, drained	4 oz.	236	28	0
Shark, breaded and fried	4 oz.	258	21	7
Tuna, light, canned in oil, drained	4 oz.	225	33	0
Tuna, white, canned in oil, drained	4 oz.	211	30	0
Shellfish				
Clams, breaded and fried	4 oz.	229	16	12

Fat/Sat Fat (g)	Chol (mg)	Fiber (g)	Sugars (g)	Sodium (mg)
4/1	38	0	na	1651
15/4	92	1	na	317
14/4	95	t	na	394
11/3	31	t	na	484
14/3.5	125	0	na	652
13/2	161	0	0	573
16/4	67	0	na	138
9/2	20	0	0	401
9/2	35	0	0	449
13/3	69	na	na	413

Fish (cont.)	Serving	Calories	Prot (g)	Carb (g)
Crab cakes, fried	2 cakes	186	24	t
Oysters, breaded and fried	4 oz.	223	10	13
Scallops, breaded and fried	4 oz.	241	20	11
Shrimp, breaded and fried	4 oz.	274	24	13
Squid, fried (calamari)	4 oz.	198	20	9

Fat/Sat Fat (g)	Chol (mg)	Fiber (g)	Sugars (g)	Sodium (mg)
9/2	180	0	na	396
14/4	92	na	na	473
12/3	68	na	na	520
14/2	201	t	na	390
9/2	295	0	na	347

LOW-RESPONSE COST, LOW-YIELD FOODS: FROSTINGS AND TOPPINGS

Food	Serving	Calories	Prot (g)	Carb (g)
Frostings				
Chocolate, ready-to-eat	2 tbsp	163	t	26
Coconut-nut, ready-to-eat	2 tbsp	151	t	19
Cream cheese-flavor, ready-to-eat	2 tbsp	137	t	22
Vanilla, ready-to-eat	2 tbsp	159	t	26
Toppings				
Dessert topping, frozen	½ cup	119	t	8.5
Dessert topping, pressurized	½ cup	92	t	5.5
Dessert topping, powdered, prepared with ½ cup milk	½ cup	75	1.5	6.5
Butterscotch or caramel topping	2 tbsp	103	1	27
Marshmallow cream topping	¼ jar	159	t	39
Nuts in syrup topping	2 tbsp	167	2	22

Fat/Sat Fat (g)	Chol (mg)	Fiber (g)	Sugars (g)	Sodium (mg)
7/2	0	t	24	75
9/2.5	0	t	15	71
6/1.5	0	0	21	63
6/2	0	0	24	67

9.5/8	0	0	na	9.5
8/7	0	0	na	21.5
5/4	4	0	na	26
t/t	0	t	na	143
t/t	0	0	23	24
9/1	0	1	na	17

Frostings (cont.)	Serving	Calories	Prot (g)	Carb (g)
Pineapple topping	2 tbsp	106	t	28
Strawberry topping	2 tbsp	107	t	28

Fat/Sat Fat (g)	Chol (mg)	Fiber (g)	Sugars (g)	Sodium (mg)
t/t	0	t	na	26
t/t	0	t	na	9

LOW-RESPONSE COST, LOW-YIELD FOODS: FRUITS, FRUIT DRINKS, AND PUNCHES

Food	Serving	Calories	Prot (g)	Carb (g)
Fruits				
Applesauce, canned, sweetened, w/ salt	½ cup	97	t	25
Applesauce, canned, sweetened, w/o salt	½ cup	97	t	25
Apricots, canned, extra heavy syrup, w/o skin, solids and liquids	½ cup, whole, w/o pits	118	1	31
Apricots, canned, heavy syrup, w/o skin, solids and liquids	½ cup, whole, w/o pits	107	1	28
Apricots, canned, light syrup, w/ skin, solids and liquids	½ cup, halves	80	1	21
Blueberries, frozen, sweetened	1 cup, thawed	186	1	50
Candied fruit	100 grams	321	0	83
Cherries, sour, red, canned, in heavy syrup, solids and liquids	½ cup	116	1	30

Fat/Sat Fat (g)	Chol (mg)	Fiber (g)	Sugars (g)	Sodium (mg)
t/t	0	1.5	na	36
t/t	0	1.5	na	4
t/t	0	2	na	16
t/t	0	2	na	14
t/t	0	2	na	5
0/0	0	5	45	2
0/0	0	2	81	98
0/0	0	1.5	29	9

Fruits (cont.)	Serving	Calories	Prot (g)	Carb (g)
Cranberry sauce, canned, sweetened	½ cup	209	t	54
Fruit cocktail, canned, extra heavy syrup, solids and liquids	½ cup	114	1	30
Fruit cocktail, canned, heavy syrup, solids and liquids	½ cup	91	t	23
Fruit cocktail, canned, light syrup, solids and liquids	½ cup	69	t	18
Fruit salad, canned, extra heavy syrup, solids and liquids	½ cup	114	t	30
Fruit salad, canned, heavy syrup, solids and liquids	½ cup	111	1	29
Fruit salad, canned, light syrup, solids and liquids	½ cup	73	t	19
Grapefruit sections, canned, in light syrup, solids and liquids	½ cup	76	.5	20

Fat/Sat Fat (g)	Chol (mg)	Fiber (g)	Sugars (g)	Sodium (mg)
t/t	0	1	na	40
t/t	0	1	na	8
t/t	0	1	na	7
t/t	0	1	na	7
t/t	0	1	na	6
t/t	0	2	na	3
t/t	0	1	na	8
0/0	0	.5	19	2

Fruits (cont.)	Serving	Calories	Prot (g)	Carb (g)
Grapes, Thompson seedless, canned, in heavy syrup, solids and liquids	½ cup	93	1	25
Peaches, canned, extra heavy syrup, solids and liquids	½ cup, halves or slices	126	1	34
Peaches, canned, heavy syrup, solids and liquids	½ cup	97	1	26
Peaches, canned, light syrup, solids and liquids	½ cup, halves or slices	68	1	18
Peaches, canned, extra light syrup, solids and liquids	½ cup, halves or slices	52	t	14
Peaches, spiced, canned, extra heavy syrup, solids and liquids	½ cup, whole	91	1	24
Pears canned, extra heavy syrup, solids and liquids	½ cup, halves	129	t	34
Pears canned, heavy syrup, solids and liquids	½ cup	98	t	26

Fat/Sat Fat (g)	Chol (mg)	Fiber (g)	Sugars (g)	Sodium (mg)
t/t	0	.5	na	6
t/t	0	1	na	10
t/t	0	2	na	8
t/t	0	2	na	6
t/t	0	1	na	6
t/t	0	2	na	5
t/t	0	2	na	7
t/t	0	2	na	7

Fruits (cont.)	Serving	Calories	Prot (g)	Carb (g)
Pears canned, light syrup, solids and liquids	½ cup, halves	72	t	19
Pears canned, extra light syrup, solids and liquids	½ cup, halves	58	t	15
Pineapple, canned, extra heavy syrup, solids and liquids	½ cup, crushed, sliced or chunks	108	t	28
Pineapple, canned, heavy syrup, solids and liquids	½ cup, crushed, sliced or chunks	99	t	26
Pineapple, canned, light syrup, solids and liquids	½ cup, crushed, sliced or chunks	66	t	17
Pineapple, frozen, chunks, sweetened	½ cup, chunks	104	t	27
Plums, canned, purple, extra heavy syrup, solids and liquids	½ cup, pitted	132	t	34
Plums, canned, purple, heavy syrup, solids and liquids	½ cup, pitted	115	t	30

Fat/Sat Fat (g)	Chol (mg)	Fiber (g)	Sugars (g)	Sodium (mg)
t/t	0	2	na	6
t/t	0	2	na	2
t/t	0	1	na	1
t/t	0	1	na	1
t/t	0	1	na	1
t/t	0	1	na	2
t/t	0	1	na	25
t/t	0	1	na	25

Fruits (cont.)	Serving	Calories	Prot (g)	Carb (g)
Plums, canned, purple, light syrup, solids and liquids	½ cup, pitted	79	t	21
Prunes, canned, heavy syrup, solids and liquids	½ cup	123	I	33
Prunes, dried, stewed, w/ added sugar	½ cup, pitted	154	I	41
Rhubarb, frozen, cooked, w/ sugar	½ cup	139	t	37
Strawberries, frozen, sweetened, whole	I cup	199	I	54

Fruit Drinks and Punches

	Serving	Calories	Prot (g)	Carb (g)
Apple raspberry cherry juice cocktail, ready-to-drink	I cup (8 fl. oz.)	130	t	33
Apricot nectar, canned	I cup (8 fl. oz.)	141	I	36
Cranberry-apple juice drink, bottled	I cup (8 fl. oz.)	164	t	42
Cranberry-apricot juice drink, bottled	I cup (8 fl. oz.)	157	t	40

Fat/Sat Fat (g)	Chol (mg)	Fiber (g)	Sugars (g)	Sodium (mg)
t/t	0	I	na	25
t/t	0	4	na	4
t/t	0	5	na	2
t/t	0	2	na	I
0/0	0	5	48	3

0/0	0	na	25	13
t/t	0	1.5	na	8
0/0	0	t	na	5
0/0	0	t	na	5

Fruits (cont.)	Serving	Calories	Prot (g)	Carb (g)
Cranberry-grape juice drink, bottled	1 cup (8 fl. oz.)	137	t	34
Cranberry juice cocktail, bottled	1 cup (8 fl. oz.)	144	0	36
Cranberry juice cocktail, frozen concentrate, prepared w/ water	1 cup (8 fl. oz.)	138	0	35
Fruit punch drink, canned	1 cup (8 fl. oz.)	117	0	30
Fruit punch drink, frozen concentrate, prepared w/ water	1 cup (8 fl. oz.)	114	0	29
Fruit punch, ready-to-drink	1 serving	99	0	26
Fruit punch-flavor drink, powder, w/ added sodium, prepared w/ water	1 cup (8 fl. oz.)	97	0	25
Fruit punch-flavor drink, powder, w/o added sodium, prepared w/ water	1 cup (8 fl. oz.)	97	0	25
Grape berry punch, ready-to-drink	1 serving	116	0	31

Fat/Sat Fat (g)	Chol (mg)	Fiber (g)	Sugars (g)	Sodium (mg)
t/t	0	t	na	7
t/t	0	t	na	5
0/0	0	t	na	8
0/0	0	t	29	55
0/0	0	t	na	10
0/0	0	0	25	21
0/0	0	0	na	37
0/0	0	0	na	10
0/0	0	0	30	35

Fruits (cont.)	Serving	Calories	Prot (g)	Carb (g)
Grape juice drink, canned	1 cup (8 fl. oz.)	125	t	32
Lemonade mix, with vitamin C	1 portion, 1/8 cap/tub	64	t	18
Lemonade, pink, frozen concentrate, prepared w/ water	1 cup (8 fl. oz.)	99	t	26
Lemonade, powder, prepared w/ water	1 cup (8 fl. oz.)	103	0	27
Lemonade, white, frozen concentrate, prepared w/ water	1 cup (8 fl. oz.)	99	t	26
Lemonade-flavor drink, powder, prepared w/ water	1 cup (8 fl. oz.)	112	0	29
Orange and apricot juice drink, canned	1 cup (8 fl. oz.)	128	1	32
Papaya nectar, canned	1 cup (8 fl. oz.)	143	t	36
Peach nectar, canned	1 cup (8 fl. oz.)	134	1	35
Pear nectar, canned	1 cup (8 fl. oz.)	150	t	39

Fat/Sat Fat (g)	Chol (mg)	Fiber (g)	Sugars (g)	Sodium (mg)
0/0	0	t	na	3
t/t	na	na	15	13
0/0	0	0	na	7
0/0	0	0	na	13
0/0	0	t	na	7
0/0	0	0	na	19
t/t	0	t	na	5
t/t	0	1.5	na	13
t/t	0	1.5	na	17
t/t	0	1.5	na	10

Fruits (cont.)	Serving	Calories	Prot (g)	Carb (g)
Pineapple and grapefruit juice drink, canned	I cup (8 fl. oz.)	118	1	29
Pineapple and orange juice drink, canned	I cup (8 fl. oz.)	125	3	30
Sports drink, lemon lime flavor mix, powder	¾ scoop	58	0	15
Tropical punch, ready-to-drink	I serving	90	0	24
Tropical punch, powder, prepared w/water	I serving	64	0	16

Fat/Sat Fat (g)	Chol (mg)	Fiber (g)	Sugars (g)	Sodium (mg)
t/t	0	t	na	35
0/0	0	t	na	8
0/0	0	0	14	96
0/0	0	0	23	29
0/0	0	0	16	2

LOW-RESPONSE COST, LOW-YIELD FOODS: GRAINS, PASTA, AND NOODLES

Food	Serving	Calories	Prot (g)	Carb (g)
Rice				
Rice noodles, cooked	½ cup	96	1	22
White rice, w/ pasta, cooked	½ cup	123	3	22
White rice, short-grained, cooked	½ cup	121	2	27
White rice, medium-grained, cooked	½ cup	121	2	27
White rice, long-grained, cooked	½ cup	103	2	22
White rice, long-grained, instant, cooked	½ cup	81	2	18
White rice, long-grained, parboiled, enriched, cooked	½ cup	100	2	22
Pasta and Noodles				
Alfredo egg noodles in creamy sauce, dry mix	1 serving	259	10	39

Fat/Sat Fat (g)	Chol (mg)	Fiber (g)	Sugars (g)	Sodium (mg)
t/t	0	1	na	17
3/1	1	3	na	574
t/t	0	na	na	0
t/t	0	t	na	0
t/t	0	t	na	1
t/t	0	.5	na	2
t/t	0	t	na	3

7/3	69	0	na	1097

Grains (cont.)	Serving	Calories	Prot (g)	Carb (g)
Fresh-refrigerated, plain	½ cup	149	6	28
Homemade, made w/o egg	½ cup	141	5	29
Macaroni, elbow	½ cup	99	3	20
Macaroni, spiral	½ cup	94	3	19
Macaroni, shells	½ cup	81	3	16
Pasta, w/ sliced franks in tomato sauce, canned	I serving	262	9	30
Spaghetti, w/ salt	½ cup	99	3	20

Fat/Sat Fat (g)	Chol (mg)	Fiber (g)	Sugars (g)	Sodium (mg)
l/t	38	na	na	7
l/t	0	na	na	84
t/t	0	l	na	l
t/t	0	l	na	l
t/t	0	l	na	l
12/4	23	2	na	1215
t/t	0	l	na	70

LOW-RESPONSE COST, LOW-YIELD FOODS: GRAVIES AND SAUCES

Food	Serving	Calories	Prot (g)	Carb (g)
Gravies				
Au jus, canned	2 tbsp	5	t	1
Beef, from jar	2 tbsp	13	1	2
Beef, canned	2 tbsp	15	1	1
Brown gravy, canned	2 tbsp	12	t	2
Chicken, canned	2 tbsp	24	1	2
Mushroom, canned	2 tbsp	15	t	2
Sausage gravy, ready-to-serve	2 tbsp	48	1	2
Turkey, canned	2 tbsp	15	1	2
Sauces				
Adobo fresco	1 tbsp	41	0	3
Barbecue sauce	2 tbsp	24	1	4
Barbeque sauce, hickory smoke	2 tbsp	39	t	9
Bearnaise, dehydrated, dry	1 pkt	91	4	15
Cheese sauce, ready-to-serve	¼ cup	110	4	4

Fat/Sat Fat (g)	Chol (mg)	Fiber (g)	Sugars (g)	Sodium (mg)
t/t	0	0	na	15
t/t	2	na	na	189
1/t	1	t	na	163
t/t	1	na	na	176
2/t	1	t	na	172
1/t	0	t	na	170
4/1	7	t	t	118
1/t	1	t	na	172

Fat/Sat Fat (g)	Chol (mg)	Fiber (g)	Sugars (g)	Sodium (mg)
4/1	0	0	0	3087
1/t	0	t	na	265
t/t	0	t	7	418
2/0	0	0	na	847
8/4	18	t	t	522

Gravies (cont.)	Serving	Calories	Prot (g)	Carb (g)
Golden cheese sauce, ready-to-serve	¼ cup	139	7	2
Creole sauce, ready-to-serve	¼ cup	25	1	4
Fish sauce, ready-to-serve	2 tbsp	13	2	1
Hoisin sauce, ready-to-serve	2 tbsp	70	1	14
Hollandaise, w/ butterfat, dehydrated, prepared w/ water	1 pkt	188	4	11
Jalapeno cheese sauce, ready-to-serve	¼ cup	81	2	8
Lemon sauce, ready-to-serve	2 tbsp	43	t	10
Mild nacho cheese sauce, ready-to-serve	¼ cup	119	5	3
Nacho cheese sauce, ready-to-serve	¼ cup	128	5	4
Nacho cheese sauce, w/ jalapeno peppers, mild, ready-to-serve	¼ cup	122	1	7

Fat/Sat Fat (g)	Chol (mg)	Fiber (g)	Sugars (g)	Sodium (mg)
11/6	29	1	t	501
1/t	0	1	3	339
0/0	0	0	na	2779
1/t	1	1	na	517
16/9	41	1	3	1232
5/2	6	0	t	571
t/t	0	0	8	3
10/4	20	.5	0	492
10/6	29	t	t	580
10/3	4	t	2	551

Gravies (cont.)	Serving	Calories	Prot (g)	Carb (g)
Plum sauce, ready-to-serve	2 tbsp	70	t	16
Sharp cheddar cheese sauce, ready-to-serve	¼ cup	133	5	2
Stir fry sauce, ready-to-serve	1 tbsp	16	t	2
Sweet and sour sauce, dry	1 pkt	222	1	55
Sweet and sour glaze, ready-to-serve	2 tbsp	51	t	12
Sweet and sour sauce, ready-to-serve	2 tbsp	40	t	8
Tartar sauce	1 tbsp	74	t	2
White sauce, homemade, thin	¼ cup	66	2	5
White sauce, homemade, medium	¼ cup	92	2	6
White sauce, homemade, thick	¼ cup	116	2	7

Fat/Sat Fat (g)	Chol (mg)	Fiber (g)	Sugars (g)	Sodium (mg)
t/t	0	t	na	204
12/5	23	l	t	473
l/t	0	0	l	233
0/0	0	l	na	587
t/t	0	0	8	229
l/t	0	t	7	116
8/1	6	na	na	103
4/1	5	t	na	205
7/2	4	t	na	221
9/2	4	t	na	233

LOW-RESPONSE COST,
LOW-YIELD FOODS: ICE CREAM

Food	Serving	Calories	Prot (g)	Carb (g)
Ice Cream				
Butter almond	½ cup	167	3	14
Butter pecan	½ cup	175	3	16
Cherry vanilla	½ cup	144	2	16
Chocolate	½ cup	175	2	16
Chocolate chip	½ cup	166	2	17
Chocolate/vanilla swirl	½ cup	161	3	17
Coffee	½ cup	149	3	14
French vanilla	½ cup	185	4	19
Fruit bar	1 bar	44	0	11
Frozen yogurt, chocolate, soft-serve	½ cup	115	3	18
Frozen yogurt, vanilla, soft-serve	½ cup	114	3	17
Fudge bar	1 bar	45	1	9
Ice cream sandwich	1 bar	159	3	21
Neopolitan	½ cup	150	3	17

Fat/Sat Fat (g)	Chol (mg)	Fiber (g)	Sugars (g)	Sodium (mg)
11/5	25	0	13	110
11/5	50	0	13	70
8/5	20	0	16	30
12/7	44	0	na	58
10/6	25	0	16	35
9/5	25	0	15	40
9/5	25	0	14	35
11/6	78	0	na	52
0/0	0	0	8	5
4/3	4	0	na	71
4/2	1	0	na	63
t/na	na	na	na	na
7/4	20	0	15	70
8/na	50	0	11	35

Ice Cream (cont.)	Serving	Calories	Prot (g)	Carb (g)
Rocky road	½ cup	182	2	21
Sherbert, orange	½ cup	122	1	26
Sherbert, rainbow	½ cup	122	1	26
Sorbet	½ cup	120	0	30
Strawberry	½ cup	127	2	18
Vanilla	½ cup	259	4	24
Vanilla, soft-serve, ice milk	½ cup	164	4	24
Vanilla ice cream w/ dark chocolate coating	1 bar	166	2	12

Fat/Sat Fat (g)	Chol (mg)	Fiber (g)	Sugars (g)	Sodium (mg)
10/5	20	.5	17	25
1.5/1	5	0	19	35
1.5/1	5	0	20	35
0/0	0	0	28	15
6/3	19	0	na	40
17/11	98	0	22	153
6/4	28	0	na	92
12/7	14	0	9	34

LOW-RESPONSE COST, LOW-YIELD FOODS: LAMB, VEAL, AND ORGAN MEATS

Food	Serving	Calories	Prot (g)	Carb (g)
Lamb				
Retail cuts, lean and fat, trimmed to ⅛" fat, choice, cooked	4 oz.	307	29	0
Rib, lean and fat, trimmed to ⅛" fat, choice, broiled	4 oz.	385	26	0
Rib, lean and fat, trimmed to ⅛" fat, choice, roasted	4 oz.	386	25	0
Rib, lean and fat, trimmed to ¼" fat, choice, broiled	4 oz.	409	25	0
Rib, lean and fat, trimmed to ¼" fat, choice, roasted	4 oz.	407	24	0
Lamb, ground, broiled	4 oz.	321	28	0
Veal				
Breast, point half, lean and fat, boneless, braised	4 oz.	281	32	0

Fat/Sat Fat (g)	Chol (mg)	Fiber (g)	Sugars (g)	Sodium (mg)
20/8	109	0	0	82
30/13	111	0	0	87
31/13	109	0	0	84
34/14	112	0	0	86
34/14	110	0	0	83
22/9	110	0	0	92
16/6	129	0	0	75

Lamb (cont.)	Serving	Calories	Prot (g)	Carb (g)
Breast, whole, boneless, lean and fat, braised	4 oz.	301	31	0
Retail cuts, lean and fat, cooked	4 oz.	262	34	0

Organ Meats

Brain, beef, simmered	4 oz.	181	13	0
Brain, beef, pan-fried	4 oz.	222	14	0
Brain, pork, braised	4 oz.	156	14	0
Giblets, fried	1 cup, chopped or diced	402	47	6
Sweetbread, braised	4 oz.	362	25	0
Tripe, raw	4 oz.	111	16	0
Tongue, beef, simmered	4 oz.	321	25	t
Tongue, pork, simmered	4 oz.	307	27	0

Fat/Sat Fat (g)	Chol (mg)	Fiber (g)	Sugars (g)	Sodium (mg)
19/7	128	0	0	74
13/5	129	0	0	99

Fat/Sat Fat (g)	Chol (mg)	Fiber (g)	Sugars (g)	Sodium (mg)
14/3	2328	0	0	136
18/4	2261	0	0	179
11/2	2892	0	0	103
20/5	647	0	na	164
28/10	333	0	0	131
4/2	107	0	0	52
24/10	121	0	na	68
21/7	165	0	0	124

LOW-RESPONSE COST, LOW-YIELD FOODS: LUNCH MEATS AND SAUSAGES

Food	Serving	Calories	Prot (g)	Carb (g)
Lunch Meats and Sausages				
Beerwurst, beef	1 slice	76	3	t
Beerwurst, pork	1 slice	55	3	.5
Blood sausage	1 slice	94	4	0
Bologna, beef	1 slice	87	3	t
Bologna, beef, Lebanon	1 slice	112	11	t
Bologna, pork	1 slice	69	4	t
Bologna, pork and beef	1 slice	87	3	1
Bratwurst, beef and pork, smoked	2 oz.	168	7	1.5
Bratwurst, pork, cooked	1 link	256	12	2
Bratwurst, veal, cooked	2 oz.	194	8	0
Braunschweiger	1 slice	65	2.5	.5
Cheesefurter, cheese smoke	1 link	141	6	1

Fat/Sat Fat (g)	Chol (mg)	Fiber (g)	Sugars (g)	Sodium (mg)
7/3	14	0	na	236
4/1.5	14	0	na	285
9/3	30	0	0	170
8/3	16	0	na	275
7.5/3	35	0	1.5	773
6/2	17	0	na	332
8/3	15	0	1	285
15/3	44	0	0	480
22/8	51	0	na	473
18/8.5	45	0	0	34
6/2	28	0	na	206
12/5	29	0	1	465

Lunch Meats (cont.)	Serving	Calories	Prot (g)	Carb (g)
Hot dog, beef and pork	1 hot dog	135	5	1
Hot dog, pork	1 hot dog	204	10	t
Knockwurst	1 link	221	8	2
Liverwurst	1 slice	59	2.5	t
Pork sausage links	2 links	165	8	.5
Pork sausage patties	2 patties	199	11	.5
Pork sausage, Italian	1 link	216	13	1
Pork sausage, Polish	1 sausage	740	32	4
Pork and beef sausage, cooked	2 links	103	4	1
Pork and beef sausage, cooked	2 patties	214	7.5	1.5
Salami, beef	2 slices	204	10	t
Salami, beef and pork	2 slices	115	6	1
Summer sausage, w/ cheese	2 oz.	242	11	1

Fat/Sat Fat (g)	Chol (mg)	Fiber (g)	Sugars (g)	Sodium (mg)
12.5/5	23	0	0	504
18/7	50	t	0	620
20/7	43	0	na	670
5/2	28	0	na	155
15/5	37	0	t	401
17/6	45	0	na	699
17/6	52	0	na	618
65/23	159	0	na	1989
9/3	18	0	na	209
20/7	38	0	na	435
18/5	39	0	t	930
9/4	30	0	na	490
21.5/6	50	t	t	841

Lunch Meats (cont.)	Serving	Calories	Prot (g)	Carb (g)
Swisswurst, pork and beef, w/ Swiss cheese, smoked	1 serving (2.7 oz)	236	10	1
Vienna sausage	7 links	315	12	2

Fat/Sat Fat (g)	Chol (mg)	Fiber (g)	Sugars (g)	Sodium (mg)
21/8	47	0	0	637
28.5/10.5	59	0	na	1077

LOW-RESPONSE COST, LOW-YIELD FOODS: MILK, MILK PRODUCTS, CREAM, AND YOGURT

Food	Serving	Calories	Prot (g)	Carb (g)
Milk and Milk Products				
Chocolate milk	1 cup	208	8	26
Chocolate-flavored beverage mix, prepared w/ whole milk	1 cup	226	9	31
Chocolate milk, prepared w/ whole milk and chocolate syrup	1 cup	257	9	36
Eggnog	1 cup	343	9	34
Eggnog-flavored mix, prepared w/ whole milk	1 cup	261	8	39
Hot cocoa, homemade	1 cup	193	10	29
Malted drink mix, prepared w/ whole milk	1 cup	236	9	30
Milk, canned, condensed, sweetened	½ cup	491	12	83
Milk shake, chocolate	8 fl. oz.	270	7	48

Fat/Sat Fat (g)	Chol (mg)	Fiber (g)	Sugars (g)	Sodium (mg)
8/5	30	2	na	150
9/5.5	32	1	na	165
9/5	34	1	na	147
19/11	150	0	na	137
8/5	33	1	na	163
6/4	20	2	na	128
9/5	34	t	na	172
13/8	52	0	na	194
6/4	25	1	na	252

Milk (cont.)	Serving	Calories	Prot (g)	Carb (g)
Milk shake, vanilla	8 fl. oz.	254	9	40
Milk substitutes, fluid, w/ hydrogenated vegetable oils	1 cup	149	4	15
Strawberry-flavored beverage mix, prepared w/ whole milk	1 cup	234	8	33
Whole milk	1 cup	156	8	11

Cream

	Serving	Calories	Prot (g)	Carb (g)
Creamer, nondairy, w/ hydrogenated vegetable oil and soy protein	1 tbsp	20	t	2
Creamer, nondairy, w/ lauric acid oil and sodium caseinate	1 tbsp	20	t	2
Half-and-half	1 tbsp	20	t	1
Liquid, coffee or table	1 tbsp	29	t	1
Whipping, heavy	1 tbsp	52	t	t
Sour cream	1 tbsp	26	t	1

Fat/Sat Fat (g)	Chol (mg)	Fiber (g)	Sugars (g)	Sodium (mg)
7/4	27	0	na	216
8/2	0	0	na	190
8/5	32	0	na	128
9/6	34	0	na	120

2/t	0	0	na	12
2/1	0	0	na	12
2/1	6	0	na	6
3/2	10	0	na	6
6/3	21	0	na	6
3/2	5	0	na	6

Milk (cont.)	Serving	Calories	Prot (g)	Carb (g)
Yogurt				
Frozen yogurt, hard, lowfat, all flavors	½ cup	140	2.5	26
Frozen yogurt, chocolate, soft-serve	½ cup	115	3	18
Frozen yogurt, vanilla, soft-serve	½ cup	114	3	17
Fruit-flavored, creamy style, lowfat (1% milkfat)	1 cup	232	9	45
Fruit-flavored, lowfat (1% milkfat)	1 small container (4.4 oz.)	135	4	27
Fruit-flavored, lowfat (1% milkfat)	1 cup	218	9	41
Fruit-flavored, whole milk	1 cup	252	11	38
Plain, whole milk	1 cup	179	19	11
Yogurt fruit smoothies, bottled	1 bottle (10 fl. oz.)	270	8	52

Fat/Sat Fat (g)	Chol (mg)	Fiber (g)	Sugars (g)	Sodium (mg)
3/na	na	0	na	na
4/3	4	2	na	71
4/2.5	1	0	na	63
2/1	20	1	39	125
1/.5	11	t	24.5	56
2/1	20	.5	39.50	118
6/2	13	0	na	156
7/na	na	0	na	na
3.5/2	15	0	50	130

LOW-RESPONSE COST,
LOW-YIELD FOODS: NUTS AND SEED PRODUCTS

Food	Serving	Calories	Prot (g)	Carb (g)
Nuts and Seed Products				
Almonds, honey roasted	I tbsp	53	2	2.5
Almonds, oil roasted, w/ salt	I tbsp	60	2	2
Almonds, oil roasted, w/o salt	I tbsp	60	2	2
Almond butter, w/ salt	I tbsp	101	2	3
Almond butter, w/o salt	I tbsp	101	2	3
Cashews, oil roasted, w/ salt	I tbsp	47	I	2
Cashews, oil roasted, w/o salt	I tbsp	47	I	2
Cashew butter, w/ salt	I tbsp	94	3	4
Cashew butter, w/o salt	I tbsp	94	3	4
Coconut cream, canned	½ cup	284	4	12

Fat/Sat Fat (g)	Chol (mg)	Fiber (g)	Sugars (g)	Sodium (mg)
4/t	0	1	na	12
5/t	0	1	t	33
5/t	0	1	t	0
9/1	0	1	na	72
9/1	0	1	na	2
4/1	0	t	t	25
4/1	0	t	t	1
8/1.5	0	t	na	98
8/1.5	0	t	na	2
26/23	0	3	na	74

Nuts (cont.)	Serving	Calories	Prot (g)	Carb (g)
Coconut meat, dried, not sweetened	1 tbsp	94	1	3
Coconut meat, dried, sweetened, flaked, canned	½ cup	171	1	16
Coconut meat, dried, sweetened, flaked, package	½ cup	175	1	18
Coconut meat, dried, sweetened, shredded	½ cup	233	1	22
Coconut milk, canned	1 cup	445	5	6
Mixed nuts, oil roasted, w/ peanuts, w/ salt	1 tbsp	55	1	2
Mixed nuts, oil roasted, w/ peanuts, w/o salt	1 tbsp	55	1	2
Mixed nuts, oil roasted, w/o peanuts, w/ salt	1 tbsp	55	1	2
Mixed nuts, oil roasted, w/o peanuts, w/o salt	1 tbsp	55	1	2

Fat/Sat Fat (g)	Chol (mg)	Fiber (g)	Sugars (g)	Sodium (mg)
9/8	0	2	na	5
12/11	0	2	na	8
12/11	0	2	na	95
16.5/15	0	2	na	122
48/43	0	na	na	29
5/1	0	1	na	58
5/1	0	1	na	1
5/1	0	.5	na	63
5/1	0	.5	na	1

Nuts (cont.)	Serving	Calories	Prot (g)	Carb (g)
Peanuts, oil roasted, w/ salt	1 tbsp	51	2	2
Peanuts, oil roasted, w/o salt	1 tbsp	51	2	2
Peanut butter chunk style, w/ salt	1 tbsp	94	4	3
Peanut butter smooth style, w/ salt	1 tbsp	95	4	3
Pecans, oil roasted, w/ salt	1 tbsp	49	1	1
Pecans, oil roasted, w/o salt	1 tbsp	49	1	1
Sunflower seeds, oil roasted, w/ salt	1 tbsp	58	2	1
Sunflower seeds, oil roasted, w/o salt	1 tbsp	58	2	1
Trail mix, tropical	1 cup	570	9	92
Trail mix, regular, w/ chocolate chips, salted nuts and seeds	1 cup	707	21	66

Fat/Sat Fat (g)	Chol (mg)	Fiber (g)	Sugars (g)	Sodium (mg)
4/1	0	1	na	38
4/1	0	1	na	1
8/4	0	1	na	78
8/2	0	1	na	75
5/t	0	1	t	27
5/t	0	1	t	0
5/.5	0	1	na	57
5/.5	0	1	na	0
24/12	0	0	na	14
47/9	6	0	na	177

Nuts (cont.)	Serving	Calories	Prot (g)	Carb (g)
Trail mix, regular, w/ chocolate chips, unsalted nuts and seeds	1 cup	707	21	66

Fat/Sat Fat (g)	Chol (mg)	Fiber (g)	Sugars (g)	Sodium (mg)
47/9	6	0	na	39

LOW-RESPONSE COST,
LOW-YIELD FOODS: PANCAKES AND WAFFLES

Food	Serving	Calories	Prot (g)	Carb (g)
Pancakes				
Blueberry pancakes, prepared from recipe	1 pancake (4" dia)	84	2	11
Blueberry pancakes, prepared from recipe	1 pancake (6" dia)	171	5	22
Buttermilk mini pancakes, frozen, ready to microwave	1 serving	116	4	22
Buttermilk pancakes, prepared from recipe	1 pancake (4" dia)	86	3	11
Buttermilk pancakes, prepared from recipe	1 pancake (6" dia)	175	5	22
Plain pancakes, dry mix, prepared	1 pancake (4" dia)	74	2	14
Plain pancakes, dry mix, prepared	1 pancake (6" dia)	149	4	28
Plain pancakes, frozen, ready-to-heat	1 mini pancake	23	1	4

Fat/Sat Fat (g)	Chol (mg)	Fiber (g)	Sugars (g)	Sodium (mg)
4/1	21	na	na	157
7/2	43	na	na	317
2/t	na	na	na	290
4/1	22	na	na	198
7/1	45	na	na	402
1/t	5	.5	na	239
2/t	9	1	na	484
t/t	1	t	na	51

Pancakes (cont.)	Serving	Calories	Prot (g)	Carb (g)
Plain pancakes, frozen, ready-to-heat	1 pancake (4" dia)	94	2	18
Plain pancakes, frozen, ready-to-heat	1 pancake (6" dia)	167	4	32
Plain pancakes, prepared from recipe	1 pancake (4" dia)	86	2	11
Plain pancakes, prepared from recipe	1 pancake (6" dia)	175	5	22
Whole-wheat pancakes, dry mix, prepared	1 pancake (4" dia)	92	4	13
Whole-wheat pancakes, dry mix, prepared	1 pancake (6" dia)	268	11	38

Waffles

	Serving	Calories	Prot (g)	Carb (g)
Banana bread waffles	1 serving	212	5	32
Buttermilk waffles, frozen, ready-to-heat	1 waffle (4" square)	98	2	15

Fat/Sat Fat (g)	Chol (mg)	Fiber (g)	Sugars (g)	Sodium (mg)
1/t	4	1	na	209
2/1	7	1	na	372
4/1	22	na	na	167
7/2	45	na	na	338
3/1	27	1	na	252
8/2	79	4	na	738

7/1	0	2	5	280
3/t	12	1	na	292

Pancakes (cont.)	Serving	Calories	Prot (g)	Carb (g)
Buttermilk waffles, frozen, ready-to-heat, toasted	I waffle (4" dia)	87	2	13
Frozen waffles	I serving	197	5	30
Oat waffles	I waffle (4" dia)	69	2	13
Plain waffles	I waffle (7" dia)	218	6	25

Fat/Sat Fat (g)	Chol (mg)	Fiber (g)	Sugars (g)	Sodium (mg)
3/t	8	I	na	260
6/I	12	na	na	563
I/t	0	I	I	135
11/2	52	na	na	383

LOW-RESPONSE COST, LOW-YIELD FOODS: PIZZA

Food	Serving	Calories	Prot (g)	Carb (g)
Pizza*				
Cheese, whole pizza	1 pizza (12" dia)	1122	61	164
Cheese, slice	1 slice	140	8	21
Cheese, meat, and vegetables, whole pizza	1 pizza (12" dia)	1470	104	170
Cheese, meat, and vegetables, slice	1 slice	184	13	21
Cheese, sausage, pepperoni, and onions, frozen, whole pizza	1 package	1746	62	166
Cheese, sausage, pepperoni, and onions, frozen	1 serving	337	12	32
Crispy crust pepperoni, frozen, whole pizza	1 package	728	26	69
Crispy crust pepperoni, frozen	1 serving	364	13	35

* Includes values for whole pizzas, plus regular serving sizes.

Fat/Sat Fat (g)	Chol (mg)	Fiber (g)	Sugars (g)	Sodium (mg)
26/12	75	na	na	2681
3/1.5	9	0	na	336
43/12	164	na	na	3054
5/1.5	21	na	na	382
92/33	127	na	na	3653
18/6	25	na	na	704
39/8	23	na	na	1946
19/4	12	na	na	973

Pizza (cont.)	Serving	Calories	Prot (g)	Carb (g)
Deep dish sausage pizza, frozen, whole pizza	1 package	1576	50	164
Deep dish sausage pizza, frozen	1 serving	391	12	41
French bread pizza w/ sausage and pepperoni, frozen, whole pizza	1 package	896	35	87
French bread pizza w/ sausage and pepperoni, frozen	1 serving	448	18	44
French bread pizza w/ sausage, pepperoni, and mushrooms, frozen, whole pizza	1 package	858	32	89
French bread pizza w/ sausage, pepperoni, and mushrooms, frozen	1 serving	429	16	44
Mexican-style pizza, frozen, whole pizza	1 package	1326	43	130
Mexican-style pizza, frozen	1 serving	437	14	43
Pepperoni, frozen, whole pizza	1 package	1288	60	118

Fat/Sat Fat (g)	Chol (mg)	Fiber (g)	Sugars (g)	Sodium (mg)
80/23	63	na	na	3351
20/6	16	na	na	830
45/14	74	5	na	1720
22/7	37	2.5	na	860
41/13	67	7	na	1680
21/6	33	3.5	na	840
71/23	84	na	na	2293
23/8	28	na	na	756
64/25	160	na	na	2440

Pizza (cont.)	Serving	Calories	Prot (g)	Carb (g)
Pepperoni, frozen	I serving	400	16	36
Pepperoni, whole pizza	I pizza (12" dia)	1446	81	159
Pepperoni, slice	I slice	181	10	20
Pepperoni, stuffed sandwich, frozen	I serving	367	14	39
Pizza snacks, hamburger, frozen	I serving	231	9	26
Pizza snacks, pepperoni, frozen	I serving	385	14	39
Pizza snacks, sausage, frozen	I serving	351	14	40
Sausage, green and red peppers, mushroom, frozen, whole pizza	I package	1538	67	133
Sausage, green and red peppers, mushroom, frozen	I serving	386	17	33
Sausage and mushroom pizza, frozen, whole pizza	I package	1496	70	152
Sausage and mushroom pizza, frozen	I serving	306	14	31

Fat/Sat Fat (g)	Chol (mg)	Fiber (g)	Sugars (g)	Sodium (mg)
21/7	34	2	na	879
56/18	113	na	na	2132
7/2	14	na	na	267
18/7	41	na	na	676
10/na	na	na	na	417
19/5	31	2	na	866
15/3	24	3	na	632
83/32	147	na	na	3050
21/8	37	na	na	765
67/25	129	na	na	3509
14/5	26	na	na	718

Pizza (cont.)	Serving	Calories	Prot (g)	Carb (g)
Sausage, mushrooms, and pepperoni, frozen, whole pizza	1 package	1736	69	160
Sausage, mushrooms, and pepperoni, frozen	1 serving	344	14	32
Sausage and pepperoni, frozen, whole pizza	1 package	1389	69	120
Sausage and pepperoni, frozen	1 serving	348	17	30

Fat/Sat Fat (g)	Chol (mg)	Fiber (g)	Sugars (g)	Sodium (mg)
91/31	117	na	na	3725
18/6	23	na	na	738
70/26	175	na	na	2828
17/7	44	na	na	708

LOW-RESPONSE COST,
LOW-YIELD FOODS: PORK PRODUCTS

Food	Serving	Calories	Prot (g)	Carb (g)
Bacon				
Bacon, Canadian-style, grilled	2 slices	87	11	1
Bacon, fried, drained	3 slices	109	6	t
Pork				
Boston blade, roasted	4 oz.	305	26	0
Ham, cured, whole, roasted	4 oz.	275	24	0
Ham, patties, grilled	1 patty, cooked	205	8	1
Cutlet, cooked	4 oz.	284	32	0
Ground, cooked	4 oz.	336	29	0
Loin blade (chops), bone-in, lean and fat only, braised	4 oz.	366	25	0
Loin blade (chops), bone-in, lean and fat only, broiled	4 oz.	363	25	0

Fat/Sat Fat (g)	Chol (mg)	Fiber (g)	Sugars (g)	Sodium (mg)
4/1	27	0	na	727
9/3	16	0	na	303

Fat/Sat Fat (g)	Chol (mg)	Fiber (g)	Sugars (g)	Sodium (mg)
21/8	97	0	0	76
19/7	70	0	0	1345
19/7	43	0	0	638
17/6	96	0	0	64
24/9	108	0	0	84
29/11	96	0	0	62
28/11	97	0	0	79

Pork Products (cont.)	Serving	Calories	Prot (g)	Carb (g)
Loin blade (chops), bone-in, lean and fat only, pan-fried	4 oz.	388	24	0
Loin blade (chops), bone-in, lean and fat only, roasted	4 oz.	366	27	0
Loin, country-style ribs lean and fat only, braised	4 oz.	335	27	0
Loin, country-style ribs lean and fat only, roasted	4 oz.	372	27	0
Shoulder, arm picnic, lean and fat only, braised	4 oz.	373	32	0
Shoulder, arm picnic, lean and fat only, roasted	4 oz.	359	27	0
Shoulder, blade roll, lean and fat only, roasted	4 oz.	325	20	t
Spareribs, cooked	4 oz.	448	33	0

Fat/Sat Fat (g)	Chol (mg)	Fiber (g)	Sugars (g)	Sodium (mg)
31/12	96	0	0	76
28/10	105	0	0	34
24/9	99	0	0	67
29/10	104	0	0	59
26/10	124	0	0	100
27/10	107	0	0	79
27/9	76	0	na	1103
34/12	137	0	0	105

LOW-RESPONSE COST,
LOW-YIELD FOODS: POULTRY PRODUCTS

Food	Serving	Calories	Prot (g)	Carb (g)
Poultry				
Chicken w/ skin, roasted	4 oz.	272	31	0
Chicken, dark meat, w/ skin, roasted	4 oz.	288	29	0
Chicken, dark meat, w/ skin, fried in batter	4 oz.	334	24	11
Chicken, dark meat, w/ skin, fried in flour	4 oz.	319	30	5
Chicken breast, broilers or fryers, meat and skin, fried in batter	½ breast	364	35	13
Chicken breast, broilers or fryers, meat and skin, fried in flour	½ breast	218	31	2
Chicken drumstick, broilers or fryers, meat and skin, fried in batter	1 drumstick, bone removed	193	16	6

Fat/Sat Fat (g)	Chol (mg)	Fiber (g)	Sugars (g)	Sodium (mg)
14/4	100	0	0	92
18/5	104	0	0	100
21/6	100	na	na	330
19/5	103	na	na	100
18.5/5	119	t	na	385
9/2	87	t	na	74
11/3	62	t	na	194

Poultry (cont.)	Serving	Calories	Prot (g)	Carb (g)
Chicken drumstick, broilers or fryers, meat and skin, fried in flour	1 drumstick, bone removed	120	13	1
Chicken wing, broilers or fryers, meat and skin, fried in batter	1 wing, bone removed	159	10	5
Chicken wing, broilers or fryers, meat and skin, fried in flour	1 wing, bone removed	103	8	1
Cornish game hens, meat and skin, roasted	½ bird	335	29	0
Duck, meat and skin, roasted	4 oz.	377	21	0
Goose, domesticated, meat and skin, roasted	4 oz.	342	28	0
Pâté de foie gras, (goose liver pâté), canned, smoked	1 tbsp	60	1	1
Turkey breast, meat and skin, roasted	4 oz.	141	25	0
Turkey, canned	1 can (5 oz.)	204	30	0

Fat/Sat Fat (g)	Chol (mg)	Fiber (g)	Sugars (g)	Sodium (mg)
7/2	44	0	na	44
11/3	39	t	na	157
7/2	26	0	na	25
23/6	169	0	0	83
32/11	94	0	0	66
25/8	102	0	0	78
6/2	20	0	na	91
4/1	47	0	0	445
9/2.5	83	0	0	584

Poultry (cont.)	Serving	Calories	Prot (g)	Carb (g)
Turkey dark meat, meat and skin, roasted	1 cup	309	38.5	0
Turkey w/ gravy, frozen	1 pkg	95	8	7
Turkey leg, meat and skin, roasted	½ leg, bone removed	568	76	0
Turkey light meat, meat and skin, roasted, chopped	1 cup	276	40	0
Turkey patties, battered, fried	1 patty	181	9	10
Turkey sticks, battered and fried	2 sticks	357	18	22
Turkey wing, meat and skin, roasted	1 wing, bone removed	426	51	0

Fat/Sat Fat (g)	Chol (mg)	Fiber (g)	Sugars (g)	Sodium (mg)
16/5	125	0	0	106
4/1	26	0	na	787
27/8	232	0	0	210
12/3	106	0	0	88
12/3	40	t	na	512
22/6	82	na	na	1073
23/6	151	0	0	113

LOW-RESPONSE COST,
LOW-YIELD FOODS: PUDDINGS

Food	Serving	Calories	Prot (g)	Carb (g)
Puddings				
Banana, dry mix, instant	1 portion makes ½ cup	92	0	23
Banana, dry mix, instant, w/ added oil	1 portion makes ½ cup	97	0	22
Banana, dry mix, regular	1 portion makes ½ cup	83	0	20
Banana, dry mix, regular, w/ added oil	1 portion makes ½ cup	85	0	19
Banana, ready-to-eat	1 can (5 oz.)	180	3	30
Chocolate, dry mix, instant	1 portion makes ½ cup	89	1	22
Chocolate, dry mix, regular	1 portion makes ½ cup	90	1	22
Chocolate, ready-to-eat	1 can (5 oz.)	189	4	32

Fat/Sat Fat (g)	Chol (mg)	Fiber (g)	Sugars (g)	Sodium (mg)
t/t	0	0	na	375
l/t	0	0	na	375
t/t	0	t	na	173
l/t	0	t	na	173
5/l	0	t	na	278
t/t	0	l	17	357
l/t	0	.5	na	88
6/l	4	l	na	183

Puddings (cont.)	Serving	Calories	Prot (g)	Carb (g)
Chocolate, ready-to-eat	1 snack size (4 oz.)	150	3	26
Coconut cream, dry mix, instant	1 portion makes ½ cup	97	t	22
Coconut cream, dry mix, regular	1 portion makes ½ cup	98	t	22
Lemon, dry mix, instant	1 portion makes ½ cup	95	0	24
Lemon, dry mix, regular	1 portion makes ½ cup	76	t	19
Lemon, ready-to-eat	1 can (5 oz.)	178	t	36
Rice, dry mix	1 portion makes ½ cup	102	1	25
Rice, ready-to-eat	1 can (5 oz.)	231	3	31
Tapioca, dry mix	1 portion makes ½ cup	85	t	22
Tapioca, ready-to-eat	1 can (5 oz.)	169	3	28

Fat/Sat Fat (g)	Chol (mg)	Fiber (g)	Sugars (g)	Sodium (mg)
5/1	3	1	na	146
1/1	0	t	na	302
1/1	0	t	16	260
t/t	0	0	na	333
t/t	0	0	na	106
4/1	0	t	na	199
t/t	0	t	na	99
11/2	1	t	na	121
t/t	0	0	15	110
5/1	1	t	25	226

Puddings (cont.)	Serving	Calories	Prot (g)	Carb (g)
Tapioca, ready-to-eat	1 snack size (4 oz.)	134	2	22
Vanilla, dry mix, instant	1 portion makes ½ cup	92	0	23
Vanilla, dry mix, regular	1 portion makes ½ cup	81	t	21
Vanilla, ready-to-eat	1 snack size (4 oz.)	147	3	25

Fat/Sat Fat (g)	Chol (mg)	Fiber (g)	Sugars (g)	Sodium (mg)
4/1	1	t	20	180
t/t	0	0	19	360
t/t	0	t	16	166
4/1	8	t	na	153

LOW-RESPONSE COST, LOW-YIELD FOODS: SNACKS: CHIPS, PRETZELS, AND POPCORN

Food	Serving	Calories	Prot (g)	Carb (g)
Chips				
Banana chips	1 oz.	147	1	16
Beef jerky, chopped and formed	1 oz.	116	9	3
Beef sticks, smoked	1 oz.	155	6	2
Cheese puffs or twists	1 oz.	156	2	15
Cheese puffs or twists, low fat	1 oz.	122	2	20
Chex mix	1 oz. (approx. ⅔ cup)	120	3	18
Corn chips, barbeque-flavor	¼ bag (7 oz.)	259	3	28
Corn chips, plain	¼ bag (7 oz.)	267	3	28
Cornnuts, barbecue flavor	1 oz.	123	3	20
Cornnuts, nacho flavor	1 oz.	124	3	20
Cornnuts, plain	1 oz.	126	2	20

Fat/Sat Fat (g)	Chol (mg)	Fiber (g)	Sugars (g)	Sodium (mg)
9/8	0	2	10	2
7/3	14	1	3	625
14/6	38	0	na	418
10/2	1	0	na	297
3/1	0	3	2	363
5/2	0	2	na	287
16/2	0	3	na	378
17/2	0	2	na	312
4/1	0	2	na	276
4/1	1	2	na	179
4/1	0	2	0	155

Snacks (cont.)	Serving	Calories	Prot (g)	Carb (g)
Popcorn, caramel-coated w/ peanuts	⅔ cup	113	2	23
Popcorn, caramel-coated w/o peanuts	⅔ cup	122	1	22
Popcorn, cheese-flavored	2 cups	116	2	11
Popcorn, oil-popped	2 cups	110	2	13
Pork skins, bar-becue flavor	1 oz.	152	16	0
Pork skins, plain	1 oz.	154	17	0
Potato chips, barbeque-flavor	¼ bag (7 oz.)	243	4	26
Potato chips, cheese-flavor	¼ bag (6 oz.)	211	4	25
Potato chips, made from dried potatoes, plain	¼ can (7 oz.)	276	3	25
Potato chips, made from dried potatoes, sour cream and onion flavor	¼ can (6.75 oz.)	271	3	25

Fat/Sat Fat (g)	Chol (mg)	Fiber (g)	Sugars (g)	Sodium (mg)
2/t	0	1	na	84
4/1	1	1.5	na	58
7/1	2	2	na	196
6/1	0	2	na	194
9/2	32	0	na	753
9/3	27	0	0	519
16/4	0	2	na	371
12/4	2	2	na	337
19/5	0	2	na	325
18/5	1	1	na	356

Snacks (cont.)	Serving	Calories	Prot (g)	Carb (g)
Potato chips, plain, made w/ partially hydrogenated soybean oil, salted	¼ bag (8 oz.)	304	4	30
Potato chips, plain, made w/ partially hydrogenated soybean oil, unsalted	¼ bag (8 oz.)	304	4	30
Potato chips, plain, salted	¼ bag (8 oz.)	304	4	30
Potato chips, plain, unsalted	¼ bag (8 oz.)	304	4	30
Potato chips, reduced fat	¼ bag (6 oz.)	200	3	28
Potato chips, sour cream and onion flavor	¼ bag (7 oz.)	263	4	25
Potato sticks	1 oz.	147	2	15
Sesame sticks, wheat-based, salted	1 oz.	153	3	13
Snack mix, original flavor	1 cup	260	6	37
Tortilla chips, taco-flavor	¼ bag (8 oz.)	272	4	36

Fat/Sat Fat (g)	Chol (mg)	Fiber (g)	Sugars (g)	Sodium (mg)
20/3	0	3	na	337
20/3	0	3	na	5
20/6	0	3	na	337
20/6	0	3	na	5
9/2	0	3	na	209
17/4	3	3	na	309
10/3	0	1	0	71
10/2	0	1	0	420
11/2	1	4	na	724
14/3	3	3	na	447

Snacks (cont.)	Serving	Calories	Prot (g)	Carb (g)
Pretzels				
Cheddar cheese pretzels	10 pieces	139	3	20
Chocolate-coated pretzels	1 pretzel	50	1	8
Plain pretzel, hard, w/salt	10 twists	229	5	48
Plain pretzel, hard, w/o salt	10 twists	229	5	48
Pretzels, soft	1 large (143 grams)	483	12	99
Whole-wheat pretzel, hard	2 oz.	206	6	46

Fat/Sat Fat (g)	Chol (mg)	Fiber (g)	Sugars (g)	Sodium (mg)
5/na	2	na	na	335
2/1	0	na	na	63
2/t	0	2	na	1029
2/t	0	2	na	173
4/1	4	2	0	2008
1/t	0	4	na	116

LOW-RESPONSE COST,
LOW-YIELD FOODS: SOUPS

Food	Serving	Calories	Prot (g)	Carb (g)
Soups				
Bean w/ frankfurters, canned, prepared w/ water	1 cup (8 fl. oz.)	188	10	22
Bean w/ ham, chunky, ready-to-serve	1 cup (8 fl. oz.)	231	13	27
Bean w/ pork, canned, prepared w/ water	1 cup (8 fl. oz.)	172	8	23
Beef w/ country vegetables, chunky, ready-to-serve	1 serving	153	12	16
Beef, chunky, ready-to-serve	1 cup (8 fl. oz.)	170	12	20
Cheese, canned, prepared w/ milk	1 cup (8 fl. oz.)	231	10	16
Cheese, canned, prepared w/ water	1 cup (8 fl. oz.)	156	5	11
Chicken corn chowder, chunky, ready-to-serve	1 serving	238	7	18

Fat/Sat Fat (g)	Chol (mg)	Fiber (g)	Sugars (g)	Sodium (mg)
7/2	13	na	na	1093
9/3	22	11	na	972
6/2	3	9	na	951
4/1	24	na	na	868
5/3	14	1	na	866
14/9	48	1	na	1019
10/7	30	1	na	958
15/4	26	2	na	718

Soups (cont.)	Serving	Calories	Prot (g)	Carb (g)
Chicken, mushroom chowder, chunky, ready-to-serve	1 serving	192	7	17
Chicken, mushroom, canned, prepared w/ water	1 cup (8 fl. oz.)	132	4	9
Chicken w/ dumplings, canned, prepared w/ water	1 cup (8 fl. oz.)	96	6	6
Chicken, chunky, ready-to-serve	1 cup (8 fl. oz.)	178	13	17
Clam chowder, New England, canned, prepared w/ milk	1 cup (8 fl. oz.)	164	10	17
Cream of asparagus, canned, prepared w/ milk	1 cup (8 fl. oz.)	161	6	16
Cream of celery, canned, prepared w/ milk	1 cup (8 fl. oz.)	164	6	15
Cream of chicken, canned, prepared w/ milk	1 cup (8 fl. oz.)	191	7	15
Cream of mushroom, canned, prepared w/ milk	1 cup (8 fl. oz.)	203	6	15

Fat/Sat Fat (g)	Chol (mg)	Fiber (g)	Sugars (g)	Sodium (mg)
11/3	14	3	na	814
9/2	10	t	na	942
6/1	34	.5	na	860
7/2	30	2	na	889
7/3	22	2	na	992
8/3	22	1	na	1042
10/4	32	1	na	1009
11/5	27	t	na	1047
14/5	20	.5	na	918

Soups (cont.)	Serving	Calories	Prot (g)	Carb (g)
Cream of mush-room, canned, pre-pared w/ water	1 cup (8 fl. oz.)	129	2	9
Cream of onion, canned, prepared w/ milk	1 cup (8 fl. oz.)	186	7	18
Cream of onion, canned, prepared w/ water	1 cup (8 fl. oz.)	107	3	13
Cream of potato, canned, prepared w/ milk	1 cup (8 fl. oz.)	149	6	17
Cream of shrimp, canned, prepared w/ milk	1 cup (8 fl. oz.)	164	7	14
Cream of shrimp, canned, prepared w/ water	1 cup (8 fl. oz.)	90	3	8
Cream of vegetable, dehydrated, pre-pared w/ water	1 cup (8 fl. oz.)	107	2	12
Oyster stew, canned, prepared w/ milk	1 cup (8 fl. oz.)	135	6	10
Pea, green, canned, prepared w/ milk	1 cup (8 fl. oz.)	239	13	32

Fat/Sat Fat (g)	Chol (mg)	Fiber (g)	Sugars (g)	Sodium (mg)
9/2	2	.5	na	881
9/4	32	1	na	1004
5/1	15	1	na	927
6/4	22	.5	na	1061
9/6	35	t	na	1037
5/3	17	t	na	976
6/1	0	.5	na	1170
8/5	32	0	na	1041
7/4	18	3	na	970

Soups (cont.)	Serving	Calories	Prot (g)	Carb (g)
Potato ham chowder, chunky, ready-to-serve	1 serving	192	6	13
Sirloin burger w/ vegetables, ready-to-serve	1 serving	185	10	16
Split pea w/ ham, chunky, ready-to-serve	1 cup (8 fl. oz.)	185	11	27
Split pea w/ ham, canned, prepared w/ water	1 cup (8 fl. oz.)	190	10	28
Tomato beef w/ noodle, canned, prepared w/ water	1 cup (8 fl. oz.)	139	4	21
Tomato bisque, canned, prepared w/ milk	1 cup (8 fl. oz.)	198	6	29
Tomato, canned, prepared w/ milk	1 cup (8 fl. oz.)	161	6	22

Fat/Sat Fat (g)	Chol (mg)	Fiber (g)	Sugars (g)	Sodium (mg)
12/4	22	1	na	874
9/3	26	6	na	866
4/2	7	4	na	965
4/2	8	2	na	1007
4/2	5	1	na	917
7/3	23	.5	na	1109
6/3	17	3	na	744

LOW-RESPONSE COST, LOW-YIELD FOODS: SUGARS, SWEETENERS, JAMS, AND SYRUPS

Food	Serving	Calories	Prot (g)	Carb (g)
Sugars				
Brown	I tbsp unpacked	34	0	9
Maple	I tbsp	32	t	8
Powdered	I tbsp	29	0	7
White	I lump (2 cubes)	19	0	5
White	I packet	23	0	6
White	I tbsp	49	0	13
Honey, Jams, Preserves, Jellies				
Apple butter	I tbsp	29	t	7
Honey, strained or extracted	I tbsp	64	t	17
Jams and preserves	I tbsp	56	t	14
Jams and preserves	I packet	39	t	10
Jam, apricot	I tbsp	48	t	13
Jam, apricot	I packet	34	t	9
Jellies, all types	I tbsp	54	t	13

Fat/Sat Fat (g)	Chol (mg)	Fiber (g)	Sugars (g)	Sodium (mg)
0/0	0	0	na	4
t/t	0	0	na	1
t/t	0	0	na	0
0/0	0	0	na	0
0/0	0	0	na	0
0/0	0	0	na	0

Fat/Sat Fat (g)	Chol (mg)	Fiber (g)	Sugars (g)	Sodium (mg)
0/0	0	t	6	1
0/0	0	0	na	1
t/t	0	t	10	6
t/t	0	t	7	4
t/t	0	t	na	8
t/t	0	t	na	6
t/t	0	t	8	5

Sugars (cont.)	Serving	Calories	Prot (g)	Carb (g)
Jellies, all types	1 packet	40	t	10
Orange marmalade	1 tbsp	49	t	13
Orange marmalade	1 packet	34	t	9
Strawberry spread, all-fruit	1 tbsp	42	t	10

Syrups

	Serving	Calories	Prot (g)	Carb (g)
Blends, cane and 15% maple	1 tbsp	56	t	15
Blends, corn, refiner, and sugar	1 tbsp	64	0	17
Chocolate fudge-type syrup	2 tbsp	133	2	24
Corn, dark	1 tbsp	56	0	15
Corn, high fructose	1 tbsp	53	0	14
Corn, light	1 tbsp	56	0	15
Fruit syrup	1 tbsp	53	0	14
Malt	1 tbsp	76	1	17
Maple syrup	1 tbsp	52	0	13
Molasses	1 tbsp	58	0	15
Pancake, regular	1 tbsp	57	0	15

Fat/Sat Fat (g)	Chol (mg)	Fiber (g)	Sugars (g)	Sodium (mg)
0/0	0	t	6	4
0/0	0	0	na	11
0/0	0	0	na	8
0/0	0	na	8	4

Fat/Sat Fat (g)	Chol (mg)	Fiber (g)	Sugars (g)	Sodium (mg)
t/t	0	0	na	21
0/0	0	0	na	14
3/1.5	1	1	16	131
0/0	0	0	na	31
0/0	0	0	na	0
0/0	0	0	na	24
0/0	0	0	na	7
0/0	0	0	na	8
t/t	0	0	13	2
0/0	0	0	11	7
0/0	0	0	na	17

Sugars (cont.)	Serving	Calories	Prot (g)	Carb (g)
Pancake, w/ butter	1 tbsp	59	0	15
Pancake, w/ 2% maple	1 tbsp	53	0	14
Sorghum	1 tbsp	61	0	16

Fat/Sat Fat (g)	Chol (mg)	Fiber (g)	Sugars (g)	Sodium (mg)
t/t	1	0	na	20
t/t	0	0	na	12
0/0	0	0	na	2

LOW-RESPONSE COST, LOW-YIELD FOODS: VEGETABLES AND VEGETABLE PRODUCTS

Food	Serving	Calories	Prot (g)	Carb (g)
Vegetables				
Beans, baked, canned, w/ beef	½ cup	161	8	22
Beans, baked, canned, w/ franks	½ cup	184	9	20
Beans, baked, canned, w/ pork	½ cup	134	7	25
Beans, baked, canned, w/ pork and tomato sauce	½ cup	124	7	25
Beans, baked, canned, w/ pork and sweet sauce	½ cup	140	7	27
Beans, baked, canned, plain or vegetarian	½ cup	118	6	26
Broccoli in cheese-flavored sauce, frozen	1 cup	113	4	15
Corn, sweet, white or yellow, canned, cream style, no salt added	½ cup	92	2	23

Fat/Sat Fat (g)	Chol (mg)	Fiber (g)	Sugars (g)	Sodium (mg)
5/2	29	na	na	632
9/3	8	9	na	557
2/1	9	7	na	524
1/t	9	6	na	557
2/1	9	7	na	425
t/t	0	6	na	504
4/1	na	0	na	806
t/t	0	1	na	4

Vegetables (cont.)	Serving	Calories	Prot (g)	Carb (g)
Corn, sweet, white or yellow, canned, cream style, w/ salt added	½ cup	92	2	23
Corn pudding, home-prepared	1 cup	272	11	32
Onion rings, breaded, par fried, frozen, prepared, heated in oven	1 cup	195	3	18
Potatoes, au gratin, home-prepared from recipe using butter	1 cup	323	12	28
Potatoes, au gratin, home-prepared from recipe using margarine	1 cup	323	12	28
Potatoes, au gratin, dry mix, prepared w/ water, whole milk and butter	0.17 package (5.5 oz.)	130	3	18
Potatoes, French fried, frozen, home-prepared, heated in oven, w/ salt	20 strips	200	3	31

Fat/Sat Fat (g)	Chol (mg)	Fiber (g)	Sugars (g)	Sodium (mg)
t/t	0	1	na	365
13/6	250	0	na	138
13/4	0	1	na	180
19/12	56	4	na	1061
18/8	37	4	na	1061
6/4	21	1	na	612
8/1	0	3	na	266

Vegetables (cont.)	Serving	Calories	Prot (g)	Carb (g)
Potatoes, French fried, frozen, home-prepared, heated in oven, w/o salt	15 strips	150	2	23
Potatoes, French fried, frozen, home-prepared, heated in oven, w/ salt	15 strips	150	2	23
Potatoes, French fried, frozen, par fried, cottage-cut, prepared, heated in oven, w/ salt	15 strips	164	3	26
Potatoes, French fried, frozen, par fried, cottage-cut, prepared, heated in oven, w/o salt	15 strips	164	3	26
Potatoes, French fried, frozen, home-prepared, heated in oven, w/ salt	20 strips	200	4	32
Potatoes, hash browns, frozen, plain, prepared	1 patty, oval (3" x 1½" x ½")	63	1	8

Fat/Sat Fat (g)	Chol (mg)	Fiber (g)	Sugars (g)	Sodium (mg)
6/1	0	2	na	23
6/1	0	2	na	200
6/3	0	2	na	211
6/3	0	2	na	34
8/2	0	4	na	266
3/1	0	1	na	10

Vegetables (cont.)	Serving	Calories	Prot (g)	Carb (g)
Potatoes, hash browns, frozen, plain, prepared w/ butter sauce	1 patty, oval (3" x 1½" x ½")	52	1	7
Potatoes, hash browns, home-prepared	1 cup	326	4	33
Potatoes, mashed, dehydrated, prepared from flakes w/o milk, whole milk and butter added	½ cup	119	2	16
Potatoes, mashed, dehydrated, prepared from granules w/milk, water and margarine added	½ cup	83	2	14
Potatoes, mashed, dehydrated, prepared from granules w/o milk, whole milk and butter added	½ cup	113	2	15
Potatoes, mashed, home-prepared, whole milk added	½ cup	81	2	18

Fat/Sat Fat (g)	Chol (mg)	Fiber (g)	Sugars (g)	Sodium (mg)
3/1	7	1	na	29
22/8	0	3	na	37
6/4	15	2	na	349
2/1	2	2	na	246
5/3	15	2	na	270
1/t	2	2	na	318

Vegetables (cont.)	Serving	Calories	Prot (g)	Carb (g)
Potatoes, mashed, home-prepared, whole milk and butter added	½ cup	111	2	18
Potatoes, mashed, home-prepared, whole milk and margarine added	½ cup	111	2	18
Potatoes, O'Brian, frozen, unprepared	½ cup	76	2	17
Potato puffs, frozen, prepared	1 cup	284	4	39
Potato salad, home-prepared	1 cup	357	7	28
Potatoes, scalloped, home-prepared w/ butter	½ cup	105	4	13
Potatoes, scalloped, home-prepared w/ margarine	½ cup	105	4	13
Potatoes, scalloped, dry mix, prepared w/ water, whole milk and butter	0.17 package (5.5 oz.)	130	3	18
Potato wedges, frozen	½ cup	123	3	26

Fat/Sat Fat (g)	Chol (mg)	Fiber (g)	Sugars (g)	Sodium (mg)
4/3	13	2	na	310
4/1	2	2	na	310
t/t	na	2	na	33
14/7	0	4	na	955
20/4	170	3	na	1322
5/3	15	2	na	410
5/2	7	2	na	410
6/4	15	2	na	476
2/t	0	2	na	49

Vegetables (cont.)	Serving	Calories	Prot (g)	Carb (g)
Spinach au gratin, frozen	I serving	222	7	II
Spinach, creamed, frozen	I serving	169	3	9
Spinach soufflé, home-prepared	I cup	219	II	3
Stir-fry w/ white rice and vegetables and Oriental soy sauce, frozen	I cup	130	5	27
Succotash (corn and limas), canned, with cream-style corn	½ cup	102	4	23
Sweet potato, candied, home-prepared	I potato (2½" x 2" dia.)	144	I	29
Sweet potato, canned, syrup pack, drained solids	½ cup	106	I	25
Sweet potato, canned, syrup pack, w/ solids and liquids	½ cup	101	I	24
Tomatoes, sun-dried, packed in oil, drained	I cup	234	6	26

Fat/Sat Fat (g)	Chol (mg)	Fiber (g)	Sugars (g)	Sodium (mg)
17/8	42	2	na	654
13/4	16	2	na	335
18/7	184	0	na	763
0/0	0	2	na	636
1/t	0	4	na	326
3/1	8	3	na	74
t/t	0	3	na	38
t/t	0	3	na	50
15/2	0	6	na	293

Medical and Nutrition References

Brown, M. D., et al. 2001. "Controlling Calories—the Simple Approach." *Diabetes Spectrum* 14: 110–112.

Davis, R. B., et al. 2001. "A Review of Current Weight Management: Research and Recommendations." *Journal of the American Academy of Nurse Practitioners* 13: 15–19.

Farnsworth, E., et al. 2003. "Effect of a High-Protein, Energy-Restricted Diet on Body Composition, Glycemic Control, and Lipid Concentrations in Overweight and Obese Hyperinsulinemic Men and Women." *American Journal of Clinical Nutrition* 78: 31–39.

Jakicic, J. M., et al. 2001. "American College of Sports Medicine Position Stand. Appropriate Intervention Strategies for Weight Loss and Prevention of Weight Gain for Adults." *Medicine and Science in Sports and Exercise* 33: 2145–2156.

Jiang, H., et al. 1999. "Dietary Sodium Intake and Subsequent Risk of Cardiovascular Disease in Overweight Adults." *Journal of the American Medical Association* 282: 2027–2034.

Freedman, M. R., et al. 2001. "Popular Diets: A Scientific Review." *Obesity Research* 1:1S–40S.

Loria, C. M., et al. 2001. "Choose and Prepare Foods with Less Salt: Dietary Advice for All Americans." *Journal of Nutrition* 131: 536S–551S.

Nielsen, S. J., et al. 2003. "Patterns and Trends in Food Portion Sizes, 1977–1998." *Journal of the American Medical Association* 289: 450–453.

Nestle, M. 2003. "Increasing Portion Sizes in American Diets: More Calories, More Obesity." *Journal of the American Dietetic Association* 103: 39–40.

Roberts, S. B., et al. 2002. "The Influence of Dietary Composition on Energy Intake and Body Weight." *Journal of the American College of Nutrition* 21: 140S–145S.

Smiciklas-Wright, H., et al. 2003. "Foods Commonly Eaten in the United States, 1989–1991, 1994–1996: Are Portion Sizes Changing?" *Journal of the American Dietetic Association* 103: 41–47.

Westerterp-Plantega, M. S. 2003. "The Significance of Protein in Food Intake and Body Weight Regulation." *Current Opinion in Clinical Nutrition and Metabolic Care* 6: 635–638.

Wing, R. R., et al. 2001. "Successful Weight Loss Maintenance." *Annual Review of Nutrition* 21: 323–341.

Young, L. R., et al. 2003. "Expanding Portion Sizes in the U.S. Marketplace: Implications for Nutrition

Counseling." *Journal of the American Dietetic Association* 103: 231–234.

Zemel, M. B. 2003. "Mechanisms of Dairy Modulation of Adiposity." *Journal of Nutrition* 133: 252S–256S.

About the Author

Phillip C. McGraw, Ph.D., is the #1 New York Times bestselling author of Life Strategies, Relationship Rescue, Self Matters, and The Ultimate Weight Solution. He is the host of the nationally syndicated, daily one-hour series Dr. Phil. One of the world's foremost experts in the field of human functioning, Dr. McGraw is the cofounder of Courtroom Sciences, Inc., the world's leading litigation consulting firm. Dr. McGraw currently lives in Los Angeles, California, with his wife and two sons.

Visit his website: www.drphil.com.